The Power to Punish

The Power to Punish

Contemporary Penality and Social Analysis

Edited by

David Garland and Peter Young

Heinemann Educational Books · London
Humanities Press · New Jersey

Heinemann Educational Books Ltd
22 Bedford Square, London WC1B 3HH

Published in the USA by Humanities Press Inc.,
Atlantic Highlands, New Jersey 07716

British Library Cataloguing in Publication Data

The power to punish.
  1. Punishment
  I. Garland, David   II. Young, Peter
  364.6′01   HV8675

    ISBN 0-435-82325-6
    ISBN 0-435-82326-4 Pbk

    ISBN 0-391-02902-9 cased (Humanities Press)
    ISBN 0-391-02901-0 paper (Humanities Press)

Printed in Great Britain.

Contents

Notes on Contributors

Anthony E. Bottoms
Anthony Bottoms has been Professor of Criminology and Director of the Centre for Criminological and Socio-Legal Studies, University of Sheffield since 1976; he was previously Lecturer and Senior Lecturer in the same university. He is a co-author of *Criminals Coming of Age* (Heinemann, 1973); *The Urban Criminal* (Tavistock, 1976); and *Defendants in the Criminal Process* (Routledge & Kegan Paul, 1976); and co-editor (with R. H. Preston) of *The Coming Penal Crisis* (Scottish Academic Press, 1980). Professor Bottoms is also an editor of the *Howard Journal of Penology and Crime Prevention* and was a member of the English Parole Board, 1974–6.

Pat Carlen
Pat Carlen is Senior Lecturer in Criminology at the University of Keele. She has previously published *Magistrates' Justice* (Martin Robertson, 1976); *Sociology of Law* (University of Keele, 1976); *Official Discourse* (with Frank Burton) (Routledge & Kegan Paul, 1979); and *Radical Issues in Criminology* (edited with M. Collison) (Martin Robertson, 1980). Her latest book, *The Moment of Prison: The Meanings of Women's Imprisonment in Scotland*, will be published by Routledge & Kegan Paul in 1983.

Stanley Cohen
Stanley Cohen has taught in the sociology departments of the Universities of Durham and Essex in England. His publications include *Images of Deviance* (Penguin Books, 1971); *Folk Devils and Moral Panics* (Martin Robertson, 1972); *The Manufacture of News* (with Jock Young) (Constable, 1973); and (with Laurie Taylor), *Psychological Survival* (Penguin Books, 1972); *Escape Attempts* (Penguin Books, 1977); and *Prison Secrets* (NCCL/RAP, 1978). He is now Professor of Criminology at the Hebrew University, Jerusalem.

David Garland
David Garland is a Lecturer in the Department of Criminology at the University of Edinburgh and has taught courses in criminology and in the social analysis of penality for the past three years. He is author of a number of articles in the fields of penality, social work and criminal justice, and is currently writing a book on the political conditions of emergence of modern penality.

Thomas Mathiesen
Thomas Mathiesen was born 1933; since 1972 he has been Professor of the Sociology of Law in the Faculty of Law, University of Oslo, and was Chairman of the Norwegian prisoner's organisation, KROM, from 1968 to 1973. He has written numerous books in Norwegian, Swedish, German and English; among them are *The Defences of the Weak* (Tavistock, 1965); *Across the Boundaries of Organizations* (Glendessary Press, 1971); *The Politics of Abolition* (Martin Robertson, 1974); and *Law, Society and Political Action* (Academic Press, 1980).

Andrew Scull
Andrew Scull is an Associate Professor of Sociology at the University of California, San Diego. He previously taught at the Universities of Princeton and Pennsylvania and was an American Council of Learned Societies Fellow at University College, London, 1976–7. He is author of *Decarceration: Community Treatment and the Deviant: A Radical View* (Prentice-Hall, 1977); *Museums of Madness: The Social Organisations of Insanity in Nineteenth Century England* (Allen Lane, 1979); and editor of *Madhouses, Mad-Doctors and Madmen* (Athlone Press, 1981). He is presently at work on a study of Durkheim's sociology of law and a monograph on English ideas about insanity in the eighteenth and nineteenth centuries.

Barry Smart
Barry Smart is Lecturer in Sociology at the University of Sheffield, where he teaches courses in social theory and the sociology of culture. He is author of *Sociology, Phenomenology and Marxian Analysis* (Routledge & Kegan Paul, 1976), and editor (with C. Smart) of *Women, Sexuality and Social Control* (Routledge & Kegan Paul, 1978). He is presently completing a volume on the implications of Foucault's work for Marxism.

Peter Young
Peter Young is Lecturer in Criminology and Director of Research in

the Department of Criminology, University of Edinburgh. He is the author of a number of articles in the fields of criminology, sociology and penal relations. He is currently engaged in research on the development of monetary sanctions and is completing a book on the sociology and history of penal ideas.

Preface

This book grew out of our awareness of a somewhat paradoxical situation not uncommon in social science. Typically, advances in new areas of knowledge proceed not by an ordered and systematic progression, but rather by the production of diffuse and isolated pieces of work. Thus paradoxically those areas of greatest intellectual excitement and interest may also be those which are least accessible. The subject-matter of this book is one such area.

The great diversity of types of analysis and of angles of approach to 'the power to punish' make research and the production of useful knowledge uneven and fragmented. Moreover, our experience of teaching undergraduate and postgraduate courses in this area testifies to the difficulty of communicating and developing a knowledge which is nascent and often incoherent. The aim of this book is to introduce some coherence and stability in this regard. By covering what we take to be some of the most important and controversial theoretical, empirical and political issues concerning penality, we hope to provide a valuable text for current use in teaching and one which will open up further inquiry.

The essays included in this volume exhibit this diversity and difference. Indeed, they often take dispute one with another. However, there are certain themes and common ground which underpin them. First, the essays endeavour to provide an explanatory and not merely a descriptive approach to penality. Second, they ground their explanations within the terms and concepts of socio-political discourse. Third, they are committed to a conception of theoretical work which promotes progressive political intervention. These themes are visible in each contribution, even though the focus and level of analysis varies from the conceptual arguments presented in the first section of the book to the more concrete and explicitly political essays which follow on from this.

Finally, a word about the title of this volume. 'The Power to

Punish' is intended to signify a shift away from traditional moral and technical penology towards a political and social analysis of the institutions, practices and techniques through which that power is exercised. However, it should not be thought that penality is exclusively 'political' or that there exists, behind the penal complex, a newly discovered subject of history – 'power' itself.

The editors would like to thank the contributors for their co-operation and encouragement throughout the course of this project. We are indebted to Lydia Lawson, Isobel Crawler and Jeanette McNeill for their help in the production of this volume, and to the past and present staff of the Department of Criminology, Edinburgh University for their continuing advice and support.

The articles by Andrew Scull and Thomas Mathiesen are based upon earlier articles published by Academic Press. We gratefully acknowledge their permission to publish them here.

David Garland and Peter Young
Edinburgh

1 Towards a Social Analysis of Penality
David Garland and Peter Young

In recent years the study of punishment has undergone a remarkable transformation. Central to this development has been a fundamental shift in what are perceived to be the basic parameters of analysis. From being a technical, administrative discipline – epitomised by the notion of penology – the study of punishment is now increasingly considered to be an area of legitimate, even central, sociological concern. Although this development is welcome – indeed it is one of the purposes of this book to record it – it should not be imagined that the resulting product exhibits the degree of internal coherence or systematic nature which would warrant heralding it as a new discipline. Rather, the infusion of social theory has followed a more complex path and, as a consequence, has thrown up a number of often competing modes of explanation. As this book demonstrates, analyses run from those inspired by the work of Foucault, to those premised in a critical reading of more standard sociological classics such as Durkheim and Marx.

This state of ferment and debate is common in social science; indeed social science is by legend apparently unable to demonstrate or determine a framework which all its practitioners would hold in common. Whether this is inherent in the nature of social study or emanates from the possibly idiosyncratic proclivities of social scientists is not, for the moment, of tremendous importance. Of far greater significance is one of its ramifications which may be considered deleterious. This ferment and debate – or contestability – often subordinates what should be a central, indeed a logically prior question for any social analysis: under what conditions does its specified subject-matter become an object of knowledge? Too often, social analysis proceeds by taking it as obvious or as common sense that what it purports to investigate is naturally, and without further reflection, a genuine and self-evident object of knowledge; that social science proceeds by the gradual and ceaseless appropriation of one natural, empirical object after another.

An empiricist or positivist version of social science would, of course, find such procedures perfectly respectable. Indeed, for an empiricist this is the only way of conducting true science. However, it is an irony that the very state of social science as described above, which is often most lamented by empiricists, seems to belie this version of it. The very contestability of social science suggests that its objects of knowledge are not simple reflections of naturally occurring events, but that social science creates its own objects by a process of theoretical and, we would claim, practical relevances and reflections. As a type of knowledge, social science does not advance by reproducing snapshots of reality and explaining the connection between parts of them. Rather, for us, social science is a critical discipline in as much as the knowledge that it produces is subjected to a set of theoretical and practical criteria. Moreover, the authority of the criteria does not rest upon the correspondence they have with an immutable social world. An important impetus behind the work of all major theorists has been the possibility to talk of alternative social arrangements – that the prime reason for investigating the social is the desire to change it. In this sense, all social reflection is, as Hirst (1979) claims, a type of political calculation that imagines certain effects.

If this is accepted, then the crucial questions become ones defined not so much by the 'scientific' status of social inquiry and its 'practical implications', but ones surrounding the process by which objects – be they crime, punishment, law or sex – are generated as genuine fields of inquiry and the alternative social arrangements inherent and imagined in this. A central part of this process involves analysis of the conditions under which knowledge is produced, for it is only through an understanding of these conditions that it becomes possible to apprehend and assess both the status of the object – in this case, penality – as a genuine field of inquiry and to discern the nature of those alternative social arrangements envisaged.

From penology to the social analysis of penality

As mentioned earlier, this transformation in the study of punishment can be summarised as a development from penology to the social analysis of penality. To appreciate the profound nature of this transformation it is necessary to describe the nature of traditional penology as a form of knowledge, indicating its social foundations and its preferred explanatory form.[1] One issue that arises in such a description is the culturally specific nature of penology. Although British penology does share broad characteristics with similar types of endeavour in the United States and in Europe, its precise nature is bounded by a quite specific concatenation of social conditions. In a very profound sense, British penology is a determinate form of knowledge. It is a product of a complex interaction between a compromised positivistic conception of knowledge – the hegemony of jurisprudential and philosophical discourse and the pragmatic demands of an administrative framework, on the one hand, and a tradition of voluntary, charitably-based social work, on the other. Out of this complex has emerged a form of knowledge which can, at one and the same time, be both precise and infinitely flexible. British penology has been able both to exclude certain types of thought or social policy as irrelevant, yet offer, as an alternative, a type of knowledge which achieves its hegemony by its very obscurity, plurality of purpose and indefiniteness. In short, British penology legitimates itself both by denying its status as ideology and more simply, by fudging issues.

The positivism of British penology is compromised by two considerations. First, positivism in British intellectual life rarely had the stark features of scientism that are associated with the work of European theorists like Ferri (1917), or American reformers such as Healy (1922) or Wines (1895). Rather, positivism was received into British culture by a process of dilution and extension. The radical scientism and individualism of European positivism were transposed into a form of practice, 'opting for the promotion of progress through conciliatory reform rather than full scale social upheaval' (Carson and Wiles, 1971). The potentially revolutionary effects of systematically applying (even positivist) 'science' to all social or penal issues thus were mitigated by an overlay of traditional British pragmatism and empiricism. The empiricism of British intellectual life – its peculiarity – eschewed adherence to any 'philosophy' that seemed to demand the advocacy of singular causes or programmes. Instead, British penology absorbed positivism by relegating it to one of the possible modes of inquiry available in which to discuss particular problems or issues. Systematic corrections or treatment – the outgrowth of a purer positivism – find little place in the history of British penology or penal policy. For example, the Gladstone Committee, normally taken as the agency which introduced treatment to the British penal system, did not perceive treatment in its positivist guise; rather, 'treatment' is rendered as reform, evoking an evangelical and utilitarian tradition, not a scientific one. Moreover, reform was to be one of the *concurrent* aims of the system, not its sole or singular one. Again, as Rodman (1968) has argued, it is not really the case that 'treatment' or reform were suddenly adopted or emerged anew at a particular point in the history of penal policy. Rather, deterrence and reform were joint aims which were advocated simultaneously and coherently as early as Bentham and the 1779 Prison Act; British penology and penal policy have continually oscillated between the two, at one time privileging one, at another time the other.

The second consideration that compromises British penology has been, and still is, its genuflections to legal and jurisprudential thinking.

If treatment or reform are discussed, then this is in a context set by legal discourse. For British penology, the penal system is, above all, a legal institution. Law and legal decisions are given the right to define – even in theory – the character and possible significance of punishment, be it justified as reform, retribution or deterrence. The putatively scientific discourse of penology thus is made subject to the yoke of legal imperialism. As Rusche and Kirchheimer (1939) put it, there is a still prevalent tendency to endeavour to explain 'punishment' by its legally defined ends. Now, logically, there is nothing within positivism that required such compromise. Positivism – taken to one of its natural conclusions – must reject a legal definition of crime and punishment (see Garofalo, 1914). Crime and punishment (or treatment) ought to be behaviourally defined types of action, not limited to, or based upon, a prior legal definition.

As a consequence of these two conditions, British penology is best understood as a hybrid. Its empiricism, combined with the structures of legalism, results in a pragmatic, piecemeal form of knowledge that feeds on an assumed but broad consensus on 'the way ahead'. Although British penology may exhibit these pragmatic characteristics, it should not be thought that this results in it being completely open or formless. Rather, the scope and range of the 'discipline' is limited by, and tied to, quite specific demands emanating from the requirements of governments, the penal bureaucracy itself and the activities of charitably-based reformers (later to be social workers proper). On these occasions, when definite ideas of policy are promoted, they become subordinated to the details of the internal workings of organisations. For example, although a policy of classification of prisoners for treatment or reform did emerge in the last decades of the nineteenth century, the actual implementation of these classifications followed the demands of good prison discipline rather than individual treatment. As Sparks (1971a) has remarked of the present prison system, the day-to-day operation of that system is established more by the expedient provision of finance, staffing and other resources, than by any ideology on how one ought to deal with crime. Specific ideologies become sometimes distant modes of legitimation, secondary to the more general and overwhelming ideological emphasis on 'efficiency' and administration.

British penology carefully reflects this priority. It discusses crime and punishment 'scientifically' and legally, yet ties this to an ideology of administration that is remarkable for its facility to be infinitely flexible and variable, adopting that which functions to maintain its unchallenged credibility. As a consequence, British penology has a marked tendency to treat all questions as matters of technical efficacy rather than as constituting possible choices between substantively different ends. British penology thus is defined in terms of technique; but a technique which is not exhausted by any one particular justification. The flexibility of its notion of administration allows it to pay regard to any number of differing, even competing, theories and ideologies and turn them to its own purpose.

Rooted in this consensus, the practice and teaching of penology became, and in many ways remain, marginal to any attempt actually to explain the nature of the penal system. If these basic parameters are assumed, then the only viable questions become ones of description and improvement; of establishing techniques that allow the illusion of rational choice between other techniques. That such a stance is charged with politics is forgotten; technique and administration neutralise and castrate the political – they represent the political as irrelevant, the ideological as non-ideology. The theoretical boundaries of traditional penology therefore were (and, where it is still practised, remain) set by description, and its practice was limited by consensus. Questions concerning the social foundations of the penal realm and the possibility of legitimately exploring other foundations or different practices became, literally, unimaginable.

The move to the social analysis of the penal realm may be described as an attempt to break this mould by arguing, first, for an explanation of the social foundations of penality and second, by contending that an alternative range of practices is possible. Furthermore, as in traditional penology, it is proposed that the explanatory and the practical inter-mesh. Although the thrust to establish this social analysis emanates mostly from academics, it is characterised by a healthy appreciation of the need to discuss policy, to intervene in the practical. The essence of this social analysis therefore can be defined by dual objectives; the need to explain, and the conception that this is irrevocably tied to practice. Moreover, it is assumed that these are unified in the very process of producing knowledge.

The origins or social conditions underlying the emergence of this movement are complex and often paradoxical. In Britain, they begin in the late 1960s and early 1970s. In this period, criminological thinking was subjected to a number of challenges. First, 'labelling theory' challenged the traditional explanatory parameters of criminology. In particular, it suggested that explanation of crime was logically bound up with the explanation of social control. As Lemert (1967) put it, social control should not be regarded as a dependent variable following movements in criminal activity, but an independent one, having its own causal efficacy. This challenged orthodox criminology by making it necessary to consider social control in any explanation of crime, and also by reconnecting the links between crime and the political that orthodox criminology so easily severed.

As an analysis of control involves contemplation of law and law-making and of the function of control agencies (albeit within the limits set by conceptions like secondary deviance, and deviancy amplification), the connection between crime, punishment and politics becomes more easily apparent and therefore necessary to consider.

The criminology of the late 1960s and early 1970s thus became more 'political', in the sense of appreciating the theoretical and empirical links between crime and control. This appreciation was re-emphasised and extended by the emergence of radical or critical criminology (see Taylor, Walton and Young, 1973 and 1975). Basing itself within Marxism, critical criminology not only continued the challenge to orthodox criminology already begun by labelling theory and by bodies such as the National Deviancy Conference, but it also extended the challenge to a critique of these bodies themselves. Critical criminology asked for a further theoretical and empirical widening of scope and also for a more radical politics. Crime, it suggested, was not only to be analysed in the context of the low-level interactions conceived of by labelling theory, but within the political economy of capitalism. Crime, economy and the state are connected. Moreover, the problematic infusion of Marxism led to calls for a practice consummate with it. Crime could 'be solved' by a transposition in the mode of production; radical criminological politics are centred upon the possibility of a society in which 'socialist diversity' exists. As J. Young put it, 'images of deviance, are images of freedom' (Young, 1975).

Although this radicalisation of criminology was an essential pre-condition to the emergence of a desire to provide a social analysis of the penal realm, it cannot fully explain this development. An irony of this radicalisation is that, although it brought 'control' to the centre of the stage and called for forms of political practice linked to this, it never followed through the full implications of either position. First, though they may have called for an analysis of control, labelling theory and radical criminology never produced systematic accounts of it. Rather, the appreciation of control was tied to the traditional question of its significance in relation to crime. Control was important, but only as a vague 'force' which is logically entailed in explaining crime; the question of 'control' remained secondary to the question of crime. Second, the radical politics of these movements proved to be mostly limited to the written page or conducted in abstract. As Cohen (1979a) has pointed out, although criminology was reconceived of as politics, it never engaged the concrete issues and debates surrounding penal issues. The penal complex operates just as it did before, without regard to this movement. In other words, the 'progress' made by radical criminology was never played back into an account of the actual nature of the penal system – except in broad generalities – nor into changing penal policy. Questions of penal policy remained the property of the very traditional penology that we have described. The findings and politics of radical criminology seem to evaporate before the reality of that which it says is central and abiding; the politics of control. This is all the more surprising as this period witnessed in many countries the emergence of a number of struggles and radical movements in the area of penality – prisoners' rights litigations, PROP, RAP, KRUM – and saw general talk of a crisis in penal affairs.

Radical criminology thus put a theme upon a general agenda; it did not provide answers. The social analysis of penality could not, and cannot, be founded within such a criminology. What radical criminology could not provide was a framework which took the penal realm, rather than some general concept of control, as its object of knowledge. The subsequent development of this new framework of social analysis has been stimulated by a number of intellectual traditions. First, there has been a return to already established, but partially forgotten, texts such as Rusche and Kirchheimer's *Punishment and Social Structure* (1939, reissued 1968). *Punishment and Social Structure* has provided an early, but quite seminal influence upon the range of issues and mode of analysis deployed. As we argue later, the reductionism of this text makes it increasingly unsuitable as a vehicle for analysis, but it did, and possibly still does, constitute one of the best arguments for taking penality as a discrete object of knowledge. Rusche and Kirchheimer's basic contention, that 'there is no such thing as punishment, but only concrete systems of punishment', indicates both a general predisposition towards analysis as well as implying the need for concrete, historically specific investigations into particular penal practices.

Classical sociological work, in particular Durkheim's, has not been utilised to any great extent. This is surprising – and yet, given the prevailing and somewhat misguided predilection to regard Durkheim only as a functionalist, and to regard all functionalism as wrong – only to be expected. Notwithstanding this attitude, Durkheim's work on law and punishment amounts to a major argument for taking penality as a central concern for sociology. For Durkheim, punishment is not simply a minor or ephemeral part of social order; it is a defining characteristic. Sociality or solidarity can only be conceived of once a framework of norms and sanctions has been evolved. Garland's paper in this volume is one of the few attempts to come to terms with this tradition, yet also to argue for its limitations.

One of the major stimuli in this movement to construct a social analysis of the penal has been the work of Foucault. Although it emanates from a quite different intellectual tradition, Foucault's *Discipline and Punish* (1977a) now amounts to an orthodoxy for much work in the area. As Smart indicates in Chapter 3, there are a number of problems in this incorporation, not least the consideration that, in a very profound sense, the penal realm does not constitute a special object of knowledge for Foucault. Rather, for Foucault, the object of analysis is power, of which penality – be it discipline or torture – is but one representation. Moreover, there are good grounds for contending, as Bottoms does in Chapter 8, that Foucault's work is partial and distorts the nature of contemporary penality. However, even given this, any account of attempts to analyse penality would be seriously incomplete, if it did not pay attention to Foucault's work.

The appeal of Foucault's writing, perhaps, is the apparent utility of his work in solving an abiding sociological problem – how to connect a special object, like penality, with what are taken to be general and central sociological concepts like social structure or power. As Smart argues below, Foucault does this by the employment of genealogical analysis. The crucial question is whether Foucault's solution amounts to a general one for social analysis, or whether it is restricted to the internal coherence of his original scheme.

If these have been the major intellectual stimuli underlying the emergence of the social analysis of penality, it would be misguided to imagine that one can account for it only as an autonomous movement in the realm of ideas. The 1970s has been a period of profound crisis in the penal systems of the capitalist world. The insistent struggles of prisoners and inmates, the collapse of the belief in rehabilitation, the fiscal and discipline problems of the penal system, the possibility that we are undergoing a major transformation in penality (see the chapters by Cohen, Mathiesen and Scull below) have conjoined to make penality a highly political issue. The various intellectual traditions outlined above were not forged in isolation from these wider concerns. Either implicitly or explicitly, investigations of penality are irrevocably tied to a reflection on the political consequences of their analysis. Later in this essay, we outline the variety and nature of these consequences and their implications. At this stage, it is important to note that an essential theme in this tradition is a concern with the possibility of intervention, of the possibility and problems of practice. The social analysis of penality must be understood, as should social theory in general, as a form of political analysis and calculation.

This movement from penology to the social analysis of the penal realm is neither complete nor does it exclude the continued and profound influence of the former. Traditional penological reflection is still a powerful and consequential intellectual tradition. Moreover, as must be apparent from even the most cursory reading, this new form of analysis is one of potential; it does not, as we argued earlier, constitute a homogeneous discipline. On the contrary, at the moment, it amounts more to a commitment to a general type of analysis. In the following sections we review some of the problems that arise in constructing such analyses, and we attempt to offer some possible solutions.

Theorising 'punishment'

Once 'punishment' is installed as a serious object of theoretical and political analysis, the immediate problem which emerges is how to conceive of this object. What are the concepts and categories which will allow a knowledge of this phenomenon to be produced? Equally, what kind of knowledge will allow political interventions in this area to be promoted?

The formal characterisation of 'legal punishment' and the 'penal system' is not itself a major difficulty.[2] Although there is no doubt that terms such as 'criminal' or 'penal' present some ambiguities (for example, in the institutions of juvenile justice, or where 'rehabilitative' practices are concerned), for practical purposes it is possible to determine fairly precisely the formal parameters of the penal realm. The matrix of criminal and quasi-criminal sanctions imposed in law, and the institutions, practices and agencies which exercise and enforce these sanctions, are in fact quite clearly defined and identifiable *in legal terms*. Thus in this formal-legal sense, the field of study is already clearly demarcated.

The real difficulty arises when formal description gives way to redescription, explanation and analysis – at the point where the search for the social meaning and significance, or for the 'determinants' and 'conditions of existence', of these legal institutions begins. At this point, the agreed formal description is often quietly displaced in the analysis by a much more contentious conception which rethinks the phenomenon in its own theoretical terms.

Of course there can be no objection to this process whereby the legal or common-sense definition of the object gives way to a theoretical description. This is precisely the nature of critical social analysis. However, if we look closely at the various analyses which embark on this task of theorisation, we find that their theoretical constructs of 'punishment' are frequently quite different in nature and scope from the formal-legal definition that formed their starting-point. This difference is not merely a change of understanding in which the legal and common-sense knowledge of 'punishment' is replaced by a sociological, political or critical knowledge of the object. What also happens is that in this process of theorisation, part of the object is left behind, ignored or passed over without comment, while other aspects are seized upon, expanded and given pride of place in the theoretical analysis. In other words, the overall configuration of the 'penal system' is ignored, but particular sanctions or meanings are accorded a privileged place as somehow representative or expressive of the essence of 'punishment' itself. By this means, an analysis of particular penal aspects undergoes an unwarranted generalisation and claims to speak of 'punishment' as such.

This kind of theoretical operation faces a number of difficulties. Most obviously, it fails to 'account for all the facts': analyses which promote one particular aspect (for example, the prison, or 'discipline') to dominance have little to say about other features which are equally deserving of the term 'punishment' and which may threaten the privileged explanation. Secondly, in presenting this partial and selective vision, focused upon particular practices at the expense of others, the analysis may misrepresent the significance, function and effects of certain sanctions, because it fails to present them in their proper context. Specific institutions depend for their effects upon other institutions and practices which operate alongside them. Moreover, since significance is largely dependent upon difference, the meaning of a particular penal category or sanction will be determined in part by the alternative sanctions and categories which were not in fact used. (For example, the significance of a prison sentence for a young offender today, in the face of the large number of alternative dispositions such as probation, Borstal, detention centre, community service and intermediate treatment, is quite different from the significance of a similar prison sentence in the nineteenth century.) Thirdly, and in consequence, the power of these analyses can be easily undercut by means of a simple shift in focus. The analysis insists that 'punishment' has a particular character or significance; the critique points to a penal practice passed over in the analysis and shows it to have a different significance and the result is that the standing of the former analysis is seriously questioned.

This problem, however, is by no means peculiar to the study of 'punishment'. It is an abiding problem of any form of analysis which seeks to produce general patterns, connections and explanatory statements. However, this problem has been more serious than usual in the analysis of 'punishment'. Despite the fact that most of the available analyses have little hesitation in presenting their theories as applicable to 'punishment in general' (either by explaining it all, or else by revealing its true essence), very few of these analyses take the trouble to examine the institutions of 'legal punishment' in all their different aspects, or else to argue why this is unnecessary. We believe that the reason for this central failing has been the manner in which questions and investigations about 'punishment' have been posed.

Philosophy, sociology and 'punishment in general'
Leaving aside the tradition of technicist penology discussed above,[3] which deals only with the technical efficacy of specific practices and

abjures more abstract or critical questions, there are two main types of analysis undertaken in regard to 'punishment' – the philosophical and the sociological.

Normally the philosophical analysis is not in the least concerned with the specifics or mundane details of penal practice (Hart, 1968; Acton, 1969; Honderich, 1976). Its self-appointed task is to question 'punishment in general' in the hope of establishing some rationale or justification for the 'right to punish' (see Chapter 9). In order to do so, it begins with the (stated or unstated) recognition of a universal necessity to punish and control, then by a process of abstraction it elevates the discussion to one of the state, the individual and the general problem of coercion (incidentally reducing the problem to the base currency of liberal discourse). Having taken the side of this or that moral imperative, the problem is then resolved, still at this very general level, by stating the conditions which render 'punishment' morally sound, for example, punishment must be in accordance with the norms of retribution and just deserts (Bradley, 1927; Kant, 1965; Von Hirsch, 1976) or must promote the greatest good for the greatest number (Bentham, 1962) or must be undertaken for the benefit of the individual offender (Hegel, 1967; Plato, 1981) or some combination of these three (Hart, 1968; Rawls, 1972; Ball, 1979).

Of course this prescriptive moral position could then be used as a means to a detailed critique of the existing system. Perhaps significantly, it rarely is.[4] But the important point for our purposes is that within all of these philosophical texts, 'punishment' is presented and discussed as a singular, unitary phenomenon. The actual practices, institutions and sanctions are disregarded as mere empirical 'accidents' and manifestations – the object of analysis is seen as 'punishment itself'. A whole tradition of philosophical writing and debate conspires to present 'punishment' as something we can talk of and refer to in the singular, whilst disregarding the plurality and complexity of its empirical supports. Indeed, the fact that we continue to talk of the realm of penal sanctions in the singular term 'punishment' (and not 'corrections' or social defence) not only signifies the influence of penal philosophy in shaping our attitudes to the phenomenon, but also indicates which strand of philosophical argument has prevailed in British culture. The word 'punishment' bears the definite connotation of a retributive penalty for wrong-doing – a general connotation which is quite out of place with regard to a large number of the 'welfare sanctions', 'rehabilitative' practices and financial penalties which make up the modern system. (For a fuller discussion of this tradition, see Garland, 1983.)

When we turn to the various sociological analyses of 'punishment', we discover the same problem in a slightly different form. In contrast to the philosophical analyses, some effort is made to identify and examine the empirical practices and institutions of 'punishment' and to show how these empirical objects can be theorised and 'made sense of' in theoretical terms. Nevertheless, up to the present, there have been very few sociological analyses which have seriously attempted to deal with the whole empirical range of penal sanctions and practices. Instead, particular aspects of punishment are singled out, examined and made to do duty for the whole field. Thus Rusche and Kirchheimer (1939) focus upon those institutions, such as galley-slavery, the House of Correction, the early prison and the modern fine, which can be shown to have direct implications for the state's exploitation of labour power and its 'fiscal interests'. At the same time they denegate the significance of institutions and sanctions which fall outside the terms of this 'materialist' explanation – sanctions such as corporal punishment or solitary confinement are deemed unworthy of social explanation, and are presented instead as the contingent consequences of 'irrationality' or 'sadism'. Likewise, Durkheim (1964) singles out the elements of penal practice which can be termed 'retributive', arguing that penal law is the retaliatory public expression of the *conscience collective*. As for those sanctions and practices which might appear to operate according to a non-retributive logic, his theory denies their significance in advance by means of a stipulative definition of the essence of punishment (see Chapter 2). Pashukanis (1978) is equally partial in regarding (bourgeois) penal sanctions as determined by the form of equal and proportionate exchange conducted between the state and the offender on the model of a retrospectively constituted contract. Essentially the same criticism is applicable to Foucault (1977a) who ultimately presents 'discipline' as the essence or model of modern penal practice, to Ranulf (1964) and his concept of 'resentment', and to Sellin (1976) on the idea of slavery which is said to be both the origin and the essence of modern 'punishment'.

Why is it that these theories, each of which claims to be dealing with the same empirical object and to be dealing with it in its entirety, can be so consistently partial and limited as general theories of penal practice?

It seems to us that these limitations derive from the fact that in each case a more general sociological theory (historical materialism, Durkheim's sociology, Pashukanis' general theory of law, etc.) is being 'applied' to a particular empirical object ('punishment'). Because this procedure is adopted, it inevitably occurs that the pre-given propositions and statements of the general theory do damage to the integrity of the empirical object – focusing upon some of its features, explaining some of its aspects, at the cost of others. Of course in the normal run of things, such is the price that has to be paid for the insights and knowledge which emerge when a theory of general connections and relations is brought to bear upon a particular object or event. No general theory can ever exhaust the significance of a particular object – its utility lies in its powers of explanation, the ability it has to reveal connections, determinants and significance. In this sense all sociological knowledge is partial and limited. But once again we would argue that this problem has been more pronounced than usual in the analysis of penal practice. The general theories available are too partial, and too limited; the integrity of the object has been too readily destroyed.

This has been the case for two reasons. First, until now 'punishment' has rarely been a serious object of sociological analysis. Rather, it has formed an empirical area, tangential to the main sociological enterprise, to which various theories have been 'applied' with more or less interesting consequences. There are few sociological analyses which have begun with the phenomenon of 'punishment' as their main object of analysis, which have constructed concepts that would be appropriate to that object, or have designed questions that would pertain specifically to it. Secondly, we would argue that the intrinsic complexity of the penal realm is such that it suffers more than usual when forced into the terms of a pre-given theoretical framework. As we will see, 'punishment' inadequately references an institutional complex which supports a very wide range of social implications and effects.

Of course, it lies open to these general theories to admit that their explanations and analyses only partly explain the character of 'punishment' and then to await correction by a theory that takes into account the whole field of penality and accords significance on that basis. Or else, if such theoretical modesty is not enough, the theory in question could argue for its positions and explicitly justify focusing upon some aspects and disregarding others. Unfortunately these options are rarely adopted. Instead, the various theories in effect deny the complexity of the field of penal practices, assert the unity of 'punishment in general' and proceed to reduce it to their own particular terms.

Finally, and most importantly, this tendency to essentialism, simplification, and reductionism which we have identified also places severe limitations on the political utility of the theories in question. Practical intervention in penal issues requires that analytical knowledge of the conditions, functions and effects of penal practices is of a precise and detailed kind. The level of generality so far offered by sociological theories of 'punishment' has been altogether unhelpful in this respect.

Towards a theory of penal practice
Although we have no imperious desire to delimit in advance the kind of work that takes place in this field or to dictate a specific programme or

framework for research, we nevertheless feel that it may be worth specifying a number of points which we believe to be relevant to an adequate social analysis of penal practice. If the problems which we have identified in much contemporary penal analysis are to be overcome, the following positive principles of analysis may be of some value.

First of all, analyses should reject the question-begging notion of 'punishment' and install in its place a less tendentious term, such as the 'field of penal practices' or 'penality', which would signify a complex field of institutions, practices and relations rather than a singular and essential type of social event. Thereafter the analysis would be involved in a war on two fronts: first, against the reductionist tendency implicit in sociological and philosophical analysis, which would deny in advance the diversity and complexity of the object; and secondly, against the empiricist and technicist tendencies of conventional penology, which would narrow the field of inquiry and deny the connections and implications that penal practices have in regard to other social practices.

We are not suggesting that the only adequate analysis is one that takes in the whole field of penality and traces the whole range of its social connections and effects. Analyses are (and should be) produced in regard to specific issues from specific positions and with determinate objectives in view. But concrete analyses, for all their detailed focus and intent, must situate themselves within more general frameworks, if they are to be well founded. They must have some reasonable conception of the overall pattern within which they intervene. They must have a reasonable grasp of the relations between their specific object of study (for example, a particular sanction or institution, or a specific ideological discourse), and the other elements in the penal complex. They should also be aware of the general contours of that complex and its relations with its 'outside'. Similarly, the study that views penality only from one aspect (for example, the legal, or the economic, or the ideological) nevertheless requires some knowledge of the other aspects of the phenomenon, if only to delimit the claims and pertinence of the investigation.

Nor are we suggesting that this general theoretical framework can ever be anything more than a schematic, tentative outline which roughly constructs the parameters of the field of study, only to be redefined and reconstructed by the concrete investigations that it promises. Nevertheless, if penality is to become a coherent object of analysis, attracting systematic and sustained investigation, then a start must be made in tracing the nature of its parameters.

The problem of internal differentiation

In any analysis of penality – whether it is a specific study of a particular
practice or a more general view of the field as a whole – it is of the first
importance that the internal *differentiation* of the penal realm should
be acknowledged and respected. As we have indicated above, too many
texts discuss 'punishment' as if it was all of a piece, or else discuss one
particular element (for example, the prison, or 'rehabilitation', or 'discipline') on the unargued assumption that it is somehow representative
of the whole field.

The penal realm is not a singular, coherent unit. It is a complex network composed of a variety of different institutions, practices and relations supported by a number of agencies, capacities and discourses.[5]
This complex is made up of a multiplicity of different institutions (criminal and quasi-criminal courts, Home Office departments, prisons,
detention centres, List D schools, social work and probation services,
assessment centres, psychiatric institutions, community homes, etc.),
each of which has differential access to legal, jurisdictional, financial
and other resources and each of which produces differential penal and
social effects. Each one of these institutions is, in turn, composed of a
variety of different internal practices and procedures. The prison, for
example, does not merely incarcerate; in its various forms it subjects
inmates to practices of scrutiny, assessment and classification and
thereafter to a large number of different regimes which may involve
'training', industrial labour, solitary confinement, isolation,
'therapy', numerous forms of deprivation and prohibition, and so on.
A similar complexity of procedures operates within the other penal or
'penal-welfare' institutions.

Again, within and across these institutions there exists a large number of different agencies of decision-making (sentencing agencies,
individual prison and probation officers, prison governors, social
work teams and directors, Boards of Visitors, Parole Boards, Prison
Department officials, Home Office ministers, Parliament, etc.), each
operating according to specific criteria and forms of calculation, on the
basis of different forms of knowledge, training and 'expertise', and
with a variety of powers and objectives. And of course operating
throughout these institutional differentiations is a diverse variety of
discourses and ideologies (operational languages of classification and
categorisation, ideologies of rehabilitation and reform, of 'just
deserts' and retribution, of 'less eligibility' and legality, conceptions
of 'man management' as well as psychological and criminological discourses, social work knowledge, 'law and order' ideologies, etc.),
which overlay the penal network and find concrete expression in the
practices of institutions as well as in judicial decisions, government
policy documents, official reports and parliamentary rhetoric. One
only has to list these penal elements to make it perfectly clear that

complexity and contradiction within and between them is every bit as probable as coherence and cohesion.

Now it may be, as some would claim, that all of these differences are merely formal or superficial and that, in effect, the penal complex hangs together – whether around the logic of justice, crime control or 'discipline'. But be that as it may, it should be clear that any such unity must be argued for, evidenced and analytically demonstrated. Analyses which merely assert this unity or else presuppose it in their analytical categories by talking a priori of 'punishment in general' are fundamentally inadequate. And if, for example, it is to be claimed that certain *strategies* are operative within the penal realm (see Foucault, 1977a; Garland, 1981), then it becomes crucial to demonstrate how the various agencies and practices relate to the strategy's logic, how this is made compatible with the different forms of calculation and objectives which are present, and how the overall strategic effect is achieved and reproduced.

Before proceeding to a discussion of penality's relations to 'external' institutions and social relations, there are a number of points to be made concerning the internal characteristics of penality and the manner in which these should be regarded. First of all, reference must be made to the penal discourses (for example, the various penal philosophies and criminological theories) which operate in this realm.

It has frequently been the case that terms such as 'reformation', 'rehabilitation' or 'retribution' have been presented as analytical or descriptive concepts which can provide a framework with which to analyse and criticise penal practices (for example, Walker, 1969; Bean, 1976 and 1981). The same is true of a number of criminological discourses which specify the causes of criminality and the appropriate correctionalist response (the various forms of child psychology, behavioural psychology, social work discourse, and the positivist criminologies which condense and reformulate these knowledges) (Wootton, 1959 and 1963; Bottoms and McClintock, 1973). There can be no logical objection to analyses which take their stand upon any of these philosophical or theoretical positions in order to criticise penality from their standpoints. But we would argue that the fact of the practical inclusion of these concepts, discourses and philosophies *within* the field of penality requires that they themselves be subjected to scrutiny and analysis. For example, the term 'rehabilitation' has for nearly a century functioned as an important ideological element within government policy documents, political rhetoric and in the public presentation of penal practice. As such it demands analysis as a functioning element within the penal complex.

Analyses should not be content to ask whether or not penal practices do in fact produce the 'rehabilitative effect', or whether or not they operate according to their rehabilitative claims. They should go on to deconstruct the term itself, asking what range of meanings and implications have been signified under the sign of 'rehabilitation'? How has this term been employed in official and criminological discourses? What have been its social and ideological effects? In other words, the discursive and ideological elements of the penal complex must become objects of analysis in their own right. To analyse an institution in its own terms is always to limit radically the questions which can be asked of it and to predetermine the answers which will be given. Thus, for example, the terms provided by penal philosophies usually presuppose that penality is to be understood solely as a response to crime; likewise, the terms of the establishment penologies assume that it is to be understood primarily as a means of transforming pathological individuals (see Garland, 1983).

Precisely the same considerations apply with regard to the fragments of criminological and penological theory which have become imbricated in official penal practices and institutions. The question of the veracity of these theories, and of their penological success or failure, needs to be supplemented – and in fact preceded – by other inquiries concerning the conditions under which these knowledges became established within the penal complex. For the purposes of these inquiries, it is necessary to suspend (or at least, reformulate) the question of the scientific or epistemological standing of these knowledges and instead question their operative function, their strategic effects, and the conditions which allowed these, and not other knowledges, to become empowered. For even if we were, for the moment, to allow these doubtful criminological theories the status of 'science', the history of penal practice makes it clear that scientificity and rationality do not guarantee recognition or employment in the realm of penality.

Sanctions and representations: the two realms of penal practice
It will be clear from the above section that we consider it unhelpful to analyse penal practices solely on the basis of what these practices say about themselves. The public presentation of the prison in terms of 'rehabilitation' or 'training' or even 'humane containment'; of probation in terms of 'welfare' and 'caring supervision'; of detention centres in terms of 'physical discipline' and 'short sharp shocks', etc. should be treated first of all as precisely that – a *public (re)presentation*. Far from disregarding this, or else using it unquestioningly as a basis for analysis, analyses should scrutinise these representations, asking how they operate at the ideological level, how they function to shape political and public consciousness, and what effects they have in structuring the available social knowledge of penal affairs.

Indeed we might go so far as to suggest that in conceptualising the penal complex, it is necessary to introduce a radical distinction between the operational realm of sanctions, institutions and physical practices and the public realm of representations, significations and symbolic practices. (However, this must be understood as an *analytical* distinction and not a real one – the structure of physical institutions, like the materiality of physical sanctions, produce their own ideological effects; see Carlen (1976) on the symbolic effects of court rooms, and Foucault (1977a) on prison buildings and corporal sanctions.) This second level of analysis, the realm of representation, should be regarded not as the 'theory' of the practical level, nor as its ideational reflection, but rather as a separate realm of penal discourse composed of policy statements, political rhetorics, penal philosophies and institutional propaganda. It is in this public realm of signification, quite removed from the less visible practices of the institutions themselves, that public knowledge about penal practice is primarily formed, specific problems are defined, possibilities are constructed and legitimations are offered. The form of analysis appropriate to this realm is consequently a form of *reading*. It requires that its elements (texts, utterances, theoretical discourses, rhetorics, signs) be differentiated and analysed in terms of their structures, their chains of reference and social meaning, and their ideological effects (see Chapter 5 of this volume; also Burton and Carlen, 1979). This reading would involve analysis of a number of different kinds of text (the official and unofficial, the public document and the in-house report, the theoretical and the rhetorical, etc.) in relation to a number of different audiences (penal functionaries, Parliament, the general public, etc.), and the problem of tracing the ideological effects would also involve a number of different levels (for example, the offender, his/her family, the morale of penal agents, the terms of political debate, 'public opinion', etc.).

The form of analysis appropriate to the realm of actual sanctions is also a form of reading, but of course its materials are quite different. This realm is the sphere of institutions, practices and practical discourses and the initial problem is to describe the concrete, detailed nature of these practices in order to allow a reading of their social effects. As was implied above, the official descriptions of the nature and objectives of these practices should not be uncritically accepted: the actual practices of the prison cannot be deduced from the Prison Rules (Rule No. 1: 'encourage prisoners to lead a good and useful life') any more than the objectives of probation can be summarised in the statutory imperative to 'assist, advise and befriend'. The objectives, purposes and effects of specific practices can only be identified on the basis of concrete empirical analyses.

This (potential) difference between official objectives and objectives-in-operation has a number of causes. First, the practical objectives which structure penal practices are rarely stated explicitly in the rhetorics and representations which accompany them. It is not only that official discourse misrepresents official practice, or that in practice institutions displace or transform their initial objectives, although both of these tendencies certainly occur (Blumberg, 1974; Carlen, 1976; Foucault, 1977a). In addition, the terms in which these objectives are officially stated, for example, as 'rehabilitation', 'training' or 'care and supervision', are so indefinite that they leave everything to empirical elaboration – the precise meaning of these terms can only be identified at the concrete level of practice. And relatedly, practices such as probation work or social supervision leave a good deal to the particular agents and functionaries involved. Before the objectives and practical ideologies of probation and social work can be properly described, it is necessary to pay close attention to the variations and possibilities which have been explored within these frameworks: for example, the attempts to practise a radical social work or a democratic psychiatry where the objectives-in-operation may be subversive of the official objectives (Corrigan and Leonard, 1978; Probe, 1980; Basaglia, 1981; Bolger *et al.*, 1981; Walker and Beaumont, 1981). Only on the basis of this kind of information and analysis can one begin to evaluate particular practices and to examine their contradictions and potential for transformation.

In addition to describing the ideologies and practical objectives which are set in motion in the various penal practices, an important problem for penal analysis is to trace and describe the techniques and modes of control which operate at the various levels of the complex. We see no reason to assume that the penal network uniformly relies on a singular mode of control, and would argue that a plurality of modes can be identified, each of which operates in a particular fashion and with specific conditions and effects. Thus in line with the contemporary work of Foucault (1977a) and Donzelot (1980), we would point to *disciplinary* modes and techniques (that is, practices of physical *dressage*) identifiable in detention centres, prison regimes, Borstals, etc. and to the various techniques of *normalisation* utilised in probation work, social casework and through the various residential welfare institutions. But these modes and techniques are by no means exclusive or omnipotent, and we would argue that alongside them exist a number of other forms. These include forms of *financial control* (particularly through the fine, compensation orders, restitution, etc.), which operate by quite different means to produce a form of self-discipline and internalised control in an 'automatic' manner, without the requirement of personal intervention by a penal agent (see Chapter 8). Another common mode of control works by means of *incentive schemes* that reward the 'good behaviour' of inmates with minor privileges – which in an atmosphere of deprivation can take on major subjective importance – and prevent indiscipline by the threat of their withdrawal (see Thomas, 1972). This particular technique also operates *between* institutions (for example, the network of mental institutions of more or less rigour, the movement from 'hard' to 'soft' prisons, and then to semi-release or 'open' regimes) and since the 1890s has formed an important aspect of the penal network's operation.

Again, we would point to the persistence of the *classical legal penalty*, unmarked by the modern methods of disciplinary control, which merely responds to a criminal offence with a pre-specified and 'proportionate' penalty, and has no regard to the character, conditions or needs of the offender (the use of fines in relation to corporate crime is an obvious example). No doubt empirical investigation would identify other regulatory modes (for example, of tutelage, or of behaviour modification – see Chapter 5) which could be added to this list. The problem for research (and thereafter for political practice) is to identify these modes, their contradictions and their relations one to the other. On this basis, it becomes possible to evaluate them and to investigate their potential for progressive transformation (for example, the possibilities for democratic accountability and regulation, for popular involvement, etc.) or else for abolition.

Penality and other social relations

Having dealt at some length with the internal differentiations and mechanisms of the penal complex, we now turn briefly to the question of penality's relation to its 'outside' – that is, to the multiplicity of 'non-penal' social relations and institutions which appear formally external to it (politics, ideology, the economy, power structures, etc.). Once more, we feel that it is necessary to rethink this problem in a quite fundamental way.

As we have noted above, penal practices have conventionally been dealt with either in a narrow technicist manner – as a simple response to crime – or else within the terms of a philosophical tradition which sees 'punishment' as a singular and universal kind of social event with particular moral implications. In either case, the 'social context' within which penal practices take place becomes marginal to the analysis: marginal in the first case because the problem is of a technical nature which concerns the means to a specific end; marginal in the second because the 'problem of punishment' is posed in an abstract and universalist manner. Within these two frameworks the specific social location of penal practice is of little or no significance.

As we have seen, recent developments have led to the questioning of these frameworks and to the posing of problems concerning the relationship of 'punishment' to 'society' or to 'social structure'.

However, there is a danger that this relationship between the realm of penality, on the one hand, and of society, on the other, may be seen as an *external* relationship between two separately constituted and mutually exclusive realms. Already this kind of approach appears in a number of 'social histories' of 'punishment', which conceive of the relationship in this way, and are therefore obliged to rely upon weak notions of 'influence' or the unspecifiable 'pressure' of one realm acting upon the other (Rose, 1961; Hibbert, 1963; Radzinowicz, 1966).

In contrast to this, we would conceive of penality as a specific *institutional site* which is traversed by a series of different social relations. Political, ideological, economic, legal and other social relations do not merely, 'influence' or 'shape' or 'put pressure upon' penality – they *operate through it* and are materially inscribed in its practices. Penality is thus an over-determined site which relays and condenses a whole series of social relations within the specific terms of its own practices.

In order to appreciate the complex social functions and effects of penality we must cease, once and for all, to understand it as merely a negative response to criminality. The significance of penality is not limited to technical issues of crime control, nor can its social aspect be limited to the social pressures which limit or suggest the forms which this negative response should take (Mead, 1918; Rusche and Kirchheimer, 1939; Durkheim, 1964; Erikson, 1966). Of course, crime and crime control do play some part in determining penal practice, but they are by no means the whole story. 'Crime' no more determines the character of penality than 'human need' determines the specific nature of the economy.

Of course, if one begins by asserting the existence of 'crime' or 'anti-social behaviour', then we can grant that this might necessitate – and in that sense 'determine' – some kind of regulatory or penal response. But the possibility of that response, and its precise nature, form and content, would *not* be determined in all its aspects by the 'crime problem', nor would its social functions and effects be necessarily confined to the space of crime and its control. In any case, there is no need to grant the primacy of crime, either logically or historically. We might argue just as readily that penality defines and determines criminality: in specifying the types of behaviour which are to count as crimes (through the criminal law), in identifying those actual behaviours which fall into these categories (through the courts) and in producing a social knowledge of the official significance and character of criminality (as moral, medical or legal fact).

Once we reject the notion of penality as simple negativity, the problem becomes how to specify and describe the positive characteristics which are asserted. Various writers have presented different elements as *the* positive and defining characteristic of penality (see Durkheim (1964) on social solidarity, Rusche and Kirchheimer (1939) on the exploitation of labour power, etc.), but there is no need to elect one or other characteristic of penality and proclaim it to be the one and only true significance. Rather, we would reiterate the complexity of the phenomenon and the dense and extensive social significance which it possesses. The penal complex supports a series of social relations which include political, ideological, economic, sexual, legal, educational and religious relations, not to mention its production of 'therapeutic' and 'client' relations and its underlying and pervasive relations of force. There is every reason to promote analyses which focus upon any one of these aspects. Moreover, penality often presents material of crucial importance for a number of more general studies. Thus in relation to politics, penality is perhaps the clearest and most extreme example of the state's routine coercive power and its legitimation, and we would argue that the relationship between forms of penality and forms of citizenship is of the first importance for an understanding of the nature of political relations (see Foucault, 1977a; Young, 1980; Garland, 1981). In the realm of ideology and its analysis, penality presents a vivid illustration of an ideology which forcibly sanctions its own categories (see Edelman, 1979), and its symbolism is perhaps one of the most powerful types of ideological signifiers in modern society (see Hall *et al.*, 1978). Again, when we come to ask questions about the legal significance of penality, we find that modern penal practice continually disrupts and modifies the usual legal concepts and categories (for example, the denial of the responsibility of legal subjects, the modification of categories of 'guilt' and 'right' by notions of determination and need, etc.) (Garland, 1981) and is consequently an area of some importance for legal studies.

However, although penality may be separately viewed from within any of these disciplines, and although the specific features of penality may be differentiated analytically, it is vital to recognise that in the penal realm these various relations are actually *fused* in a series of *condensed* and *complex* relations. Individual penal sanctions condense a number of different relations and it is necessary to acknowledge this, if an analysis capable of supporting political action is desired. An offender who is sentenced to imprisonment becomes the object of a relation of *force* (resistance will be met with physical coercion and violence 'if necessary'), which is at one and the same time *legal* (it is an authoritive order of the court, the prison is a legally authorised place of detention, its officers have legal powers at their disposal, the law specifies that prisoners shall not have the rights and capacities available to other citizens, etc.); *political* (the basis and limits of that authority and that force are ultimately political, as is the definition and enforcement of the criminal law; the form of the sanction is politically conditioned, etc.); *ideological* (the prison carries specific symbolic connotations which mark the prisoner, his act and his family; prison architecture and practices carry particular signifiers – isolation, work, reward, discipline, obedience, etc.); and *economic* (the prisoner will be made to labour, his family will be financially disadvantaged, his work record and national insurance contributions will be interrupted, he will have difficulty regaining employment, the 'free' labour-market will be deprived of his labour, he will be deskilled, etc.). Of course, if the offender happens to be female, she will be subjected to a number of differential practices (as indeed will certain male 'sex offenders'), indicating the real pertinence of sexual relations in this realm. No doubt the forms of assessment, classification and supervision which occur during and after the prison sentence will also invoke various criminological, psychiatric or social work knowledges and the therapeutic or client relations which these establish.

Clearly, then, the penal sanction of imprisonment is a complex condensation of a whole series of relations. The same is true of other penal sanctions. These relations are neither external nor accidental in relation to penality. They are part of its structure, of its significance and of its effects. Each type of relation at once operates through penality and at the same time links penality into a direct connection with other social realms and institutions (the political realm, the ideological formation, social policy, the legal system, the economy, etc.). The task of social analysis is to lay bare these connections and relations, to demonstrate how they enter into penal practices and policies, and to explain penality in the light of that knowledge. In political terms, this promotes the double effect of viewing penality in all its complexity *and* of reconnecting penal issues with more general political struggles.

Marxism and penality

In the following section we will consider recent endeavours to theorise and situate 'the penal question' within Marxism. We undertake this task both because Marxism constitutes one of the most powerful forms of social analysis available and because, recently, Marxism has focused quite specifically on the broad area of law, legality and penality (see Hall *et al.*, 1978; Pashukanis, 1978; Poulantzas, 1978; Edelman, 1979; Hirst, 1979). Moreover, as we will endeavour to illustrate, the theoretical, methodological and empirical problems engendered by this focus have a direct bearing upon some of the issues raised in previous sections. More specifically, we will examine the problems generated for traditional Marxist explanations by the desire to constitute law and penality as specific objects of knowledge. Broadly speaking, we will argue that these problems 'open up' the traditional Marxist metaphor of 'base and superstructure' and imply a more flexible mode of analysis than that traditionally envisaged. However, one issue that arises for us in achieving this objective is that few Marxist accounts as yet take the penal realm as their specific object of analysis. Rather, the focus on penality tends to remain implied by a more general one on ideology and law. Consequently, although some of the ensuing comments may seem general and unrelated to the question of penality, they are nevertheless necessary, if the potential of Marxism for this area is to be appreciated.

The emergence of Marxist accounts of law and penality can be traced to some quite fundamental shifts within Marxism. Recently, there has been a major theoretical and political re-evaluation of the relationships between 'base' and 'superstructure' (see Hall, 1977). Superstructural elements have been re-evaluated as of much greater significance, both in a theoretical and a political sense, than more traditional economistic versions of Marxism allow. This new priority given to the superstructure has had quite far-reaching ramifications, the full impact of which have yet to be realised. Concisely, these ramifications consist of a questioning of received Marxist ideas of casuality; if the superstructure (that is, political, legal, ideological, sexual relations, etc.) is more than an economic reflex, can the traditional notion of economic materialism be maintained? Moreover, if the causal relationship between base and superstructure is revamped, what is the continued analytical power of the architectural metaphor itself? We will return, briefly, to look at these questions later on. Our priority here is first to describe the nature and range of Marxist attempts to analyse penality.

Contemporaneously, we may discern three trends within these endeavours.

(1) A traditional economistic perspective, in which penality is linked directly with some notion of the economy.
(2) A broadly 'structuralist' response to economism associated with the work of Althusser and Poulantzas, within which prime significance is given to a re-evaluation of the political and ideological as independent or relatively autonomous entities.
(3) A humanist and/or historicist rendition of Marxism, which counterposes itself both to economism and structuralism.

Traditional economistic perspective
The economistic perspective is most closely associated with the work of Rusche and Kirchheimer (1939). Their basic thesis is that penal

measures are directly connected with the mode of production. Thus, for them, each distinct form of economy demands an equally distinctive type of penality; a slave mode of production 'requires' or necessitates penal sanctions involving slavery; capitalism necessitates the prison and the fine. For Rusche and Kirchheimer, the manifestations and meaning of the economy appear to take two forms: either penal measures are directly related to the labour-market and the exploitation of labour power, or else they are the product of 'fiscal' motives which are the real antecedent causes behind specific sanctions. For example, the 'causes' of the prison are rendered as a mode of compulsory labour in times of labour shortage. The prison is conceived of as a type of proto-factory, administered primarily for profit rather than for 'punishment'. Or again, alternatives to the prison are accounted for as attempts to offset the fiscal costs necessarily incurred by the state of imprisoning people once it no longer constitutes a profitable exercise.

As Melossi (1977 and 1979) has argued, these notions of the economic domain are unduly restrictive and are only tangentially related to a full Marxist concept of the mode of production. They include no idea of the mode of production as a social relationship and neither can they account for the emergence of the ideological forms of discipline which overlay the 'economic' functions variously associated with the prison or with alternatives to it. Rusche and Kirchheimer, thus, are reductionist in a dual sense. Not only is their concept of the economy inadequate, but their framework is unable to conceive of ideological relations let alone explain them. Both these problems become apparent in their explanation of the economic foundations of the prison. As has been stated, although Rusche and Kirchheimer attribute economic causes to the existence of the prison, they admit also that, paradoxically, the prison became the 'normal' means of punishment at that point in time when these economic causes receded. The rise of a technologically more sophisticated 'free' factory system, the more plentiful supply of free labour, the agitation of trade unions, all combined to destroy the profitable foundation to prison enterprise. Now, if the causes of the prison were purely economic – in the sense of either supply and demand of labour or fiscality – then this institution should no longer exist. As prisons manifestly still do exist, Rusche and Kirchheimer's economistic explanation is clearly limited. One obvious possible account for the continued existence of the prison could be sought within its ideological function as a form of state 'repression' and legitimation. However, as Rusche and Kirchheimer do not provide the concepts by which to adequately 'think' the state or the ideological, recourse to such an account is rendered impossible.

It should not be thought that economic-reductionist notions of penality are limited to the work of Rusche and Kirchheimer. Recently, a similarly reductionist account of penality, albeit in a more sophisticated form, has emerged from within the 'capital logic' school. John Lea (1979), for example, has recently rekindled economism by posing the valorisation of capital as the key determinant in explaining penality. The 'state form', ideological concepts of discipline, etc. are made to follow, quite directly, 'the delicate balances of monetization . . . and capital' (Lea, 1979: 89).

Although this may constitute a more sophisticated, more traditional version of the mode of production than that of Rusche and Kirchheimer, its explanatory logic is identical. A key problem for Marxism in general, and economism in particular, is to establish criteria that allow the 'economic' to be thought of as a definite and separate instance. Usually in Marxist accounts, these criteria are supplied by an appeal to or an argument from authority. Some snippet of Marx, Engels or even Lenin's writing is quoted and given authority as the point from which to proceed. This is not to assert that assumptions do not lie at the base of every explanation. Rather, the point is that when this assumption contains the very essence of the rest of the account, then the validity of the argument must rest more or less entirely on the fullness and explanatory adequacy of its premises (see Chapter 2). As the adequacy of the concept of economy is rarely discussed by Marxist explanations, many of them, in consequence, appear closed and inward looking. Revisionism is an issue precisely because it challenges this authority and makes problematic both the veracity of the explanation and the process by which it is produced.

Structuralist response to economism
One of the promises of structuralist versions of Marxism is that, on occasion they seem to lead to these challenges. The work of Althusser (1969 and 1971), though retaining a determining role for the economy 'in the last instance', marks a notable stage in the movement to reassess the significance of the superstructure. Althusser's basic argument was to contend that a mode of production or a social formation consists of a variable combination of several definite instances or elements. For Althusser, a social formation is composed of three instances; the economic, the political and the ideological. Althusser's significant contribution was to propose that domination and class struggle always operate in and through the realms of politics and ideology as well as the economy, and that moreover in a specific historical 'conjuncture', it need not be the economic instance that is 'dominant'; rather, the ideological or political could take precedence.

Fidelity to traditional Marxism was maintained both by conceiving of the possibility of the economic, in certain circumstances, being the superordinate level and in retaining a 'last instance' determining role for it.

The 'superstructure' therefore plays a far more important role in structuring relationships than reductionist forms of Marxism allow. In particular, the state is given a vital role as the instance which is responsible for the reproduction of the conditions of continued capitalist expansion. Both Althusser and Poulantzas have endeavoured, with varying degrees of system, to construct a theory which describes the precise nature of the state, its 'functions' and its relationship with the economy. The state is described as 'relatively autonomous', as being either the site of class struggle or guaranteeing reproduction and, therefore, as serving certain vital functions. For Althusser, the state's reproductive functions are, in part, secured by the operation of two kinds of apparatus – the repressive and the ideological. Law and penality traverse these apparatuses; they are conceived of as operating both by coercion and by ideological representations. Similarly, for Poulantzas (1973 and 1978), albeit with a more systematic theory, law and penality are absorbed into and explained in terms of the functions of the capitalist state. The state's 'relative autonomy' makes it, at one and the same time, both the condensation of class forces, yet also, able to resist instrumental manipulations and use by direct class (or economic) intervention. The capitalist state thus appears as institutionally neutral, and therefore legitimate, but this neutrality is circumscribed by its 'in the last instance' class basis. Moreover, this relative autonomy and 'neutrality' are important because they allow room for alternative forms of politics not envisaged by conceptions of pure and instrumental class forces.

The new significance lent to the superstructure by Althusser and Poulantzas has both a theoretical and a political import. Theoretically, it leads to a revision, or at least a questioning, of the literal economism of the base–superstructure metaphor. If the superstructure is not a simple reflection of economy, then some new notion of causality is suggested. At present, Marxism seems unable or unwilling to follow through the implications of this suggestion. Politically, the independence of the superstructure constitutes it as a potential forum for political activity and possible change. Conscious political intervention thus does not fall instant victim to unyielding and immutable economic forces.

The renewed interest in the work of the Soviet legal theorist Pashukanis (see Pashukanis, 1978; Fine *et al.*, 1979) has extended this revisionism or questioning of the utility of traditional Marxist explanations in two ways. First, Pashukanis's emphasis upon the legal form, and upon its role in constituting basic capitalist, economic categories, takes further the ramification of structuralist thinking. Pashukanis argues that fundamental economic categories – private property, individual rights, contract, etc. – are not naturally occurring phenomena, but are historical and *legal* constructions. Private property is a legal, not simply an economic conception; similarly, capital is embedded in a legal framework, it does not operate in the market in purely 'economic' terms. Second, Pashukanis contended that criminal law and 'punishment' epitomise the capitalist legal form; they are defined in terms of the atomic, legally recognised, right-bearing subject; they are composed of an exchange relationship analogous to the exchange of commodities (the fine – that is, monetary exchange or transfer – being the exemplary form).

Apart from the obvious specific relevance of Pashukanis's work to an analysis of penality, his work extends this tendency to dissolve traditional Marxist explanatory metaphors. If there are no self-sustaining epistemological criteria upon which to demarcate the economic as an independent social realm, then the very idea of a social formation divided into instances, categories or elements becomes otiose. In terms of what we have argued earlier in this paper, this has important implications.

Earlier we identified one crucial problem in establishing a framework for the social analysis of penality. This was how to focus upon the penal realm as a specific object of knowledge, yet also to analyse its relationship to other institutions and types of relationship. One of the problems of employing existing explanatory schemes is that, although they may place the penal in a 'social context', they do so at the expense of destroying its specificity as an object of analysis; there exists a constant and apparently irredeemable tension between the particular (object) and the general (explanatory form). The recent developments in Marxism which we have reviewed exhibit some of the consequences of this tension. Their continual qualification of the base–superstructure metaphor, at points, despite their unwillingness to follow through the logic of their approach, are object lessons for the theorist. They raise acutely the question of how to resolve this tension between general and particular, possibly suggesting that the solution may lie in a serious revision of the general.

Humanist/historicist versions

The third strand of Marxism – the humanist/historicist – on occasions appears to advocate just this solution. E. P. Thompson (1975 and 1978) has argued systematically that the base–superstructure metaphor, especially in its application to detailed historical research on law and class, is of restricted utility. Thompson perceives its major deficiency to be its supposed proclivity to destroy the dynamic and the contingent in history by portraying historical events as determined and necessary. For Thompson, history is a contingent possibility rooted in the consciousness of actors who struggle. Law and penality are not restricted to a particular level, but, as Thompson declares in his investigation of eighteenth-century law, they are 'every bloody where'. No neat distinction can be maintained between legal, economic or political instances; all are intermeshed and inseparable. Thompson seems to recognise that one consequence of this argument is to compromise any clear and general concept of causality between 'forces' or factors in the history of societies. Rather, 'cause' is transposed to the level of consciousness and action played out against a backdrop of the need to control or expropriate the material means of existence. Thompson's recent, apparently unqualified, approval of what other Marxists regard as the epitome of the repressive bourgeois legal form – the 'rule of law' – becomes, in these terms, comprehensible. For Thompson the rule of law is a defence and protector of consciousness and humanity – the motor forces of history.

One can accept Thompson's rejection of the base–superstructure metaphor without endorsing his preferred alternative to it – an almost romantic invocation of humanism and the British empirical mode of historical consciousness. What is of salience for us is Thompson's refusal to sort out 'society' into preconceived layers, between which certain necessary and pre-given patterns of causality hold, before a detailed examination of the object in question – penality – has commenced. The specificity of the penal realm can only be captured by regarding its relationship to other parts of the social formation as one of the topics to be demonstrated and explained, not simply assumed.

In this light, the potential of Marxism to provide a framework for the social analysis of penality has yet to be realised. We have endeavoured to demonstrate how recent attempts to focus on law and penality have raised questions of quite fundamental significance for Marxism. The promise of it as a general theory can only be realised once those questions are resolved and its analyses are developed through concrete investigations of penality.

Theory and practice

It has long been an objective of social science to unify theory and practice. Indeed, one of the very purposes of sociological theorising has always been not only to analyse the social world but also to change it. The desire to 'change the world', to solve 'social problems', is as basic to Weber and Durkheim's work as it is to Marxism. Our earlier contention that theorising penality should be concerned with the practical is thus no innovation; we are simply reactivating an abiding tradition of social thought. However, although this may be the case, it is equally true to observe that this desire has had a dismal history; seemingly no sooner are we offered a version of enlightenment, than it is followed by recourse to a deep despair.

It is beyond the scope of this essay to account fully for these failures. Our aims are more limited. In this final section we shall focus first upon the potential of a social analysis of penality to be 'practical', and second, briefly to comment on those issues which might appear on an alternative agenda of penal reform.

Much of the discussion surrounding theory and practice is founded upon the assumption that the theoretical and the practical constitute quite distinctive forms of knowledge; that theoretical knowledge inhabits a realm of discourse that is ontologically quite separate from the practical. Questions of the potential to unify these thus became ones of how to bridge a gap; of how to harness the absolutes of abstract or factually verified knowledge to the more fleeting realm of the mundane, the practical. Posed in this way the debate becomes one of how not only to arrange a marriage between opposites, but, moreover, to enforce their consummation. There have been many attempts to provide fertile grounds for this imagined coupling. Often, the status of theory is redefined, either by perceiving it to be a form of 'practice' within knowledge (Althusser's notion of theoretical practice), or by viewing it as having roots in prior, commonly unargued, political and moral assumptions. Again, some practitioners see the solution as residing in a type of pragmatism; if the definition of truth becomes related to a particular context, then within the confines of this, theory and practice become organically combined.

The central problem with these solutions is that they either unduly restrict the notion of practice, or they do not provide grounds for the bridge to be constructed. The actual relationship between theory and practice thus remains indefinite, residing more in an act of faith than in clear substantiation or demonstration. In consequence, questions of the unity of theory and practice remain continually at the level of potential, rather than fulfilment.

The question that arises from this conclusion is whether this situation is inevitable and social science is apparently doomed to remain partial or impotent. We would suggest that an alternative way of approaching the issue resides not so much in assuming a difference between theory and practice, but rather asking the substantially different question of on what grounds, and under what conditions, this distinction is made in the first place? Why is it that social science should distinguish between theory and practice as two ontologically separate forms of activity? It is our contention that this distinction is founded within empiricism and that its generality in social science is an index of the tyranny of this philosophy and its associated ideologies. Further, that an alternative conception of theorising is possible in which, rather than endeavouring to close the gap between theory and practice, no ontological distinction is made between them at all.

The idea that theory and practice are different forms of knowledge rests upon the advocacy of the distinction between fact and value; that science is founded upon a purely factual basis as this forms the only ground upon which it is possible to supply guarantees to knowledge. A science based upon the careful observation and recording of overt phenomena, it is contended, leads to conclusions which all must recognise. However, issues of practice, although they may involve reference to factual propositions, are not based upon them; thus, there can be no sureties offered in the realm of practice. Metaphysics, values, assumptions can all 'creep in' and form the foundation of action.

One of the central tensions within social science, in general, is that it has either adopted this version of science as its own, or at least worked in distant subjugation to it, while, at the same time, wishing to seek a harmony between theory and practice. As the two orders of knowledge are, within empiricism, logically irreconcilable, social science remains caught in an ironical dilemma: either it claims a unity between theory and practice – which results in compromising that most valued and ideologically significant of symbols – the scientist; or it retains an internal logical coherence, which in separating theory and practice, leaves the relationship between them as one of immanence and potential, rather than fulfilment.

Forms of knowledge, however, are not tidy and hermetically sealed units. Although empiricist-cum-positivist forms of knowledge reserve a special and superordinate place for science as factual truth, they do not completely reject involvement in the practical. For example, the strain created by endeavouring to marry science with practice, in positivist criminology, led to a tension that was easily fractured by changing social circumstance. It was only the prevailing ideological consensus that underpinned the emergence of correctionalism in the twentieth century which made it possible for theorists to ignore this tension. Once this ideological consensus was challenged, as in the 1960s – ironically enough, in part by the findings of positivist criminology itself – the political implications of the discipline became increasingly open to challenge and debate. Indeed, the very institutionalisation of positivism heightened this critique. The fact that positivism was seen as an official or state knowledge was, and still is, a precondition for the radical or alternative critiques of it that have littered the 1970s and 1980s.

The critique of positivism thus cannot be that it discussed practical issues (although one is sometimes left with this impression), but that it did this in a way that was, first, internally inconsistent with its logical foundations, and second, in a manner that was adjudged to be politically unacceptable. One of the features of existing radical alternatives is that they seem content to restrict themselves to the latter criterion, but only at the expense of robbing themselves of any basis upon which to develop a theory or a politics that does pose an alternative. The result is that positivism – as Cohen (1979a) has argued elsewhere – still holds sway as the form of knowledge that monopolises talk of penal affairs.

The implications of our argument are that the potential of theory and practice can only be realised by rethinking one of the fundamental conceptions of the nature of social science. Specifically, we must abandon the search for what Althusser has called a philosophy of guarantees; a framework that produces results which – because of their immutability – all must recognise, and upon which to found our practice. Rather, the theoretical and the practical must be seen as inseparable, as ontologically equivalent. In other words, analysis, evaluation and theorising are properly understood as inherent, necessary and irremovable elements in any social practice – whether these practices conserve existing social arrangements (as in the case of technicist penologies), or revolutionise them. This is more than a call for practitioners to recognise the political or 'domain' (Gouldner 1971) assumptions of their work; this type of critique does little except tell us that scientists are putative social beings. Rather, in proposing that theory and practice are inseparable aspects of any social practice, we are arguing that no sensible ontological distinction can be drawn between them; there can be no privileges given to 'science' as a vehicle of the truth.

Although social science has been dominated by empiricist conceptions of science, there has been a subterranean, but important, tradition which poses an alternative to it. In this tradition, which views knowledge in the manner we advocate, the very purpose of producing knowledge about the social world is to change it. Knowledge is not regarded as neutral, either in regard of its consequences or its mode of production. Within analyses of penality, this tradition has re-emerged, for example, in the work of Thomas Mathiesen. Mathiesen's notion of 'action theory', of seeking for the alternative through the proposing of the unfinished, constitutes one of the few attempts to follow through the implications of this subterranean tradition. His work illustrates one of its features which merits special emphasis: its concern with the problem of emancipation, of how to replace present social conditions with those that are more free. We have certain disagreements with Mathiesen's *Politics of Abolition* (1974) – not least with his notion that there can be a form of revolutionary politics which involves generalisable principles and guarantees, and his reluctance to confront 'public opinion' with a series of concrete penal alternatives – but we fully endorse his project of constructing a progressive penal politics and, incidentally, the utility of many of the tactics he describes. (For Mathiesen's own revision of these positions, see Mathiesen 1980a.)

What we are proposing is a form of penological investigation in which one of the central issues is the question of how to construct alternative forms of penality which are more socialist, more popular, more democratic – which aspire to the paradox of a liberative penality. There are several qualifications to be entered here. First, we have been careful not to define penality simply in terms of repression or the exercise of state-based coercion. This is not to deny an intimate connection between penality and power; rather, it is to assert both that power is not to be defined only in terms of the state and that penality need not always be conceived of as the property of a centralised and national state. This is of great import. If these arguments were to be conceded, then it would be impossible to imagine forms of regulation that were not located in or defined by the state. Second, and underpinning this, we have argued that the relationship between 'basic' social conditions and penality is not absolutely given or necessarily determinate (in the Marxist sense) and, consequently, penality must be conceived of as a set of possible social relationships and institutions to be constructed. This entails the suggestion that there is a space, even within a society dominated by a capitalist mode of production, to create more progressive and emancipatory forms of penality. For example, as Carlen argues in Chapter 9, the extension of popular participation in decision-making could begin to socialise and transform the existing means of producing 'justice' and penality in Britain (and elsewhere) today. Moreover, there already exist numerous points at which the penal complex is open to progressive intervention (by lay magistrates, juries, children's panel members, radical social workers, prisoners' groups, civil-rights groups, etc.), if only alternative ideologies and positions could be made available. Thirdly, it ought to be clear that we are not proposing a simple continuum between repression and freedom. Such a proposition carries with it the unacceptable thesis of a form of sociality without regulation: the surrealist's dream that 'social coercion has had its day'. The crucial question is not one of regulation versus non-regulation – penality is *always* the other side of social organisation – but, rather, one of the specific nature of regulatory conditions. This is a specific and concrete question, not a general and abstract one. It is best answered in the process of creating the forms of emancipatory penality of which we are talking.

In such a process, our conception of the social analysis of penality would play a vital pedagogical role. To begin with, it would demonstrate the political and social significance of penality as a form of power and a technique of social politics which, in a powerful and significant sense, contributes to the (re)production of contemporary forms of class division and domination. In other words, it would present penality as a positive political issue – a crucial site for struggle and progressive social politics. Moreover, it would facilitate such a politics by identifying the specific points at which intervention is both possible and desirable. It would thus be concerned to render visible – and therefore open to challenge – such features as the ideological relations implicit in penal practice (its rampant individualism, the class divisions it both presupposes and reproduces, its racism and sexism, the 'popular opinion' it constructs accordingly), its political forms (of unaccountable 'expertise', hierarchy, exclusion, secrecy), the economic relations of inequality and deprivation which it feeds upon and recreates, and the legal isolationism imposed by separating the institutions which 'deal with' offenders from those which can intervene to transform the offenders' social conditions. All of these identifications can form the basis for an informed political practice which challenges unacceptable ideologies, institutions and techniques and which mobilises people around an alternative programme of penal reform. And while the difficulties and limitations of such a politics should not be underestimated, it should none the less be borne in mind that up to now this political space has been virtually abandoned by progressive forces (Hunt, 1981) and that, moreover, the extent of popular disaffection in regard to the *efficacy* of current penal regulation in preventing social harm presents a possible basis of support for alternative policies.

At a more fundamental level, the social analysis of penality could also challenge the very basis upon which penal relations are currently established. Such a challenge, although it poses immense difficulties, is absolutely crucial, if an alternative socialist programme and ideology of penality is to be constructed. At present, socialists and progressive forces concerned with issues of penality are paralysed by a lack of any alternative basis upon which to think forms of penal regulation. Tied to the conventional modes of discourse regarding 'individual guilt', 'responsibility', 'rights' and 'punishment', the socialist alternative is presently limited to appeals to a more humane, more caring or more equitable penality which, when translated into popular debate, appears altogether impotent – either to convince people that such a system would be more effective, or to establish that it would, in any fundamental sense, be different. We would argue that this conventional, individualistic discourse must be rejected (see Carlen, 1980).

The issues at stake in penal regulation need not always be constructed in terms of a state/individual relation of guilt and sanction, as they are at present. The very terms of this formula (the state, the individual) and the form of their relationship (an operation of censure, isolated from other social relations) can and should be attacked and transformed by a progressive penal politics. As we have indicated above, there is no reason to suppose that penal regulation must always be statist in form; popular involvement, community discipline, local and informal sanctioning are possibilities (and have occasionally been actualities in China, Cuba and elsewhere) with a progressive potential to be developed. (The fact that these forms of organisation carry with them their own specific problems and conditions of existence need not undercut this potential.)

Similarly, there is no reason to follow legal ideology and individualistic psychologies in always locating 'responsibility' at the level of the individual: there are alternative means of ascribing social accountability (which could be applied to corporate entities, firms, public agencies, etc. as well as individuals), which do not rely upon this process of individualisation. Such a system would ensure that 'corporate crimes' and the social harms promoted by public agencies were no less real and amenable to intervention than the trespasses of individuals.

Finally, as Carlen indicates in Chapter 9, there is no reason why questions of penal regulation need always be privatised affairs limited to the sanctioning of guilty subjects. Since criminality does not reside solely in the hearts of individuals, institutions of penality could be 'opened up' and given a jurisdiction to investigate and intervene in the social conditions which promote the kinds of unacceptable conduct in question. The current impotence of social workers, children's panels or criminal courts to deal with the conditions which produce their individual 'problem cases' is a question of political organisation – not a universal imperative which condemns them to deal always with social casualties and never with their causes. In other words, criminality and penality could be relocated within the matrix of social relations and struggles from which they have long been isolated, and this return would provoke social transformations as well as individual corrections. It is essential that penal analysis and penal politics take seriously these questions of social regulation, 'crime' and 'punishment' (Cohen, 1979a). But it is equally essential that the basis of these questions and the terms of penal debate be analysed, challenged and transformed.

Our conception of the inseparable relationship of the theoretical and the practical should not be taken to suggest that all social practice consists solely in 'theory' or 'discourse' (any more than it is reducible to the 'practical' or the 'non-discursive'). We are under no illusion that theoretical or analytical developments of the type we suggest can, by themselves, produce a new dawn in the realm of penality. Social transformations require critical knowledge certainly, but they also demand social forces, political mobilisations and material struggles. But as we have argued above, *without* the appropriate knowledge, such forces are formless, without direction, politically paralysed. Indeed, they are unlikely to be realised at all.

If the project described in this volume is carried through, then analyses and knowledge of penality will be transformed, both in terms of their objectives and the methods used. From being an esoteric subject of limited concern to social science, it will be transposed into a topic for general political discussion and progressive political practice. However, we are fully aware that this project exists more at the level of potential than of completion. The analyses which are presented here, and the practices which they promote, thus inhabit the realm of possibility; they should not be interpreted as providing programmatic statements or finalised versions of the social analysis – and transformation – of penality.

Notes

1   By 'traditional' or 'technicist' penology, we mean the corpus of texts, studies and research findings generated by, for example, the Home Office Research Unit, the Cambridge Institute of Criminology and the *British Journal of Criminology*. Works in this tradition include such texts as Mannheim and Wilkins (1955), Hood and Sparks (1970), West (1972).

2   It should be noted that our discussion throughout is limited to the sanctions imposed by the institutions of 'criminal justice' and their ancillary agencies. This focus should not be taken to deny the existence, or political importance, of other, non-legal, forms of sanctioning such as occur in, for example, domestic, educational or employment relations. In particular, it should not be read as a denial of the significance of other, non-criminal, forms of legal sanctioning implicit in the regulation of health and safety at work, taxation, company law, social security claims, etc. The division between criminal and non-criminal — between 'bourgeois illegalities' and 'proletarian crimes' — is of immense political and ideological importance.

3   We include in this category the various psychological studies of punishment and its effect (for example, Walters, Cheyne and Banks, 1972), which form an important ancillary of the technicist endeavour.

4   Important exceptions include Bentham (1962), Walker (1969) and Von Hirsch (1976).

5   The notion of 'penal process', as opposed to 'penal system', has been suggested by writers such as Bottemley (1973) and Bottoms and McClean (1976). However, the term 'process' usually remains a descriptive rather than an analytical category, and in any case carries definite connotations of an effective unity.

2 Durkheim's Theory of Punishment: a Critique[1]
David Garland

Introduction: critical practice

The work of Emile Durkheim has traditionally been the central reference point for the sociology of punishment. Whenever theoretical questions are posed as to the form, historical trajectory or social significance of punishment, the concepts and analyses of Durkheim present themselves as the most adequate or developed responses available.

This essay interrogates these concepts, and questions both their coherence and their ability to open up the social analysis of penal practice. After a brief exposition of Durkheim's position(s) on the subject, the paper argues, first, that these positions, and the arguments which support them, are often incoherent, essentialist or presumptive, and secondly, that these Durkheimian concepts arbitrarily close off certain crucial questions concerning punishment.

These 'closures' are shown to be at once illogical or arbitrary, and yet are required by Durkheim's arguments. They are also shown to be of considerable political significance in that they limit the kinds of questions (and struggles) which can otherwise be advanced in regard to penal practices.

The paper is therefore engaged in the business of critical analysis, of exposition and critique. But before entering upon that venture, perhaps a word or two is necessary on the question of criticism and its credentials.

The predominant modes of criticism currently undertaken in reference to Durkheim may be characterised in the following way:

(1) the 'empirical' critique;
(2) the 'theoretical' critique;
(3) the political/ideological critique.

Although any one article or analysis may include a combination of these types, it is generally the case that these modes or 'levels' of critique are seen as separable, and to some extent distinct. These modes of criticism, as I will describe them, share a fundamental misconception of the nature and status of theory. The first type wrongly construes the relation of theory to the category of the empirical; the second type confuses the relation of one theory to others; and the third misrepresents the relationship of the author to his or her theoretical discourse.

The 'empirical' critique

The so-called 'empirical' critique referred to here (see Schwartz and Miller, 1964; Sheleff, 1975; Spitzer, 1975a; Clarke, 1976) may be more properly described as *empiricist*. This critique proceeds by transforming the theoretical discourse in question into a number of 'propositions' or 'hypotheses' which relate to empirical objects. These propositions are then measured against the facts, in so far as these have been separately and 'objectively' ascertained, and any discrepancy discovered between these two realms supposedly signifies the inadequacy of the theory in question. Within this framework, theories are no more than inductivist generalisations and 'abstractions' which are generated by a close scrutiny of the empirical data. And since empirical reality is the source and foundation of theoretical knowledge, it must also be its measure – all theories must ultimately submit to judgment by the facts themselves.

The problem with this mode of criticism is that it misrepresents the production of knowledge by completely denegating the place of theory. By proposing that the validity of a theory should be tested by reference to an external realm outside discourse (that is, to reality: the pre-theoretical facts), empiricism wrongly supposes the possibility of a direct access to the real world. The experiential 'facts' which make up this empirical realm are *not* simply given by reality; no matter how receptive or impartial the observer; they are always the product of definite theoretical and ideological practices. Language itself, in constructing our means of knowing the world, ensures that all knowledge is already a social and historical product. The 'facts' which appear in theoretical discourses are not only tainted by this original linguistic sin, they are also selected, classified, redefined and set into relations with one another – a process which leaves them far from innocent. It follows, therefore, that the process which this critique characterises as a reference to 'reality' is , in effect, a reference to empirical statements about reality produced by a different, privileged and unspecified theoretical system. In other words, this type of criticism functions by contrasting two discrete sets of theoretical propositions, one of which has been arbitrarily assigned the status of 'reality'.

The only legitimate 'empirical' critique is, strictly speaking, always also a theoretical critique. Since 'concrete facts' – or rather, our knowledge of them – are produced by the particular theory in question (by its concepts, its methods, the sources it deems appropriate, etc.), such a critique would involve demonstrating that the assertions relating to concrete objects arising within the theory are in contradiction with other axioms of that same theory. In other words, the process of empirical validation or refutation must be *internal* to the theory itself.

The 'theoretical' critique

The second type of critique in question is that one which criticises a specific theory for neglecting questions and issues which other theories demonstrate to be 'of importance'. Thus Durkheim is reproached for failing to adequately 'take account of' the existence of conflict, class struggle, the economy, etc. (see Chambliss, 1976; Therborn, 1976; Hunt, 1978). In so far as these neglected 'issues' are seen as being real objects or 'facts', we are back within the empiricist framework which attempts to measure theory directly against the real. In so far as they are conceived as objects of knowledge then the criticism is, by itself, of questionable authority; it attempts to dismiss Durkheim because he is not something other than a Durkheimian. The fact that other theories dealing with 'society' or 'punishment' propose different concepts and theories with which to grasp their specific object does not imply an inadequacy in Durkheim's work.

Durkheim's theoretical system, like any other, must first be assessed on its own terrain. It should be examined in terms of its own forms of argument and conceptualisation, in relation to its own specific object and to the questions which are asked of that object, and finally with regard to the *limits* of that terrain. It is only by denying the specificity of different theoretical systems (that is, the differences in their premises, questions, objects, etc.) and reducing them to so many bundles of 'insights' about a common, given reality that this process of measuring Durkheim's 'lack' with respect to other theories can proceed.

The political/ideological critique

Finally, the political/ideological critique commences by locating the author within the spectrum of contemporary politics, tracing the author's activities either in national politics or in ideological struggle in some other arena (for example, Durkheim's activities in the field of education) and then going on to demonstrate how these same ideological and political positions are to be found, for good or bad, in the author's work itself (see especially Zeitlin, 1968; but also Richter, 1964; Taylor *et al.*, 1973). The problem with this kind of critique is that it reduces a theoretical text to a mere elaboration of the prejudices of its author – theory becomes merely the continuation of ideological struggle by other means. In so doing, it makes two related errors.

First, it fails to separate out the author from 'his' or 'her' theoretical text. The latter is not simply a medium whereby the mental conceptions of the thinker are recorded. What makes it a theoretical text and not a rhetoric, a casual remark or a drunken stream of consciousness is its systematicity, and its forms of elaboration. Such a text is, in fact, the expositional form of a theoretical discourse, in which concepts are deployed in a particular mode of reasoning which develops answers to certain questions posed within a specific theoretical system. As such it has a status independent of its author and his or her politics. If certain political and ideological positions are present within Durkheim's theoretical work (and they are), then this is rarely a simple expression of its author's prejudices. As Hirst points out:

> No amount of ideological motivation on the part of an author can provide certain positions with a place and function in a discourse if they have no theoretical conditions of existence there. Such positions, if they are present become mere opinions. (Hirst, 1973: 32–3)

Secondly, by reducing theory and theoretical texts to the status of ideological elaborations, this type of critique implicitly accords itself the same status – as one moral position disdaining another. And although there can be no objection to the adoption of moral standpoints, this should not be allowed to lead to relativism and the abandonment of proper theoretical criticism. It is rarely productive to say of a knowledge simply that one dislikes it.

In contrast to the modes of criticism described above, this paper will endeavour to judge Durkheim's theoretical system first and foremost on its own terms. It will examine the object of that system, the concepts developed and the modes of reasoning employed there, in an attempt to identify contradictions, weak argumentation and silences (such as suppression of logically necessary questions) which are internal to it. The objective of the critique is to demonstrate that Durkheim's categories, and in particular his method of explaining penal phenomena, cannot be simply taken over and used by others without the necessary entailment of the contradictions and problems internal to the logic of this discourse.

It should be noted that an example of this type of critique already exists, in Paul Hirst's text *Durkheim, Bernard and Epistemology* (1975a), where Hirst examines Durkheim's claim to have provided a scientific basis for a sociology. The present paper builds upon Hirst's discussion, taking for its object not Durkheim's epistemology, but instead a substantive theoretical area – 'punishment'. And although

Durkheim's epistemology will have certain discursive effects within these texts, the intention is not to reiterate the point that Durkheim's claim to scientificity is an empty one, but rather to examine the theoretical effects of his basic concepts and method.

I shall begin with a short exposition of Durkheim's general sociology and of his conceptualisation of law, punishment and the state.

Durkheim's sociology: a science of ethics

Durkheim's sociology is conceived in a break with previous moral philosophies. It attempts to succeed where they have failed in the quest for a knowledge of the laws of morality. Its success is premised upon its scientific method which substitutes for metaphysical questions concerning eternal moral laws a new set of questions which seek to determine the specific conditions of existence of determinate historical moralities, that is, of social facts. In his appendix to *The Division of Labour*, he dismisses the method of humanist philosophers such as Kant, regarding it as essentialist and speculative in so far as it proceeds by deducing moral rules from a particular conception of 'man'. Such a conception is not, says Durkheim, 'the product of a scientific elaboration', but is merely the outcome of the moralist's 'beliefs and personal aspirations', and as such is open to simple refutation by a different set of premises and deductions. It falls to science to lead the study of ethics out of this cycle of deaths and rebirths in which it has been trapped by classical philosophy.

History has shown that 'what was moral for one people was immoral for another' (Durkheim, 1964: 423). Durkheim argues that this was so, not because some societies were deceived about the true nature of 'man', but instead because different conditions of social existence necessitate different ethics:

> If the ancient Romans had not the wide conception of humanity we have today, it is not the result of an error due to the narrowness of their understanding, but simply that such ideas were incompatible with the nature of the Roman world . . . The moral law, then, is formed, transformed, and maintained in accordance with changing demands; these are the only conditions the science of ethics tries to determine. (Durkheim, 1964: 33)

The object of study, then, is the relationship between social morality and its conditions of existence.

Morality, for Durkheim, is intrinsically *collective* and signifies everything which tends to bind the individual to the collectivity: 'Everything which is a source of solidarity is moral' (Durkheim, 1964: 398). Since the collectivity, though possessing its own *sui generis* reality, lives in and through individuals (in specific forms of association), Durkheim's sociology becomes the study of 'the relations of the individual to social solidarity' (Durkheim, 1964: 37). However, this sociology is not to be an individual psychology which explains social phenomena in terms of the will and needs of individuals. It is a distinct science with an object of its own (the 'social') which corresponds to a reality in the world. Social facts, even though they consist of ideas and 'representations', are nevertheless *real* and have *effects*, and therefore they must be treated by the sociologist as 'things'. But how do we know that these ideas and representations are indeed real? What is their nature and effects? How do we recognise them?

Durkheim answers our questions by revealing the necessary clue:

> A social fact is to be recognised by the power of external coercion which it exercises or is capable of exercising over individuals, and the presence of this power may be recognised in its turn by the existence of some specific sanction or by the resistance offered against every individual effort that tends to violate it. (Durkheim, 1966: 10)

So, for example, languages, currencies, technical organisations of material production, moral rules, laws and customs all share this quality of being social facts, and are recognised by their external effects of constraint. The social fact of *solidarity*, Durkheim's central object, is likewise to be studied through its external effects:

> social solidarity is a completely moral phenomenon which, taken by itself, does not lend itself to exact observation nor indeed to measurement . . . we must substitute for this internal fact which escapes us an external index which symbolises it and study the former in the light of the latter. The visible symbol is law. (Durkheim, 1964: 64)

The position and function of the category of 'law' in Durkheim's discourse is thus fixed by the relation of expression which holds between it and the real (but invisible) object of inquiry. We study law because through it we view solidarity.

It turns out that social solidarity is of two distinct types: mechanical solidarity based upon resemblances between individuals, and organic solidarity founded on complementary differences between them – solidarities of like and unlike. It follows from this that two types of law can also be distinguished: *repressive (penal) law* which both reflects and reinforces mechanical solidarity by harshly repressing difference and dissent; and *restitutive (co-operative) law* which reflects and facilitates organic solidarity by organising and regulating exchange relations between the different individuals and sectors of complex social types. It is Durkheim's basic thesis in *The Division of Labour* that organic solidarity and its complementing legal form become more predominant as the division of social labour advances through time, bringing about the specialisation and development of the occupations and personalities of individuals.

The theory of punishment in the division of labour

> punishment results from crime and expresses the manner in which it affects the public conscience. (Durkheim, 1973: 300)

For Durkheim, penal law is essentially a reaction to crime, and crime consists in those acts which 'shock . . . sentiments which for a given social system are found in all healthy consciences' (Durkheim, 1964: 73); that is to say, crime is an act which violates the *conscience collective*. In *The Division of Labour* Durkheim argues that social cohesion is maintained in simple segmental societies by means of a set of shared sentiments and beliefs held in common. Whenever these collective sentiments are breached, the solidarity and cohesion of the social whole is threatened. This threat, in turn, necessitates a collective response against the offender in order to revenge and repair the injured *conscience*. At the same time, the process of public vindication serves to reinforce these sentiments. The beliefs and representations which form the collective consciousness derive their force and power from the fact that they are common to everybody. Deviance disturbs this commonality and necessitates an act of punishment to renew the mutual assurance of agreement.

The social repression of acts which offend common sentiments varies in degree and intensity according to the importance and sanctity of the injured representation; sanctions are diffuse in the case of moral rules, and organised where the sentiment is embodied in the penal law. A predominance of penal laws in the juridical system of any society may therefore be taken as an indication of the strength of the *conscience collective* and the mechanical nature of that society's solidarity. In addition, penal laws may sanction offences directed not against the *conscience collective*, but instead against the government or its functionaries. However, this is merely a special case of the relation established above, since, as Durkheim points out, the directive organ of government is the symbol and living expression of the *conscience collective*. Offences against the state are treated as crimes because the state 'is the collective type incarnate' (Durkheim, 1964: 84).

Durkheim conceptualises punishment as the expression of a particular form of social relationship – a solidarity based upon resemblances and maintained by the enforcement of collective beliefs. It is essentially a mechanism whereby the domination of the social over the individual is reproduced:

> Punishment consists, then, essentially in a passionate reaction of graduated intensity that society exercises through the medium of a body acting upon those of its members who have violated certain rules of conduct. (Durkheim, 1964: 96)

This characterisation of punishment as public vengeance is not confined to simple mechanical societies; it is also intended to refer to penal law in modern organic society. Although the relative importance of the *conscience collective* and penal law have greatly diminished with the development of the division of labour, and despite modern penal theories to the contrary, for Durkheim the 'essential elements of punishment are the same as of old' (Durkheim, 1964: 88). Whatever the conscious intentions of those who apply penal sanctions, their essence still consists in the principle of public retaliation.

'The two laws of penal evolution'
In *The Division of Labour* Durkheim insists that the essential nature of punishment does not change in the transition from mechanical to organic society. However, he does allow that the forms and intensity which this retaliation displays have altered, and he suggests that this change is due to a certain rationalisation and enlightenment:

> Today, since we better understand the end to be attained, we better know how to utilize the means at our disposal; we protect ourselves with better means and, accordingly more efficiently . . . we are faithful to the principle of retaliation, although we apply it in a more elevated sense than heretofore. We no longer measure in so material and gross a manner either the extent of the deed or of the punishment. (Durkheim, 1964: 87, 89)

In a later essay, 'The two laws of penal evolution', this explanatory appeal to 'progress' is replaced by a more solid argument, which explains the diminishing intensity of punishment in terms of the changed nature of the collective sentiments which have been violated.

The collective sentiments typical of mechanical society are collective in a double sense: they have a collectivity as their subject (they are found in the majority of individual consciences) *and* they have collective things as their object (they concern religion, tradition, public authorities, etc.). Offences against these sentiments – crimes of the 'religious' or collective type – have the character of sacrilege, being perceived as offences against a transcendent and superhuman entity, and consequently the sacrilegious act demands a particularly intense punishment. On the other hand, the collective sentiments of the more secular and modern organic society are of a different type. They tend to be less 'collective' in both respects, since few beliefs are held in common by everyone, and those which are common usually display a more individualistic character, involving norms of individual freedom, privacy, property, etc. Their object is not the 'collective', but the 'individual'. Offences against these sentiments – which Durkheim terms human criminality – do not spark off the same heights of moral outrage: 'The offence of man against man cannot arouse the same indignation as an offence of man against God' (Durkheim, 1973: 303). Neither do they forbid the display of sentiments of pity for the offender. Human criminality thus evokes mercy – a trait which must remain absent where the dignity of an offended deity is at stake. The outcome is a move towards 'leniency' in punishment, caused by a declining sentiment of outrage and an increasing sentiment of mercy. Thus the progressive weakening of the intensity of punishment is no longer vacuously explained by reference to progress. Instead, it is now seen as the inevitable consequence of the decline in religiosity and the elevation of individuality which accompany the development of the division of labour:

> Seeing as, in the course of time, crime is reduced more and more to offences against the person alone, while religious forms of criminality decline, it is inevitable that punishment on the average should become weaker. This weakening does not come from the fact that morals become less harsh, but from the fact that religiosity, which was earlier imprinted in both the penal law and the collective sentiments which underlay it, steadily declines. (Durkheim, 1973: 303)

A particular consequence of the tendency of the 'quantity' or intensity of punishment to decrease as societies become more developed was the necessity of abandoning practices such as executions, mutilations, tortures, etc. and replacing them with less severe measures. The new institution which tends to replace these sanctions as the normal means of social control – the prison – is, according to Durkheim, itself the product of the same processes which tend to decrease the severity of punishment. The breakup of segmental societies and the progress of individualisation ended the ethic of collective responsibility, necessitating the use of places of detention for offenders awaiting trial. At the same time differentiation of the organs of government began to manifest itself in the construction of functional buildings (the manorial castle, the royal palace, fortresses) separate from the rest of the community and offering the architectural conditions for incarceration. Thus the social need for a place of detention became marked at the same time (and from the same causes) as the material conditions for such an institution. Once established, the prison lost its purely preventive character and took on more and more the character of a punishment in itself. Gradually, says Durkheim, it became the 'necessary and natural substitute for the other punishments which were fading away' (Durkheim, 1973: 299).

In general, then, punishment is determined by the nature of the social type in which it is found, and penal evolution is explained in terms of the broader process of change from mechanical to organic solidarity and, in particular, by reference to the secularisation and individuation that accompany this transition. However, in the 'Two laws' essay, Durkheim introduces an additional, 'independent' causal factor:

The intensity of punishment is the greater the more closely societies approximate to the less developed type – *and the more the central power assumes an absolute character.* (Durkheim, 1973: 285; my emphasis)

According to Durkheim the emergence of an absolute power tends to revive or reinforce the transcendental nature of the state and its laws, and consequently amplifies the gravity of criminal offences. These take on, once more, an aspect of sacrilege and are therefore more harshly repressed:

whenever the government takes this form, the one who controls it appears to the people as a divinity. When they do not make an actual God of him, they at the very least see in the power which is invested in him an emanation of divine power. From that moment, the religiosity cannot fail to have its usual effects on punishment. (Durkheim, 1973: 305)

It is important to note that this discussion of absolute power is not presented as merely an elaboration of the previously established relation between social type and penal practices. The emergence and effects of absolute power are, says Durkheim, independent of any particular social type:

This special kind of political organisation is not . . . a consequence of the fundamental nature of the society, but rather depends on unique, transitory and contingent factors. This is why these two causes of the evolution of punishment – the nature of the social type and of the governmental organ – must be carefully distinguished. For being independent, they act independently of one another, on occasion even in opposite direction. (Durkheim, 1973: 288)

This characterisation of the state/social type relation as one of autonomy and contingency has given rise to a great deal of confusion and misplaced criticism in subsequent commentaries on Durkheim's work; to be fair, this confusion often mirrors the unsystematic manner of Durkheim's own exposition of his theory of the state and its relation to the 'fundamental nature of society'. The following section attempts to outline and clarify some aspects of that theory.

Durkheim's theory of the state
Implicit in Durkheim's work is an untheorised distinction between *state-form* and *political type.* The state-form refers to the extent to which the state apparatus is differentiated and developed, to the range and number of its social functions, generally that is, to the sphere and complexity of state action. Far from being a contingency, the state-form is determined by the social type in which it is located, becoming enlarged and more complex with the increasing division of labour and the more extensive range of exchange and interaction betweeen individuals characteristic of organic society:

The greater or lesser extent to which the central directive organ is developed only reflects the development of social life in general, just as the extent of the individual's nervous system varies with the importance of the organic exchanges. The society's directive functions accordingly are only rudimentary when the other social functions are of the same type; and thus the relationship between them remains constant. (Durkheim, 1973: 288)

Distinct from the question of state-form and its determinants is the question of *political type*. This refers not to state functions, but to the actual political control and direction of these functions. It indicates the locus of power within the state and the constitutional framework through which this power is exercised (for example, monarchist, republican, parliamentary or absolutist regimes). Thus conceived, the specific political organisation of a society is not a consequence of that society's 'fundamental nature' (for Durkheim, its form of solidarity), but rather, it 'depends on unique, transitory and contingent factors' (Durkheim, 1973: 288). Thus the political type or regime may vary (cf. the constitutional history of France from 1789 to the present) without any accompanying change in the fundamental nature of the social type or its form of state.

Using this state-form/political-type distinction, we can clearly see that Durkheim's discussion of absolutism falls within the latter category. Absolute governmental power, characterised by an absence of countervailing 'checks and balances' and by a property-like relation between state and subject, is a specific type of political organisation which may appear within *any* social type:

> one may find such a government as often in an extremely complex society as in very simple ones, it is no more tied exclusively to primitive societies than to other types. (Durkheim, 1973: 288)

However, if the political type is not causally related to the social type concerned, Durkheim nevertheless suggests that certain types of political organisation are more 'appropriate' than others in specific societies. Thus he argues in *Professional Ethics and Civic Morals* that (his conception of) democracy is the political organisation 'best suited' to organic society and its cult of the individual. Similarly, although absolutism is, strictly speaking, possible in any social type, there is good reason to suppose that its emergence in complex organic society tends to have disruptive and 'pathological' effects; effects which would not be registered in mechanical social types.

In chapter 2 of *The Division of Labour* Durkheim describes the state as the symbol and living expression of the *conscience collective*; as 'the collective type incarnate' (Durkheim, 1964: 84). In mechanical society, where the collective sentiments are immensely powerful and authoritative, the state, in formally expressing these sentiments in laws, etc., directly partakes of this authority. Governmental power becomes 'an emanation of the inherent life of the collective conscience' (Durkheim, 1964: 195 ff.). In so far as a transcendental or

religious quality is attributed to these sentiments, this will also extend
to the authority of the state (*whatever* its political type). This is why
Durkheim argues that the authority of the state over its citizens will
tend to be greatest 'in the lower societies' (Durkheim, 1964: 85).

However, in organic social types the state is more than a simple
expression or reflection of a unified, all-embracing and authoritative
conscience collective. The advent of social differentiation ensures
that no such common consciousness exists; sentiments become partic-
ularised and not general. With the exception of the common respect
for individuality, beliefs and moralities become *specific* to classes,
groups, occupations and individuals. Consequently, the role of the
state is no longer one of simple and unmediated expression. It must
now actively interpret and co-ordinate the diverse currents of
opinion, its task being to *create* a higher unity. In a later discussion of
organic society, Durkheim recognises this explicitly:

> It is not accurate to say that the State embodies the collective conscience
> for that goes beyond the State at every point. In the main that conscious-
> ness is diffused: there is at all times a . . . vast number of social sentiments
> and states of . . . mind of all kinds, of which the State hears only a faint
> echo. The State is the centre only of a particular kind of consciousness, of
> one that is limited but higher, clearer and with a more vivid sense of itself
> . . . we can therefore say that the State is a special organ whose respon-
> sibility it is to work out certain representations which hold good for the
> collectivity, these representations are distinguished from the other collec-
> tive representations by their higher degree of consciousness and reflection.
> (Durkheim, 1957: 37)

If the state is indeed the 'social brain' that Durkheim suggests, then in
organic society that brain is more developed and is called upon to
make interpretations, to synthesise diversities, to 'think harder'.

The result is that the state's authority in organic society is reconstituted on a more secular and rational basis. The majority of laws –
in this case restitutive laws – 'correspond to no sentiment within us';
however, the state – subject relation is necessarily modified by the cult
of the individual and the norms of formal equality which derive from
contractual exchange. Given these developments, the emergence of
the absolutist political type is doubly pathological in the context of the
organic social type. First, it recalls the religious state-worship of a
previous form of solidarity, and secondly, it defiles the individual by
reducing him or her to a status resembling that of a chattel – the
property of the state-power.

A critique of Durkheim's 'social science'
The theoretical shortcomings which will later be identified in
Durkheim's analysis of punishment – namely, the denegation of the
specificity of punishment, the reduction of the phenomenon to a

simple expression of a unitary essence, the contradictions implicit in his theory of the state and its consequences for penal law, the suppression of the question of social ideologies – are not peculiar to this particular area of analysis, but are rather the substantive effects of problems which are located at a much more fundamental level in Durkheim's sociology. To understand fully the nature and origin of these 'shortcomings' as they appear in the theory of punishment, it is therefore necessary to undertake a preliminary (and schematic) discussion of the basic structure of Durkheim's theoretical sociology.

The epistemological argument with which Durkheim founds his theory of sociological knowledge is a *realist* one (see Hirst, 1975a). He deems a particular realm of visible social facts to be the external and observable expressions of an underlying reality. Thus, for example, social facts such as law and morality are the phenomenal expressions of the 'internal' fact of solidarity. For Durkheim this realm of observable social phenomena is not a contingent one. On the contrary, it is a realm *given to observation* by the underlying structure of the real, and is therefore necessary. Durkheim thus proposes a principle of expressive causality which connects the visible traces of the real with the as-yet-undiscovered and deeper order of the real itself. These tangible and observable facts 'are our only clue to reality' (Durkheim, 1966: 35), and consequently the method of the scientist must be to 'substitute for this internal fact which escapes us an external index which symbolises it and study the former in the light of the latter' (Durkheim, 1964: 64). On closer examination this epistemological foundation turns out to be of doubtful validity, resting as it does upon a circular and speculative philosophical argument. Contrary to Durkheim's assertions, the 'givenness' of the realm of social facts is quite spurious. 'Visible' facts are not simply given to perception by the real. As we have seen, the definition of specific phenomena as 'perceivable' and as worth perceiving is a product of theory. These facticities are given to us not by the real, by means of pure perception, but as products of a definite theoretical system – the same system which characterises these 'facts' as expressions of an underlying essence. Proof of the existence of the essence in terms of arguments from the facts is therefore inherently tautological. As Hirst points out, the 'facts' are 'hand picked' by the theory which has already thought the existence of the deeper reality and pre-established the relation between the two categories.

Durkheim tells us that the essence of social reality, 'social life itself', consists in social *representations* (Durkheim, 1966: xliv). That is to say, even though these representations may be embodied in, and therefore studied through, material objects, social life is essentially a realm of consciousness. However, as we saw before, social life has certain conditions of existence. It only exists in and through *individuals*, and each individual carries with him or her a series of individual representations, ideas and interests, derived from his or her relations with the external world. Consequently, social life exists only in so far as social representations and individual representations can 'fit together' in a satisfactory manner. This problem of the articulation of social and individual representations is the problem of *solidarity*.

This definition of the social essence and its mode of existence serves to establish the central questions and categories of Durkheim's sociology. It ensures that this 'sociology' in fact resembles a work of collective psychology which addresses material objects and relations, but only to the extent that these latter have some significance for either individual or collective psychology. Thus, for example, the division of labour is worthy of investigation only in so far as it creates differentiation among individuals and thereby necessitates a new type of solidarity and a new series of social representations. Hence, too, the oft-noted absence of structural categories and concepts. For Durkheim social structure is merely the expression and 'crystallisation' of a particular type of consciousness. Articulated social structures, like free currents of thought and opinion, 'are simply life, more or less crystallised' (Durkheim, 1966: 12). Likewise, Durkheim's social typology and his historical periodisation derive directly from this basic question of solidarity. The 'mechanical' and 'organic' social types are defined not in relation to the types of economic, political, sexual or legal structures they manifest, but solely with reference to the type of solidarity they possess. Indeed, for Durkheim the structures and institutions of any society are but mere expressions of the dominant form of social consciousness:

> When the way in which men are solidary becomes modified, the structure of societies cannot but change. The form of a body is necessarily transformed when the molecular affinities are no longer the same (Durkheim, 1964: 174)

The weaknesses and contradictions which I wish to identify in Durkheim's theoretical system relate to the structure of the essentialist argument as such, rather than simply to the specific content which Durkheim gives to the social essence. Contrary to the implications of critics such as Zeitlin, Hunt and Therborn, who castigate Durkheim for 'attributing too much importance' to the 'ideological community', the substitution of a material essence in place of Durkheim's 'idealist' one would retain exactly the same theoretical defects. A *philosophical* inversion is not in itself a *theoretical* advance. Whether materialist or idealist in substance, the essentialist form of argument retains its weaknesses, which in Durkheim's case take the following form.

We are told that social facts are the expression of an underlying essence, but we are never told how this essence is accounted for or explained. To say that this essence consists of representations, and that these are not reducible to the biology or psychology of individuals, does not in any way explain its existence. It is simply a *given* in Durkheim's discourse, as indeed is the extra-social individual and his or her 'psychology'. At no point does he pose the question as to how this essence comes into existence. By refusing to examine the mechanisms which produce and establish these social representations, Durkheim subverts the question of who or what controls the means and the forms of their production: the question of *social ideologies*.

He can perform this theoretical sleight of hand because in his theory social representations, beliefs and attitudes are merely the expressions of something else – namely, the social essence. So the problem is displaced to a lower level and we must reserve our questions until such time as he discusses and argues for this vital concept of social essence (*conscience collective*) from which all else derives. The problem is that such a time never arrives. Instead Durkheim simply presents us with this concept, unargued, unexplicated and unabashed, as if it were self-evident that 'society' is centred, unitary and devoid of contradiction, discontinuity or social division. That being the case, of course, our questions about social ideologies, about the place of power in the production of knowledge, about the role of the state in shaping social sentiments would be altogether out of place. But it is very far from being the case, and Durkheim says nothing at all which might change our opinion on the matter.

The essence given in Durkheim's theory is a unitary one, the product of society-as-a-whole. He establishes this unity and its communal source in a completely arbitrary fashion, but this arbitrariness is concealed in the distracting context of a continuing polemic against methodological individualism. Thus a typical example is the following:

> A moral or juridical regulation essentially expresses then, social needs that society alone can feel; it rests in a state of opinion and all opinion, is a collective thing, produced by collective elaboration. (Durkheim, 1964: 5)

So we can rest assured that moral or juridical rules are 'collective' and not merely 'individual'; but of course the real problem remains: how universal, consensual or representative are these 'collective' entities? Again and again, Durkheim ignores this problem and formulates the central opposition as being that between the social and the individual. Meanwhile he simply assumes the unity of the former category. Contrary to the common criticism, this does not involve Durkheim in a blind conservatism, seeing only consensus, when 'in reality' conflict rages. Durkheim can and does conceive of social conflict, as the most cursory glance at *The Division of Labour* will confirm. But the conflict 'in society' is always the outcome of a disjunction in the relations between 'the social' and its *external* conditions of existence: it is never internal to the social essence itself. Thus all forms of social disruption (some of which are 'a good thing' in Durkheim's view) have their source in individuals or else their natural-material environment, for example, crime, social change, the transition from one social type to another, etc. As Hirst remarks:

> 'Society' has no contradiction within itself but it must not contradict that which is external to it, the constitution and needs of its human materials. Durkheim's doctrine of the normal and the pathological discovers the source and the necessity of pathology in the a-social individual. By individualising the source of pathology it de-socialises the pathological in society. (Hirst, 1975a: 120)

The substantive theoretical (and political) effects of this position are clearly evident in Durkheim's conceptualisation of the state, punishment, morality, etc. as more or less simple expressions of a unitary collective consciousness.

Durkheim's sociology specifies the existence of a social essence and a realm of social facts through which this underlying reality is expressed. These facts are thus constituted as the necessary and given field of study of sociology – as the reality which gives this new science its specific object. Penal law is one such social fact. Punishment is constituted as an object of study because of its expressive relation with the social essence (that is, it is 'hand picked'), and is then subsequently explained in terms of that same essence. Clearly, then, the theory of punishment is only valid in so far as Durkheim's general theory of the social essence and its phenomenal expressions can also be shown to be respectable. As was shown above, it cannot. The arguments utilised to demonstrate the existence of any essence are circular and rest upon vain appeals to extra-theoretical 'observation'. The explanation for such an essence is nowhere given, but its nature is arbitrarily specified as both unitary and communal. The actual mechanisms and forms of representation which somehow achieve the authentic expression of this essence are likewise assumed without argument. The central foundation upon which Durkheim's theory of punishment rests is thereby shown to be speculative, rather than 'scientific'. With this in mind we can proceed to a more detailed examination of the specific problems inherent in this theory.

A critique of the theory of punishment

> crime shocks sentiments which, for a given social system, are found in all healthy consciences. (Durkheim, 1964: 73)

The discussion of crime reproduces all the circularity of Durkheim's basic arguments. We are told that crime consists in acts 'universally disapproved by members of each society' (Durkheim, 1964: 73). Clearly, as an empirical statement this is questionable; one must presume that the offenders themselves do not wholly partake in this universal spirit of disapproval. However, Durkheim tells us that he refers only to healthy consciences, that is, to those which share the sentiments of the collective conscience. But since violation of the collective conscience is the very quality which gives certain acts the attribute of criminality, the appeal to 'healthy consciences' as a proof is an empty form of tautology.

Nevertheless, even if we allow that crime and its punishment do indeed arise out of the violation of collective beliefs and sentiments, how can we be sure that positive penal law, as legislated by the state, does in fact adequately express this *conscience collective*? This brings us back to the question of how the social essence is actually represented or expressed – and to Durkheim's theory of the state and its effectivity. This problem is dealt with explicitly at an early point in *The Division of Labour* where it is stated that:

> It is true that, in other cases the power is wielded by a privileged class or by particular magistrates. But these facts do not lessen the demonstrative value of the proceeding, for, simply because collective sentiments are enforced only through certain intermediaries, *it does not follow* that they have ceased to be collective while localising themselves in a restricted number of consciences. (Durkheim, 1964: 77; my emphasis)

Durkheim 'sees' the problem, but peremptorily dismisses it. Of course it 'does not follow' that the state will distort the collective sentiments in its legislation. But neither does the opposite case follow in logic – unless we already know that the state and law are merely *expressions* of the collective conscience. As we saw earlier, this is precisely the position Durkheim adopts. Whatever the *form* of state, be it simple or developed, its laws are always faithful expressions of the collective conscience (or of social representations arising from a division of labour) more or less reflectively 'interpreted'. The question of *political type*, of actual political structures and forms of representation, is deemed to be a secondary and non-fundamental one. But since social representations evidently cannot simply form themselves into law, but in fact require a specific mechanism of recognition, interpretation and legislation, one must assume that this mechanism will have an effectivity, the specific effects of which will depend upon its constitution and structure. In noting that the absolutist type of state affects the religiosity of social sentiments about crime, Durkheim *admits* just such an effectivity. The state *is* more than a mere cipher without effects, and yet Durkheim's theory also *denies* this when it characterises positive law as an index-expression of 'social life':

social life, especially where it exists durably, tends inevitably to assume a definite form and organise itself, and law is nothing else than this very organisation in so far as it has greater stability and precision. (Durkheim, 1964: 65)

Of course penal law is an index-expression of the collective conscience *or of absolute state power*, but this latter variable is introduced as a special case, to do with the properties of *absolutism* and not *state power*. It remains a special explanation versed in terms of religiosity, and not the first part of a theory of political types and the effectivity of their specific modes of representation. A vitally important aspect of penal law – its constitution in and through political state structures – is thus closed off from investigation.

It is worth adding that, if we take the trouble to scratch the surface of this explanation, it turns out to be less 'special' than it at first seems. In the absence of a fuller discussion, it is difficult to accept Durkheim's argument that absolute power is indeed an 'independent variable', even in his own terms. Since no reference is made to any deliberate attempt by the sovereign to actively inspire and create this renaissance of the religious *conscience collective*, we must assume that such religiosity is simply a constant, spontaneous aspect of absolutism. To suggest that the sovereign had any hand in the creation of this renaissance would throw serious doubt upon Durkheim's basic premise that the *conscience commune* and its expressions are essential, unitary and communal, *that is*, it would introduce the question of social ideology and the effects of power in structuring social facts and sentiments. Given Durkheim's general causal scheme, it would be reasonable to suppose that, if absolutism and religiosity are co-present, then the sovereign is absolute *because* the *conscience collective*, for some unspecific reason, has reverted to a prior religiosity. This, in effect, reduces Durkheim's dual explanation for quantitative penal evolution to a singular one based, as before, solely upon changes in the nature of the *conscience collective*.

As we have already noted, there exists a variety of 'empirical' critiques which contest Durkheim's substantive assertions about penal law and the 'facts' which he uses to demonstrate them. Writers such as Clarke, Spitzer, Hunt and Sheleff refer to various anthropological research findings and use these to throw doubt upon, for example, the prevalence of repressive law in 'simple' societies, or the general pattern of legal development, as described in Durkheim's work. In the introduction, I outlined the conditions under which an 'empirical' critique may legitimately proceed, and in fact the authors mentioned here by and large fail to meet these conditions. As Cotterrell (1977) and Baxi (1974) point out, the 'data' upon which these critiques base their cases are not generally the product of

Durkheimian concepts, nor have they been reorganised into the forms which these concepts demand, and they are therefore unable to refute or confirm Durkheim's arguments. However, a more rigorous and 'sympathetic' use of Durkheim's categories would still seem to produce certain problems when faced with the (theoretically conceived) empirical history of penal law in the twentieth century. Thus, for example, in terms of the 'observable social facts' as recorded in laws, sentencing statistics, policy statements, institutional practices, etc., it would appear that a degree of 'rehabilitation' and individualised treatment was prevalent in most penal systems in the decades after 1945. Furthermore, virtually every state in Western Europe, the USA and the Soviet bloc has, since the end of the nineteenth century, introduced some form of indeterminate 'reformatory' sentence, as well as psychiatric orders for offenders, probation orders, parole, social-inquiry reports and specialised 'welfare-oriented' tribunals for juveile offenders. Indeed this penal-welfare development would seem prima facie to be, in Durkheim's terms, a *normal* social fact of modern organic social types, in that 'it is present in the average of the societies of that type at the corresponding phase of their evolution'. Yet this apparently normal fact runs contrary to Durkheim's characterisation of punishment as public retribution directed at acts which offend the collective conscience. Durkheim tells us that the proof of his theory of punishment as public vengeance 'lies in the minute precautions we take to proportion punishment as exactly as possible to the severity of the crime' (Durkheim, 1964: 88). But whatever else can be said of the 'welfare sanction' in its various forms – and its meaning and effects are complex and often far from liberalising – it is *not* simply or essentially retributive. In fact it ceases altogether to take the crime or the criminal act as its object, and instead directs itself to the individual. The penal system is not a hierarchy of increasingly severe penalties, minutely geared in exact proportion to the severity of the offence. It was in Durkheim's time, and remains to this day, a differentiated grid of sanctions and dispositions irreducible to the single sign of 'public vengeance'.

We might also note in passing that this point reveals the theoretical worthlessness of Durkheim's concepts of 'penal severity' and 'intensity' (see Sorokin, 1937 and Grabosky, 1978). These concepts require that we conceive of punishment as a simple continuum of retributive pain (as well as requiring a means of measurement which Durkheim fails to provide). Without the benefit of such notions, Durkheim's central practical concepts become little more than unstable, retrospective evaluation.

If Durkheim were the inductivist which his empiricist critics take him for, he would indeed have problems. The new fact of individ-

ualised punishment would disprove his theory and necessitate a new
process of factual correlation and theoretical induction. But for
Durkheim there is no basic equality among facts: on the contrary,
only facts which truly express the social essence are of real importance
for science:

> It is not true that science can institute laws only after having reviewed all
> the facts they express . . . the true experimental method tends to substitute
> for common sense facts . . . *decisive* or crucial facts, which by themselves
> and independently of their number, have scientific value and interest
> (Durkheim, 1966: 79)

Thus the new fact of rehabilitation could well be disregarded as irrelevant – as merely a mistaken 'humanitarian' notion of the true nature
and function of punishment. As Durkheim points out, 'the nature of
a practice does not necessarily change because the conscious intentions of those who apply it are modified' (Durkheim, 1964: 87). No
doubt he could point to other, more 'decisive' evidence which suggests the persistence of a retributory criterion in sentencing and term
this as the *true* reality of punishment. However, the theory-saving
circularity of this argument and the hostile, tangible evidence that
individualised treatment has been more than a 'conscious intention'
(having formed the theoretical basis for a large number of practices,
apparatuses and institutions), might elicit a different Durkheimian
response.

Thus Durkheim, or his epigones, might argue that this phenomenon exists, and even that it exists in all such societies, but that it is,
nevertheless, a *pathological* development which subverts the real
function of punishment and thereby disrupts solidarity. This argument is open to them because the real evidence of a social fact's
'normality' is not statistical prevalence, but rather that fact's connection with the fundamental nature of the social type. Exactly this
type of argument is used by Durkheim to explain away the widespread
existence of a forced division of labour as 'pathological', having no
connection with the basic conditions of existence of organic social
types.

Thus the phenomenon is either completely ignored as epiphenomenal or else is explained away as pathological (that is,
resulting from extra-social causes *not* bound up with the fundamental
nature of society and punishment). In effect, Durkheim's theory must
always *reduce* punishment (and the other social facts) to a simple
expression of a social essence. The essentialist argument thereby
denies the specificity of the particular object (in this case, penal law)
in a constant repetition of its basic speculative premises. When faced
with some specific feature of a phenomenon which appears prima

facie to be other than a simple expression of the essence, that feature is either ignored as epiphenomenal (for example, the 'conscious intentions of those who . . . punish'), or else the nature of the essence itself is refined and better described – as in the case in the 'Two laws' essay – to show how the phenomenon is, after all, *only* an expression of that essence.[2]

Outside Durkheim's theory, there is no reason to accord punishment an essence of any sort. Punishment is a generic term which refers to a differentiated field of practices with a multiplicity of meanings, purposes and effects (see Chapter 1). At the time when Durkheim identified retribution as the essence of punishment and the prison as its expressive form, the penal systems of Europe were sentencing offenders to suspended sentences, probation, fines, compensations, reformatories, public works, transportation, inebriate asylums, labour colonies and any number of other sanctions whose significance is not exhausted by any simple notion of retribution. Imprisonment itself can hardly be reduced to a retributive singularity: how can 'retribution' explain preventive detention, conditional licensing, the details of prison regimes (which were not confined to the exaction of pain and suffering), the discourses, rhetorics and techniques of 'reform', or even the overarching utilitarian calculus of 'prevention' and 'deterrence'? The purpose of theory must be to open up such complexities to analysis and significance – not to banish them by decree of an imperious essence.

Durkheim does not provide a theory of punishment; instead he uses penal law as an 'empirical' support for his philosophical speculations about the essential nature of social life. His treatment of the phenomenon closes it off to questions concerning the effects of state structures and the possibility of social ideologies, even though these questions are necessarily implied in the logic of his discourse. Durkheim does not thereby neglect to supply his own answers to them – he simply provides arbitrary assertions in place of reasoned arguments.

Rehabilitating Durkheim

Up to this point we have been concerned to identify the limits, contradictions and shortcomings in Durkheim's work and to establish the consequences of these theoretical faults. In this concluding section we shall be concerned not with the question of Durkheim's theoretical guilt, but with the issue of his corrigibility. The question to be answered is this: given the accuracy of the critical charges, how is Durkheim to be dealt with?

There can be no question of accepting Durkheim's object of analysis as he presents it. As we have seen, his theorisation of punishment is a product of his general social theory. The point of that theorisation – the questions which are asked and the information which is sought – is not to discover the detailed mechanisms, ideologies and effects of punishment, but rather to elicit only those features which support his speculations about the fundamental nature of society. Punishment, for Durkheim, is not a serious object of analysis at all. It is merely a means of recognising and reaffirming the social essence which it is said to express.

The consequence, as we have seen, is a conception of punishment which is unitary, essentialist and of a singular and pre-given significance. The acceptance of such a conception forecloses empirical investigation and radically limits the questions which can be asked of the phenomenon. Anyone who would understand the complex nature of penality, its diverse practices, techniques and discourses, the variety of meanings and effects which it generates, and the institutions, strategies and tactics which constitute it, would be advised to look elsewhere. To those looking for the theoretical tools to guide political intervention, one can only say that Durkheim's theory of punishment renders any such intervention all but unthinkable.

There is, then, little prospect of a reformed Durkheimian sociology of punishment. But this said, there are none the less elements within Durkheim's work which are of such crucial importance that they should feature in any adequate investigation of punishment. There are methods, principles, positions and substantive descriptions in his writings which are well founded and which could be usefully taken up, reformulated and integrated into other analyses. Now the difficulties of theoretical translations are obviously considerable, and this is not a call for a free-ranging eclecticism. But for all that, there are progressive and important elements in Durkheim's work, and if they can be freed of their Durkheimian limitations, they may be employed to some considerable effect. The following points indicate briefly some of the elements which make Durkheim's work an indispensable resource, in spite of the flaws of his system.

At the level of method, and for all the empiricist shortcomings identified earlier, Durkheim's approach is doggedly social and historical in orientation. He refuses to treat punishment as a purely technical issue (in the manner of conventional penology). He insists instead upon the social construction and significance of penal technologies such as the torture chamber and the prison. At the same time his historical method is firmly materialist and non-functionalist in character, explaining institutions and events not in terms of functions or desires, but by facing these terms with their material conditions of possibility:

> To explain an institution it is not enough to establish that when it appeared it served some useful end; for just because it was desirable it does not follow that it was possible. (Durkheim, 1973: 297)

Most importantly, Durkheim's method insists upon viewing punishment as both *positive* and *productive*. He refuses to adopt the common-sense position that punishment is merely a reactive effect, a negative corollary of crime. On the contrary, he credits punishment with a constitutive status where crime is concerned (as the carrier of the collective sentiments it defines that which is criminal), and with positive social effects (the symbolic display of collective sentiments, the reinforcement of solidarity, the expressive release of collective emotion).

This recognition of the positivity of punishment is the necessary first principle of any social analysis of punishment. As such it is perhaps the most important contribution Durkheim has made in this field (though one which is rarely accredited, even when subsequently rediscovered by Rusche and Kirchheimer in 1968a, and then later by Michel Foucault, 1977a). Of course in Durkheim's work the principle is not given its full extension; punishment is seen as a means of expressing and reinforcing collective political sentiments, never as a strategy designed to produce them, but the principle is present nevertheless.

More substantially, Durkheim can be credited with the fullest and best elaborated account of what one might call the semiology of punishment. More than anyone else, Durkheim has recognised that punishment operates on two distinct levels: at the mundane level of behavioural or physical effects (deprivation of liberty, economic sanctions, physical pain, etc.), but also, and importantly, at the symbolic level (see Chapter 1). Durkheim's work opened up the analysis of punishment as a system of signs, and his description of penal representations (of symbolic threat, religious and secular sacrilege, treason, cultural blasphemy, etc.) remain among the best we have.

Once again, his contribution is limited by its own terms, and he fails to provide the means for an adequate political 'reading' of these signs and their effects. But none the less his recognition of the central ideological significance of penal law and its powerful symbolic connotations opens up a crucial area of analysis – particularly today when crime and punishment (or 'law and order') is one of the few issues which has the symbolic depth to generate powerful and wide-spread ideological support.

Finally, in regard to what was said before about Durkheim's characterisation of the retributive essence of punishment, it is worth repeating that the problem here is its essentialism, not its identification of retribution as an element of importance. There can be no doubt that what is called retribution forms an important part of the meaning of punishment, for example, in judicial ideology and sentencing, conservative political rhetorics and popular ideology. However, the point is that punishment, or rather *penality*, is not reducible to any single meaning. It is fundamentally complex, both in the institutional-practical realm and at the symbolic level. It exhibits both a diversity of practices and a multiplicity of meanings (and the second level is by no means a reflection of the first). For example, the official policy statements, rhetorics and declarations of the 1950s and 1960s in Britain and, to a much lesser extent, the institutional practices of that period, produced a new series of signifiers ('rehabilitation', 'treatment', 'welfare') which were linked to the broader chains of reference and ideologies of the 'welfare state'. These gave penality a new significance (or rather promoted to dominance a significance which had been evolving for some time) and a new political-ideological effect (see Garland, 1981). The theoretical task of penology must be to identify and describe these shifts in significances, practices and effects, just as the related political task is to change them. The misfortune is that having opened up this symbolic realm to analysis, Durkheim simply closes it off again lest it challenge his basic propositions.

Notes

1   I would like to thank Lindsay Paterson, Fiona Dando and Neil Hutton for their careful and helpful comments on an earlier draft of this chapter.
2   To argue that Durkheim's theory involves an inescapable principle of expressive causality does not entail the proposition that Durkheim explains social phenomena only in terms of the 'function' which they fulfil. Indeed Durkheim's explicit methodological stipulations in *The Rules* point out the absurdities of this functionalist explanation of cause by effect (see Chapter 5) and insist upon the need to specify the *efficient causes*, as well as the function, of any object of investigation. In fact, Durkheim consistently abides by this principle in his substantive work; see, for example, the *Two Laws* essay (p. 297), where he refuses to explain the emergence of the prison solely in terms of the social need for such an institution.

Nevertheless, even his most 'historical' and 'materialist' explanations are still *essentialist* in structure. Thus, for example, the material conditions of existence of the prison are themselves the expressions of the new 'organic' type of social solidarity.

There *is* one example within Durkheim's work of phenomena which cannot be explained as expressions of any underlying essence: the notable case of the demographic and environmental factors which bring about the transition from mechanical to organic solidarity. However, this exception merely proves the general rule and, indeed, is necessary to it. The field of social facts generated by each form of solidarity is a necessary and essential field, united and without contradiction, being an expression of a unitary essence. Consequently the theory of solidarity – the normal explanation for social facts – cannot explain the *transformation* of that form of solidarity itself. To account for such a transformation, Durkheim is forced to introduce 'factors' which are outside the province of expressive causality. The *ad hoc* nature of this explanation is thus necessitated by its function in the discourse (see Hirst, 1975a: 133, 134).

3 On Discipline and Social Regulation: a Review of Foucault's Genealogical Analysis[1]

Barry Smart

Although the association of punishment with imprisonment may have achieved a degree of self-evidence in the present, it is clear that their respective histories do not constitute a necessary unity. The contemporary use of imprisonment as a general form of punishment contrasts quite radically with earlier historical periods in which imprisonment represented merely one specific form of punishment for particular offences, or even less, namely, a means for detaining rather than punishing offenders. The 'colonisation of the penalty by the prison' is explicable less in terms of developments in penal philosophy than as a significant dimension of the emergence and exercise of a new type of power, a power of normalisation which operates, in addition, in such non-penal institutions as the school, the hospital, the factory and the military academy. Analysis of this new type of power, power as a productive force, constitutes a central feature of the work of Foucault.

My contribution to the theme of this volume will take the form of a review of the work of Foucault in particular, and to a lesser extent that of Donzelot and Pasquino. Although I will focus on the prison–punishment nexus, my concern will be to try to enlarge the discussion to accommodate the more general, yet no less significant or relevant, issue of the impact of the human sciences on the management, regulation and government of populations. I will begin by briefly outlining what I take to be the distinctive characteristics and most significant general features of Foucault's work. I will then proceed to discuss the genealogical character of Foucault's analyses; the conceptions of power–knowledge relations, discipline and the disciplinary society; the problem of the relationship between programmes and practices; and finally the regulation of population and the formation of 'the social'.

Constructing an overview or summary of Foucault's work is no easy matter, for it has a somewhat fragmentary character and spans a variety of topics, ranging from the evolution and institutionalisation of psychiatry, to a history of knowledge of sexuality. It seems therefore to defy systematisation; its destination and unity are far from self-evident. Yet it is possible to provide some idea of the direction of the work, to give some sense of its possible unity. For example, the analysis of the historical conditions of possibility of the human sciences and their effects constitutes a sufficiently generous theme within which to encompass Foucault's work (cf. Smart, forthcoming). It would also be appropriate to describe his corpus as essentially concerned with the historical inscription of forms of power on the body, or even to consider the principal focus as being the analysis of the emergence of specifically modern forms of regulation and administration of the social domain. Clearly these are not mutually exclusive formulations; they constitute related aspects of Foucault's work and indicate that behind the surface fragmentation there are a number of recurring themes and signs of a general project.

Although there are differences between Foucault's earlier works on the asylum, the clinic, and the *episteme* and the more recent works on the prison and on sexuality, there is an underlying continuity. This continuity takes the form of a concern with the relationship between forms of rationality, the emergence of specific forms of knowledge, and forms of domination, the exercise of specific forms of power. An explicit conception of an interdependence between forms of knowledge and apparatuses of power first appears with the study of imprisonment and punishment. The emergence of this apparently different type of analysis, embodied in *Discipline and Punish*, has licensed all manner of speculation as to shifts, breaks and continuities in his work (cf. Patton, 1979; Gordon, 1980). My comments will generally be confined to the more recent works in which the issues of power–knowledge, discipline and the regulation of populations receive an explicit formulation.

Genealogical analysis and the materiality of the body
In his interrogation of the rationality of the present, Foucault concentrates on specific events and transformations that occurred in the seventeenth, eighteenth and nineteenth centuries. Among the many developments identified as significant in this period are the emergence of new forms of knowledge, the human sciences; new forms of the exercise of power; a reversal of the 'axis of individualisation' away from a celebration of powerful individuals ('the individuality of the memorable man') and towards the collection of files, records and information on 'individuals' on and over whom power is exercised (the individuality of 'the calculable man'); and the constitution of the social domain as a target for rational social policies and political

interventions. These developments illustrate the necessary inter-dependence of power–knowledge relations, namely, that the human sciences are made possible by the emergence of new forms of the exercise of power, which through the discipline and surveillance of populations produce both new domains of objects and definite forms of knowledge (cf. Foucault, 1977a: 190–4).

A significant feature in the analysis of these developments is a conception of the body as the object or target for the exercise of power, a conception which reveals Foucault's Nietzschean legacy. This legacy also includes a specific conception of history, namely, genealogy. Genealogical analysis is differentiated from orthodox or traditional history on several counts. To begin with, genealogy is concerned with the singularity of events, rather than with the inser-tion of events into linear processes or explanatory systems. It repre-sents an orientation to history which is relatively silent on great movements, for it concerns itself instead with phenomena which are frequently considered to lack a history (for example, reason, punish-ment, sexuality). Finally, it rejects the traditional historical pre-occupation with 'the pursuit of the origin' in preference for a conception which recognises that historical beginnings reveal com-plexities, contingencies and differences.

There are two dimensions to Foucault's conception of genealogical analysis: genealogy as an analysis of descent, and genealogy as an analysis of emergence. Genealogy as descent permits a recognition of the multiplicity of factors which lie behind things, it allows for events to be maintained in their 'proper dispersion', for the accidents, devia-tions and errors from which things emerge to be identified. However, as Foucault has cautioned, the search for descent is not synonymous with the erection of secure foundations for knowledge:

> on the contrary, it disturbs what was previously considered immobile; it fragments what was thought unified; it shows the heterogeneity of what was imagined consistent with itself. (1977b: 147)

The focus of this conception of genealogical analysis, the analysis of descent, is 'the articulation of the body and history', the imprinting of history upon the body, manifested, for example, in 'the nervous system, in temperament', in desires and appetites. The other dimen-sion of genealogy – the analysis of emergence – conceptualises developments in history as merely the existing stage in a series of subjugations, as products of the prevailing relation of forces. Thus a genealogical analysis of the practice of punishment, which 'has been subjected throughout its history to a variety of needs – revenge, excluding an aggressor, compensating a victim, creating fear' (1977b: 148), focuses upon a specific form of punishment as the product of a particular stage in the play of dominations, rather than as the embodiment or realisation of an originating purpose or need.

Within traditional history events are subordinated to, or concealed within, preconceived continuities or formal systems to which a cause, purpose or design is attributed. An inevitability or necessity is attached to events and their singularity is subordinated to the broad sweep of economic mechanisms, demographic processes or a universal anthropological structure. The order thereby imposed on historical contents by functionalist or systematising thought is challenged by genealogical analysis. Through the excavation of formerly subjugated knowledges, 'blocs of historical knowledge which were present but disguised within the body of functionalist and systematising theory' (Foucault, 1980b: 82), coupled with the emergence of low-ranking, local, discredited and disqualified knowledges (for example, the psychiatric patient's knowledge, that of the offender, the prisoner, etc.), the weakness of global theories has begun to be exposed and their inhibiting effect on research eliminated.

Genealogical analysis accords priority to events. The aim of genealogical analysis is to reveal the singularity of an event, to salvage the event, to disrupt the self-evident grounds of our knowledges and practices, and then to proceed to effect what Foucault terms a causal multiplication, to consider the multiple processes which make up the event. For example, analysis of the event of penal incarceration requires that attention be given to a multiplicity of processes, including the 'penalisation' of internment, the 'carceralisation' of penal justice, and a host of other subprocesses which constitute the former. In practice, this involves a procedure of decomposition, the breaking down of the event under analysis into its smallest components (cf. Foucault, 1981).

Power–knowledge

Central to Foucault's work on the historical conditions of possibility of the human sciences and the effects of their deployment in social and institutional practices is a conception of the mutual, inextricable interdependence of power and knowledge. Power produces knowledge, they imply one another; a site where power is exercised is also a place at which knowledge is produced. If this seems strange to us, it is probably because we have become overburdened with epistemological considerations, have been preoccupied with determining the criteria for an elusive scientificity, or with the endless intricacies of disentangling what we wish to understand as 'science' from that which we dismiss or devalue as 'ideology'. Within the human sciences we have become accustomed to the seemingly self-evident proposition that knowledge is only possible where power relations are suspended.

The conception of power—knowledge relations, namely, that:

> there is no power relation without the correlative constitution of a field of knowledge, nor any knowledge that does not presuppose and constitute at the same time power relations (Foucault, 1977a: 27)

disturbs this self-evidence.

Exploration of the history of the rationality of the present has produced analyses of the discourses and practices through which madness, ill health, sexuality, crime, etc., have been constituted as objects of specific forms of knowledge and as targets for particular institutional practices. At its most general, this work traces the historical emergence of the social as a domain or field of inquiry and intervention, a space structured by a multiplicity of discourses emanating from the human sciences which, in their turn, are derived from, yet provide, a range of methods and techniques for regulating and ordering the social domain. Intrinsic to this analysis is the conception of power—knowledge relations, outlined above, and a particular conception of power to which I will now turn.

Foucault's references to power are dispersed throughout several texts and interviews. Generally his references to a conception of power are in the form of a distancing from prevailing conceptions, in particular from the juridico-discursive conception. Power, we are told, is not a property, it is not possessed; it is not the privilege, acquired or preserved, of the dominant class; furthermore, it is not exercised simply as an obligation or as a prohibition on those without power. Rather, power is exercised, it is a strategy; its effects of domination are attributable to 'dispositions, manoeuvres, tactics, techniques, and functionings'; it invests those on whom it is exercised, is 'transmitted by them and through them'; furthermore, 'it exerts pressures upon them, just as they themselves, in their struggle against it, resist the grip it has on them' (Foucault, 1977a: 26–7). In other words, power also provokes its own resistance.

Relations of power are not localized in particular relations, for example, between state and citizen, nor are they based on the border between social classes. For Foucault:

> Power comes from below . . . there is no binary and all-encompassing opposition between rulers and ruled at the root of power relations . . . One must suppose rather that the manifold relationships of force that take shape and come into play in the machinery of production, in families, limited groups, and institutions, are the basis for wide-ranging effects of cleavage that run through the social body as a whole. (1979a: 94)

Power is therefore not inevitably vested in the state, the sovereign or the law. The juridico-discursive conception formulates power as prohibition, as repression, as subjugation; it is an inherently negative conception. Although many of its forms persist to the present time, the conception neglects the positivity of power and, in particular, the new mechanisms which are irreducible to the representation of law, for example, those disciplines (hierarchical observation, normalising judgement, examination) which subject institutions such as the army, the school and the workshop to:

> a whole micro-penality of time (latenesses, absences, interruptions of tasks), of activity (inattention, negligence, lack of zeal), of behaviour (impoliteness, disobedience), of speech (idle chatter, insolence), of the body (incorrect attitudes, irregular gestures, lack of cleanliness), of sexuality (impurity, indecency). (Foucault, 1977a: 178)

These disciplinary methods are employed on all levels of the social domain and in forms that are not contained or exhausted by the state and its apparatuses.

The conclusion to be drawn from this is that, in order to understand and to analyse power within the 'concrete and historical framework of its operation', a break is required from the juridico-discursive conception of power–law or power–sovereign. Foucault proposes not only the abandonment of the juridico-discursive model of power and the substitution instead of a strategical-relational model, but in addition recommends a dissociation from the tradition which conceives of knowledge independently of power and of the renunciation of power as one of the conditions of knowledge. In their place Foucault inserts an alternative, a positive and productive conception of power and a radically different mode of analysis which examines the power–knowledge relations that invest human bodies and constitute them as objects of knowledge and domination.

A concept of the body thus assumes a significant place in Foucault's discourse. It represents the object of new forms of knowledge and it serves as the target for the exercise of power; it has been tortured, imprisoned, diagnosed and treated; its nature has been constituted in terms of its sex; and its forces have been trained and disciplined to optimise its economic value. The body, inscribed by history, serves as the fundamental material level; it is the principal target of the exercise of power.

The body not only represents the object or target of power, it also constitutes the location or site of resistance and opposition. The investment of power in and over the body may well produce an awareness of and control over bodily forces, but it also creates the possibility of a reaction against power, 'of health against the economic system, of pleasure against the moral norms of sexuality, marriage, decency' (Foucault, 1980a: 56). The exercise of power is thus accompanied by resistances and, although these do not constitute a major topic or theme of Foucault's analyses, they are not absent or insignificant. For example, the prison riots which have occurred since the late 1960s in several countries throughout the world (for example, Britain, USA, France, Australia and Italy) (cf. Mathiesen, 1974; Fitzgerald, 1977), are considered by Foucault to have been not so much about the relative adequacy of prison conditions, as about the very materiality of the prison, the prison as an 'instrument and vector of power' over the body. Furthermore, Foucault comments that it was from such revolts and resistances within the prison that he came to understand that punishment in general and the prison in particular belong to a political technology of the body. To understand more clearly the nature of the political investment of the body and the technology of power over the body, it is necessary to consider the conceptions of discipline and disciplinary society which are at the heart of Foucault's analysis of the practice of imprisonment.

On discipline

One of the problems that Foucault's genealogies have encountered is that of assimilation within the existing discourses of psychiatry, medicine, psychoanalysis, criminology and penology. His works are read as specific contributions to an understanding of the history of madness, medicine, sexuality and punishment. It is their descriptions and accounts of the history of the asylum, the clinic or the prison to which attention is devoted and, in consequence, the critical import of the work is lost. It is not that *Discipline and Punish* is not about punishment and the prison; rather, that the latter constitute instances of a practice and an institution, which serve as significant examples for showing the emergence of a new technology of power, discipline, and new forms of knowledge, the sciences of man, the human sciences, which constitute a technology of individuality.

A brief consideration of the terms of reference of Foucault's history of the practice of imprisonment might be helpful here. At the outset, through a graphic description of physical torture, we are invited to fall back on the self-evidence that contemporary forms of punishment are more 'humane', we are invited to be the 'reader–judge', to reflect upon the lesser cruelty and pain inflicted on offenders in contemporary societies. However, such a judgement may fail to detect a significant qualitative change in the object and objective of punishment. For it is no longer the body that is the direct object of punishment, but the 'knowable' individual, the soul. Beneath a relative stability of legal statutes and codes, a variety of subtle changes of practice have taken place which have introduced extra-juridical elements into the penal process:

A corpus of knowledge, techniques, 'scientific' discourses is formed and becomes entangled with the practice of the power to punish. (Foucault, 1977a: 23)

Thus the study of the practice of imprisonment constitutes 'a correlative history of the modern soul and of a new power to judge'. It encompasses not only a consideration of the complexity of penal mechanisms and their situation within the general field of technologies of power, but, in addition, is addressed to the interdependence of the humanisation of the penal system and the emergence of the human sciences upon the new technology of power.

Of the three different conceptions of ways of organising the power to punish, which existed in the eighteenth century, one conception predominated: namely, that involving the deployment of techniques for the transformation, reformation and discipline of individuals, from which imprisonment emerged as the general means of punishment. This 'event' did not emerge purely from developments in penal theory, neither did it constitute an adoption of the reforming jurists' programme. In the eighteenth century reforms were directed towards increasing the detail, regularity, constancy and effectivity of the power to punish, towards removing the inefficiencies and excesses of the old economy of the power to punish associated with monarchical law. The movement for more efficient and calculated punishment did not involve a reduction of penalty to imprisonment, but rather an index linking the idea of (a) crime to the idea of (b) punishment, for which visibility and a diversity of forms of punishment were prerequisites. Punishment was no longer to be a ceremonial of sovereignty in which vengeance was inflicted on the body of the condemned person; rather, it was to become both a procedure for requalifying guilty individuals as subjects, so that they might be able to resume their place in society, and also a means for discouraging the population of potential offenders.

For the reforming jurists, punishment clearly constituted a set of moral 'representations', the public circulation of which would convey to the ranks of the 'innocent' all the misfortunes of an immoral existence. Where imprisonment entered into their programme, it was not as a possible general form of punishment, for they were opposed to both concealed forms of punishment and the idea of a uniform penal mechanism, but as a specific penalty suitable for particular offences, a penalty which would conjure up in the minds of the public the idea of a particular crime and the consequences of its commission. How, then, are we to account for the adoption of the practice of imprisonment as the principal component of the penal system? Foucault's answer is that the transformation within the penal system of punishment into a penitentiary technique is synonymous with a political investment of the body, with the emergence of a political technology of the body, with the diffusion of disciplinary power.

Concomitant with the decline of 'ceremonial' punishment, of public torture and execution, there is a relative loosening of the hold of power over the body. However, although the body has become an instrument or intermediary of punishment, rather than its direct object, the hold over the body has not disappeared entirely, for punishment never functions without a certain bodily element. Imprisonment introduces a control over and regulation of time, space, material and human 'resources', and has a number of effects on the body (for example, a determination of diet, deprivation of desire, restriction of physical exercise and movement, and so forth). Nevertheless, it remains the case that this residue of bodily 'torture' is increasingly encompassed by the non-corporal qualities of the penal system. There has been a significant change in both the form and the object of punishment.

As I have indicated above, it was the emergence of new forms of the exercise of power and concomitant new forms of knowledge which produced the shift of focus from the body as the direct target of intervention to what Foucault terms 'the soul', or 'knowable man', conceptualised in terms of psyche, subjectivity, personality, consciousness and individuality. It is not a matter, therefore, of a negative process, a releasing of the body from the grip of power, but rather, of a positive transformation, the production, through the specific technology of power termed discipline, of a new reality and knowledge, that of the individual. To explore this reality further, we will have to turn to the common matrix which links, in the specific instance of punishment, the history of the penal law and that of the human sciences. In other words, turn directly to the question of discipline as a general formula of domination and to the event described as the emergence of a disciplinary society.

The diffusion of disciplinary methods in the eighteenth and nineteenth centuries represents one of the dimensions along which the new mechanisms of power exercised their control over the body, over life. These methods – disciplines – optimised the capabilities of the body, increased its economic utility, while at the same time producing its political docility. The second dimension along which power operates over life is that of population, specifically the regulation of population. Here the focus falls upon an aggregate body, the species body, and intervention takes the form of a supervision or regulation of the social environment within which the various dimensions and characteristics of population are formed. We may therefore differentiate between two forms of power over life: first, an 'anatomo-politics of the human body'; and second, a 'bio-politics of the population'.

It was in the course of the eighteenth century that the disciplines, the methods of observation, recording, regulation and training to which the body had long been subjected in monasteries, armies and workshops became general formulae of domination. The principal object of the disciplines was the control of individuals, through training and normalisation, and the regulation of social functions. The disciplines comprised a set of techniques: the decomposition of multiplicities into units, and units into elements (for example, groups into individuals, processes into practices, undifferentiated spaces into enclosed 'individual' units, actions into movements, etc.); the regulation and optimal development of bodily potential (production of utility/docility) through exercise; an architecture or social network of visibility (the eye of authority) which maintained individuals in their subjection (cf. Foucault, 1977a: 205); and a recomposition of multiplicities or units to maximise performance (for example, as in military units, industrial production units, where the 'whole' is greater than the sum of the constituent 'parts'). These disciplinary techniques spread from specific social institutions like the monastery, the hospital, the military academy, etc. to permeate the entire social domain. Disciplinary power is exercised on the 'whole indefinite domain of the non-conforming', on the pupil's error, the soldier's lapse of concentration, the worker's absence or inefficiency, not merely on transgressions of the legal code. Thus the exercise of disciplinary power, disciplinary 'punishment', is not reducible to judicial punishment. Disciplinary power is exercised on departures from the rule, on non-observance of imposed norms, and its aim is essentially corrective, to restore or reproduce the norm, to close the gap between the (deviant) actuality of human behaviour and the programmed norm.

Discipline, the power of normalisation, both required and produced a whole new apparatus of knowledge. The procedures of individualisation, which the disciplines introduced, constituted the roots of the human sciences, and it is from the detailed procedures of these disciplines that the sciences of psychology, psychiatry, pedagogy and criminology emerged. The consequences for the penal system were not insignificant, for the construction of *homo criminalis* constituted a new object for penal discourse and required a fundamental transformation of the conceptual relationship at its centre between law, crime and punishment. Within classical penal theory, as Pasquino (1980) has documented, there is no special conception of the individual, only a general anthropology of 'free will', of the potential, the possibility or the freedom of all to commit crime, and thereby to become subject to the process of penal justice. There is, in other words, no criminology as such, for there is no conception of the criminal. With the emergence of the conception of *homo criminalis* it is not only the rationality of penal discourse that undergoes a trans-formation, it is not merely a matter of a displacement of the concep-tual triangle of law, crime and punishment. Rather, the construction of a conception of *homo criminalis* signifies the emergence of the discourse of criminology and the permeation of the judicial process by the disciplines.

The penal process, from investigation to judgement and to the exercise of penality, has been penetrated by the disciplines and its 'tools' (for example, psychiatric expertise and 'the repetitive dis-course of criminology') to such an extent that it is no longer merely concerned with the establishment of the truth of a crime and the achievement of a just punishment, but rather, it constitutes a context within which there occurs an assessment of normality and the formu-lation of prescriptions for enforced normalisation. A series of subsidiary authorities have achieved a stake in the penal process; psy-chiatrists, psychologists, doctors, educationalists and social workers share in the judgement of normality, prescribe normalising treatment and contribute to the process of fragmentation of the legal power to punish. As Foucault has remarked, the judge, magistrate or juror is no longer alone; parallel judges are to be found virtually everywhere in our society, subjecting individuals to investigation through detached analytical observation and comparison with an inaccessible norm, as well as producing permanent records and files to support and authorise decisions or judgements. Subjecting individuals to observation is:

> a natural extension of a justice imbued with disciplinary methods and examination procedures. Is it surprising that the cellular prison, with its regular chronologies, forced labour, its authorities of surveillance and registration, its experts in normality, who continue and multiply the func-tions of the judge, should have become the modern instrument of penal-ity? Is it surprising that prisons resemble factories, schools, barracks, hospitals, which all resemble prisons? (Foucault, 1977a: 227–8)

This diffusion of the disciplinary mechanism, the extension of surveil-lance and the power of normalisation throughout the social domain, is synonymous with what Foucault has, somewhat ambiguously, described as the formation of the disciplinary society (the spread of the 'panoptic schema', the constitution of a 'carceral network'). This formation is associated, in turn, with a number of broad historical processes.[2]

The conception of a disciplinary society is open to a number of readings, to possible misinterpretations and misrepresentations. The use of the concept in Foucault's work may appear to invoke the very kind of global and totalising theoretical system that genealogy opposes, namely, a version of a functionalist theory of society within which individuals are reduced to 'cultural dopes' and human agency to a mere reflex of social structures. Modern societies thus seem to be represented as homogeneously disciplinary, to have become 'disciplined' societies, orderly, programmed realities which countenance no opposition or resistance. If this is a fair representation of certain uses of the conception in *Discipline and Punish*, it is certainly not adequate for understanding Foucault's subsequent work, which places less emphasis on the predominance of mechanisms of discipline and more on mechanisms of security and the management of population, the second dimension along which power over life operates.

However, it might be objected that the very interpretation of the disciplinary society which I have offered is amiss, for at least three reasons. First, the extension of the disciplines throughout the social body, the emergence of a generalised surveillance, constitutes a general formula of domination in contemporary society. The emphasis here is on panopticism, generalised surveillance, as a formula rather than as a practice which functions at optimum to produce a programmed society. Thus 'disciplinary society' refers to the diffusion of the formula, to the extension of disciplinary mechanisms, not to the realisation of a programme for a disciplined and ordered society. Second, although Foucault offers little comment on struggles against and around the exercise of power, it is clear that such 'events' are recognised to exist and to be of significance, as I have already observed of revolts within penal institutions, revolts at the level of the body against one specific disciplinary institution. Third, implicit in such an interpretation of the concept of disciplinary society is the idea that a neat correspondence is possible between rationalities and the functioning of institutions, that a disciplinary rationality may materialise in the form of a disciplined society. Such a conception is antithetical to the position adopted by Foucault, namely, that programmes never work out as planned, that there is no unproblematic correspondence between programmes and practices.

Programmes, practices and imprisonment

The conception of the inter-relationship between the exercise of power and the formation or production of knowledge, that 'power and knowledge directly imply one another', is a central feature of the position developed by Foucault, Donzelot and Pasquino. In their work they show that the human sciences provide for the development of programmes of social intervention through the generation of institutional practices towards specifically constituted objects, and that such interventions have consequences or effects. However, whereas within the discourses of the human sciences and, in particular, in the field of policy studies there is a conception of the social world as a potentially rational order, as a reality which may be rendered orderly through instrumental-rational conceptions of knowledge and social engineering techniques of intervention that constitute their corollary, in the work of 'the genealogists' the implied relationship between discourses, practices and effects is of a different order.[3]

It is the nature of the interplay between forms of rationality and specific institutional practices (for example, the practice of imprisonment) which is at issue here; in particular, the fact that programmes or rational schemes offering prescriptions for the reorganisation of institutions and the regulation of behaviour have not, and this understates the point, been fully embodied in social practices. In short, there has been, and indeed remains, a lack of correspondence between programmes and practices. The danger is that this formulation of a non-correspondence may be interpreted to mean that programmes are little more than models, imaginary schemes, fictions, with little or no relevance for, or relation to, 'the real'. This misrepresentation is especially likely within the human sciences, where conceptions of a correspondence (or the possibility of such) between analysis, policy and effects, or a close relationship between theory and practice, still predominate. However, a lack of correspondence does not signify the absence of any relationship between programmes and practices; rather, it indicates that there can be no general formula, the relationship is problematical and specific to each instance, to each particular programme, the specific related practices and their effects. To illustrate this point, I will briefly consider the analysis Foucault provides of the practice of imprisonment.

Put simply, Foucault's argument is that the 'penalisation' of incarceration was not in accord with the proposals advanced by the eighteenth-century penal reformers; rather, the practice of penal incarceration which emerged at the end of the eighteenth century signified the successful diffusion of a particular type of power, namely, 'discipline'. The self-evidence which imprisonment soon assumed as the generalised form of punishment was a consequence not only of the apparent appropriateness of punishing offenders through the deprivation of their liberty – a property common to, and valued by, each individual – but, more significantly, it stemmed from the fact that it employed, albeit in a more explicit and intense form, all the disciplinary mechanisms found elsewhere in the social body for transforming individuals. The central themes of the *Panopticon*, 'surveillance and observation, security and knowledge, individualization and totalization, isolation and transparency' were thus to find their most intense expression in the institution of the prison, in the event of penal incarceration.

However, in order to be able to make any attempt at normalising or transforming offender-inmates, a knowledge is clearly required: a knowledge of the offender's life and of the crime committed, a knowledge of the circumstances. Thus the prison became a site within which a knowledge was constituted: a scientific knowledge of the offence and of the offender. It is here, as I have implied above, that the emergence of criminology might be situated. It is not a matter of first the prison, then the construction of delinquent biographies, and thereafter the emergence of criminology; rather, they appeared together.

So far so good, but I have not yet broached the critical issue of the 'failure' of the practice of imprisonment: that prisons do not seem to diminish the crime rate; that incarceration appears to produce recidivism; that the prison environment facilitates exchanges amongst delinquents, and provides a context for forming organisations; that a 'cycle' of delinquency may be produced as a consequence of the destitution inflicted upon the inmate's family; finally, that the continuing surveillance after terms of imprisonment have been served condemns inmates to recidivism. These signs of the failure of the prison have been present from its very establishment as the general form of punishment within the penal system; indeed Foucault goes further and suggests that 'failure' might constitute part of the function of the prison (cf. 1977a: 234–5, 264–5, 270d; 1980c). Here we encounter an apparent lack of correspondence between the programme, the practices and their effects, to which Foucault responds with an inversion: namely, if the history of the prison has been one of perpetual 'failure', what positive value has this served?

Rather than concentrating on the apparent lack of realisation of Bentham's *Panopticon* schema in the prisons, where criminals resisted the new disciplines, Foucault suggests that attention be turned to the 'productivity' of the prison, to its effects, and to the positive strategical uses to which its 'successes' have been put. The practice of imprisonment is thereby recognised to be a mechanism for differentiating offences rather than eliminating them, for establishing and reproducing a 'politically and economically less dangerous type' of illegality (delinquency). This form of illegality is 'advantageous' in several respects (cf. 1977a: 276–82), but above all because it serves to provide a rational justification for the extension of methods of surveillance throughout the social body. The effect of prison is not therefore that of a 'failure' to reduce the number of illegal offences committed; rather, it may be considered a 'success' in so far as the form of illegality it produces has proven useful, that is to say, there has been a 'strategic utilisation of what had been experienced as a drawback' (Foucault, 1980c: 40). The formulation of the failure/success of the prison has prompted two related questions: one concerns the possibility of a latent functionalist tendency at play in Foucault's analysis; the other involves the conception of strategy.

If we consider functionalist analysis in terms of the ordering of historical contents, events, into a coherence, into global theories or formal systems, with their teleological conceptions of design, purpose and so on, then it is difficult to comprehend the classification of Foucault's work as functionalist, for his genealogical analyses stand in direct opposition to functionalist or systematising thought. This confusion possibly arises from a conflation of the respective levels of Foucault's analyses (discourses; social and institutional practices; effects) and from ambiguities surrounding some of his formulations (for example, the 'global' conception of a 'disciplinary society'). Whereas the human sciences operate in principle with, or assume, a conception of a possible correspondence between discursive formulations, social and institutional practices, and effects – a conception which implies the possibility of 'successful' social policies, policies producing intended effects, effects as programmed – Foucault's analyses proceed, as I have indicated, from the converse position. He argues that the complexities of institutions and human behaviour escape the programmatic formulation, that there is always a residual deviation from the norm and, furthermore, that the technologies charged with exercising a power of normalisation to correct or modify deviation are equally defective. In other words, rather than assume a correspondence, Foucault investigates the actuality of a non-correspondence between the respective levels.

From this point of view 'failure' is the norm for social policy. Thus, given the specific *Panopticon* programme, the practice of imprisonment may be deemed to have 'failed', but that is not the end of the matter. It is not, then, merely a case of charting a difference 'between the purity of the ideal and the disorderly impurity of the real' (Foucault, 1981: 10), but of investigating the actual effects (in institutions, in individual behaviour, in the perception and evaluation of 'objects') produced by the unrealised programme, in the specific instance with which we are concerned, the effects of the practice of imprisonment. These effects – the construction of a delinquency, an enclosed illegality, a less dangerous even useful illegality – are not anticipated in or by the programme. The programme may, as Foucault argues, anticipate its own failure; hence the business of prison reform being present at the very birth of the prison. But that is not the same thing as the programme producing latently 'functional effects' beneath its manifest dysfunctions or 'failures'. If there is any sense in which effects may be considered functional, it is not at the level of the programme, but at that of strategy.

In Foucault's analysis of discipline and the practice of imprisonment there are at least two strands: one concerns the analysis of a specific form of the exercise of power, disciplinary power, and the embodiment of this form of power and its form of rationality within the penal system, in the institution of the prison. In this way Foucault attempts to account for the birth or emergence of the prison. The second concern is that of the operation of the prison, the effects of the practice of imprisonment, and it is at this point that the issue of failure arises and, concomitantly, the possibility of its effects being retrieved as successes within an alternative strategy.

A brief digression is necessary here to avoid misunderstanding this conception of strategy. Behind the conception of strategy there lies no grand plan, no plotting subject, class, party or institution. Strategy is not formulated in advance of the exercise of power; it is a non-discursive rationality, it belongs to the level of effects, it refers to the particular field in which the multiplicity of force relations (power) take effect. It is, as Gordon has succinctly stated:

> the mobile sets of operations whereby a multiplicity of heterogeneous elements (forces, resources, the features of a terrain, the disposition and relation of objects in space—time) are invested with a particular functionality relative to a dynamic and variable set of objectives. (Gordon: 1980: 251)

Thus, strategies operate on the objects and relations formed within the social domain by programmes and technologies of power. Furthermore, specific technologies or mechanisms of power may be adopted within or embraced by distinctly contrasting strategies. Therefore, instead of referring to the effects of imprisonment (the production of a specific illegality, etc.) as functional for a specific strategy (the surveillance and management of the 'political' population), the direct implication of which is that the birth or origin of the prison may be accounted for in terms of its present strategical operation, it would be more appropriate to recognise that the technological apparatus of the prison may be adapted to different strategical roles, it may be made to function within different strategies.

A difficulty with discussing the conception of strategy in this context is that Foucault's study of discipline and the practice of imprisonment is less concerned with 'strategical questions', the various historical struggles surrounding the insertion of the prison within the penal system, than with specifying the character of the specific form of the exercise of power of which the prison represents an instance. The strategical conception of power emerges more explicitly with Foucault's work on sex and sexuality (cf. Patton, 1979; Minson, 1980b).

Bio-politics and the regulation of population

The new form of the exercise of power, which sought to maximise the 'economic' utility and 'political' docility of the human body, represented an important development; it signified the increasing predominance of a 'power over life', rather than, as had been the case under monarchical law with its extravagant public ceremonial and ritual torture and execution, a 'power over death'. Now, contrary to the impression which *Discipline and Punish* may convey, the disciplines constitute merely one of the dimensions along which the organisation of power over life was deployed. The second dimension, addressed by Foucault, Donzelot and Pasquino, concerns the exercise of power through the management or regulation of population.

At first sight the text in which Foucault begins to explore this issue, *The History of Sexuality*, might seem to be merely concerned with a rebuttal of the hypotheses of 'sexual repression' and 'sexual liberation'. However, this text is not concerned with a discovery of the secrets of sex, its 'nature' so to speak. Neither is it confined to a dissolution of the 'repressive hypothesis' through a demonstration that Victorian society revolved around talk of sexuality. Rather, its focus is sex as the pivot of the two axes, of the disciplines of the body and of the regulation of population, along which the technology of power over life is exercised. To describe this process, by which life was encompassed within rational discourse and calculation and made an object of transformation, Foucault formulates the term bio-power. We will see that one of the issues to which this refers, namely, the regulation of population, becomes an increasingly central feature of analysis for Foucault and his associates.

Foucault traces the emergence of population as a phenomenon, as a problem for government, through a chain of complex historical processes. Specifically, the regulation of population represents an issue of security, it involves 'the right of the social body to ensure, maintain, or develop its life', and therefore it ultimately becomes an issue of government. The problematic of government arises for Foucault at the intersection of two developments: the dismantling of the structures of feudal society and the subsequent emergence of centralised states; and the growth of religious dissidence with the Reformation and Counter-Reformation. These developments foment a variety of discourses which pose the problem of government. What eventually emerged from this complex historical process was an art of government for which population constituted the target of intervention, and the welfare of the population the ultimate goal of the governmental process. Management of population in all its various dimensions (birth and death rates, age structure, health, etc.) became synonymous with the maintenance or development of the life of the social body.

The phenomenon of population emerged as a possible object of government with the demographic expansion of the eighteenth century and the employment of statistical methods and techniques. Statistics, 'the science of the state', revealed that population had its own regularities, rates of increase and decrease. It became apparent that the effects of population were not reducible to the unit of the family and, in consequence, the conception of the family as the model for government was displaced by that of the family as an instrument of government. Before the advent of the phenomenon of population:

> the art of government was impossible to conceive except on the model of the family and in terms of economy conceived as the management of a family; from the moment when . . . population appears as absolutely irreducible to the family, the latter becomes secondary with respect to the population, comes to appear as an element internal to population. (Foucault, 1979b: 17)

As a consequence, as Donzelot (1980) has documented, the family became a mechanism of government, a privileged instrument for the regulation or management of population. The welfare of the population, improvement in conditions, health and wealth, began to constitute the object of a complex new form of power, that of government.

This complex new form of power, described by Foucault as 'governmentality', is a product of several developments. These include a change in the meaning of the concept of economy, from its sixteenth-century use as a form of government, specifically 'wise government of the family', to its eighteenth-century and contemporary use, to refer to a distinct level of reality where techniques of regulation and management may be applied. This political conception of economy is, in turn, related to the formation and development of a form of knowledge, statistics, which reveals the phenomenon of population, its regularities and characteristics. Finally, the exercise of this form of power is made possible by the development of new technical means for social control, apparatuses of security, insurantial technologies, which begin to achieve a pre-eminence over the other technical means for the exercise of power, namely, sovereignty and discipline.

To avoid misunderstanding, a few additional comments might be helpful here. Foucault is not postulating a linear historical development of either forms of punishment, forms of the exercise of power or forms of government. Sovereignty does not disappear; discipline is not eliminated. It is not a matter of an evolutionary substitution of one form of society for another; on the contrary:

> in reality we have a triangle: sovereignty − discipline − government which has as its primary target the population and as its essential mechanism apparatuses of security. (Foucault, 1979: 19)

However, it is argued that the tendency has been, certainly in the West, for governmentality to predominate over both sovereignty and discipline, for control to be increasingly exercised through apparatuses of security or via insurantial technologies.

In the eighteenth century the various discourses on government took the form of a science of police, the latter being a reference to the development of promotion of 'happiness' or the 'public good', rather than to the suppression of disorder, the surveillance of public space or the protection of private property, which is its contemporary reference. Police regulations constituted the beginning of the power of administration over the social body, a beginning which constituted the population as both a target for the exercise of power and as an object for a set of knowledges. It is at this point, with the emergence of particular forms of power and the growth of specific forms of knowledge around such sites as 'police, assistance, medicalisation . . . prison, sexuality-psychiatry [and] the family' (Pasquino, 1978: 52) that we encounter the orderly network of the social.

The analysis of the formation of the social, the birth or 'origin' of the social as an object of power, administration and knowledge should not be confused with or rendered equivalent to the more conventional analyses of society emanating from within the social/human sciences. There is, as Donzelot has remarked, a significant difference:

> 'the social' is not society understood as the set of material and moral conditions that characterize a form of consolidation. It would appear to be rather the set of means which allow social life to escape material pressures and politico-moral uncertainties; the entire range of methods which make the members of a society relatively safe from the effects of economic fluctuations by providing a certain security. (Donzelot, 1980: xxvi)

Thus the concept of the social is not synonymous with a sociological conception of society; for whereas the latter represents an ahistorical and universal conception of the necessary form of organisation of human existence, the former refers to a quite specific historical event, the emergence of a network or relay through which power is exercised over populations, a power of administration. The emergence of the social, the various laws and provisions directed to such dimensions of population as age, health, economic activity, education and welfare, constitutes a major development or shift in the form of the exercise of power. It denotes a relative decrease in the significance of techniques of discipline and a concomitant increase in the importance of mechanisms of insurance and security; it represents the insertion of a 'principle of cohesion' in the very fabric of society, the constitution of a particular kind of solidarity.[4]

The work of Foucault, Donzelot and Pasquino indicates that these developments, culminating in the formation of the social, have fundamentally transformed the nature of divisions, struggles and conflicts in society and that, in consequence, the conventional dichotomies and concepts which structure orthodox radical and critical analyses have become obsolete. However, a word of qualification is needed. Their denial of the continuing value of reducing divisions and conflicts within society to the universal currency of class struggle is not synonymous with the construction of a reconditioned consensus theory of society. The genealogists take the view that the telescoping of new forms of opposition and struggle, and new political subject groups (for example, women, prisoners, conscripted soldiers, hospital patients and homosexuals) into the limiting and limited conceptual framework of orthodox 'Left' political discourse, obscures the impact of new technologies of social relations, neglects the incorporation of the 'political' within the 'social', and perpetuates obsolete forms of analysis.

Concluding remarks

I have attempted to provide an account of the central features of the work of Foucault and his associates, and to indicate some of the respects in which their work might be differentiated from more conventional analyses produced within the human sciences. The recent history of these sciences suggests that a comparable claim might be made for discourses on law, crime and welfare derived from a variety of interpretations of Marxist and para-Marxist sources. Although Marxism is not directly accorded a privileged place or status within Foucault's analysis – indeed, it is considered to be fundamentally compatible with the other human sciences, in that it shares their epistemological space and conditions of possibility – the contexts in which it is explicitly addressed reveal its significance and status as the dominant form of radical theory and politics.

Although Foucault provides no clear appraisal or evaluation of Marxism, his scattered references nevertheless reveal the extent of his critical distance from historical materialist analysis and from Marxist politics. Criticisms are levelled at the preoccupation with the establishment of the scientificity of Marxism, with the investment of Marxism with a specific power; the theory–praxis relationship is rendered even more problematic, or more appropriately it is recast, by the conception of a relationship of non-correspondence between discourses–practices–effects; the fundamental principle of economic determination-in-the-final-instance is not only subjected to criticism, but shown to produce a neglect of the formation of the social and the 'socialisation' of politics; finally, although this does not exhaust the implications of Foucault's work for Marxism, the representational role accorded to intellectuals and political parties is criticised, in so far as it produces a further subordination of 'resistance to the normative criteria of a political programme' (cf. Gordon, 1980: 255–8).

The conflicts and political struggles of the nineteenth century contributed to the historical preconditions from which the methods of regulation, security, insurance and the other 'social' measures ultimately emerged. However, conceptualising these developments in terms of the growth of a monolithic state structure has proven sterile, analytically and politically, and has precluded analysis of the formation of the social. Historical materialist analyses have, directly or indirectly, reduced all the various effects of the social to the 'monstrous, uninterrupted and omnipresent genealogy of capital' (Pasquino, 1978: 43). As a consequence, the historical constitution and significance of the social has been neglected, and an appreciation of the inextricable interrelationship of the human sciences, including Marxism, with the technologies of power which lie behind the divisions of class, the power of capital and the emergence of the social domain has been obstructed.

Each of these issues, the formation of the social, the emergence of technologies of power exercised over individuals and populations, and the related contribution of the human sciences to the documentation, classification and normalisation of human behaviour, and organisation of a 'secure' population are addressed by genealogical analysis. However, the several genealogies of the sequestration of the insane, clinical medicine, sexuality and penal incarceration do not complement or compensate analyses emanating from the human sciences. On the contrary, their orientation is not to encompass specific practices within a technical explanation, it is not to grasp the whole of society in its reality; rather, genealogy aims to disrupt common conceptions about events and practices. Genealogy thus takes the form of critique, and attempts to show that specific forms of rationality and technologies of power have contributed to the production of particular historical events.

The project is a modest one, in so far as it lays no claim to universality or totality; there is no grand scheme or global principle for analysing society. Furthermore, the analyses provide no place for the universal intellectual, the social agency or party representing or 'speaking for' the people. There is no sense in which the question 'what is to be done' will receive an answer from genealogical analysis. Its politics is not that of the legislator or the prophet; it seeks to disrupt rather than to replace one 'regime of truth' with another.

Notes

1 I would like to thank Russell Hogg and David Garland for their critical and constructive comments on an earlier draft of this paper.
2 The historical processes identified by Foucault are as follows:

   (a) *Demographic*: an increase in the floating population in the eighteenth century; a change of quantitative scale in the populations to be supervised.
   (b) *Economic*: a growth in the apparatus of production, in both extent and complexity; an increase in the costs of production and a requirement therefore

      for rationalisation to improve efficiency and increase profitability.

(c)   *Juridico-political*: the emergence of a formally egalitarian juridical framework predicated on the organisation of a 'parliamentary representative' regime which masked the dominance of a particular class, the bourgeoisie.

(d)   *Scientific*: a development of disciplinary techniques to a level at which 'the formation of knowledge and the increase of power reinforce one another' (cf. Foucault, 1977a: 213–14).

3   As Colin Gordon states, 'Our world does not follow a programme, but we live in a world of programmes, that is to say in a world traversed by the effects of discourses whose object (in both senses of the word) is the rendering rationalisable, transparent and programmable of the real' (Gordon 1980: 245).

4   The social measures which have introduced a particular form of solidarity and cohesion within society may be differentiated in terms of three levels: the organisation of economic security; practices of assistance and social work; the positive integration of the bulk of the population (cf. Donzelot, 1979).

4 Sociology, the State and Penal Relations

Peter Young

In recent years one of the most urgent calls faced by the sociologist interested in the areas of law, crime and penality has been one emphasising the need to situate work in an adequate theoretical framework. Earlier accounts produced within these areas have been taken to task, not only because of their supposed empirical shortcomings, but, more significantly, because of their purported endemic lack of 'theory'. Although the halcyon days of what may be termed theoretical absolutism (a tendency to denigrate any reference whatsoever to the empirical) may be over – there being a typical counter-current stressing the concrete – it is nevertheless true to observe that practitioners now generally begin their investigations by seeking for, or working within, what is perceived to be an appropriate sociological theory. Furthermore, although this move to theory has complex roots – being founded, in part, in a critique of the tyranny of empiricism within social science and, in part, in a revitalisation of sociological traditions – its wider significance lies both in the role that theory is called upon to perform and also in the legacy it has created for the sociologist who desires to explain legal and penal phenomena.

It is the objective of this essay to describe this role and to trace its legacy by examining some sociological explanations that have recently been advanced to account for changes within the nineteenth-century penal system. Although these explanations emanate from various sociological traditions – some originating from within Marxism proper (see the collection in Fine *et al.*, 1979), others from within various admixtures of Marxism, Foucault and 'bourgeois' sociology (Scull, 1977a; Melossi, 1979; Young, 1980; Garland, 1981), and yet others arising from a more or less theoretical historicism (Ignatieff, 1978; Bailey 1981) – they all conjoin in portraying the capitalist state and the processes of political legitimation as being central to an explanation of change. The penal system is conceived of as part of the apparatuses of the state and is viewed also as an essential arena both within which differing political ideologies are condensed as well as being a crucial legitimating process in its own right. A dual thesis thus is developed, in which politics, ideology and the state figure large; penal relations are to be explained by the activities of the state, yet these very relations are conceived of as ideological determinants and effects of the precise manner in which the state is structured and by which it works (see Garland, 1981).

These accounts rarely propound a systematic theory of the nature of the state. However, there are some features or characteristics of it which appear with regularity and to which all presumably would adhere. First, these explanations eschew a theory of the state in general, focusing instead upon a specific manifestation of it – the capitalist state. It is the capitalist state, operating in historically specific conditions, which is perceived as the prime mover in explanations of penal relations. This is an important qualification, because not only does it abide by the characteristic methodological imperative to explain facts by reference to their historical relativity, but also it structures or determines the other features of the capitalist state which are subsequently highlighted. The second feature is a conception of the state as a unifying medium for the social formation. The state is ascribed both the function of political legitimation and also, on occasions, the significant one of reproducing the conditions of existence of capitalist society; the state appears as political, legal and economic guarantor. Third, the capitalist state is perceived as having quite specific relationships to the various classes within capitalism. It is conceived as an extension of bourgeois power, but not necessarily a purely instrumental one; the state unifies, in part, by claiming neutrality and independence of particular classes or factions. However, this neutrality, although it has material effects, is apparent rather than ultimately real; lurking behind this phenomenal expression are the realities of class and economic forces which combine to subjugate the working class to the disciplines of class society.

These explanations mark a significant advance and therefore are to be welcomed. Not only do they make penality a central topic of genuine sociological concern, but they do this by stressing relationships and forces considered to be at the fore of contemporary theorising. As an intimate connection is posited between the state and penality, it follows that the latter may provide a special vantage point from which to analyse the former; an investigation of penality fades into, and becomes central to, an understanding of the capitalist state in general. Moreover, these explanations seem to achieve a goal of sociology, long sought after, but rarely met. Their emphasis upon theoretical elaboration, and political institutions, tied to an area as concrete as penality, seems to unify theory and practice (that chimera

of the sociological tradition) with such ease that it obviates the difficulties normally encountered and typically experienced as insur-
mountable. However, this very obviousness and apparent success
should not blind us to the difficulties and problems engendered by
these explanations. These difficulties arise as much in their basic
constitution as they do in consideration of their finery and detail. Is it
so obvious that the state was, or is, the fundamental point of departure in explaining penality? Are the methodological protocols underpinning the use of sociological theory sufficiently clear or secure as to
justify and make tenable these explanations? What empirical or concrete grounds exist for these contentions, and can changes in the
nineteenth-century penal systems be explained upon an alternative
basis? Finally, do these accounts necessarily lead to a political
practice as fecund and effective as it is presupposed?

This essay will consider these questions by examining the grounds
upon which these explanations are constructed. Its broad conclusion
will be to contend that there is little other than a superficial foundation from which to claim such a priority for the state in explaining
penal relations. It will also propose that many of the conclusions
mistakenly proffered arise, not simply from an insufficient grasp of
empirical detail (although this is very often the case), but more from a
particular theoretical practice which tends to delimit and determine
the range of questions and problems initially posed. However, the
argument cannot be left at this point, for it is one thing to claim that
contemporary sociological explanations posit a false centrality for the
state and yet another to contend that political processes – including
the state – are quite irrelevant. Thus, the essay will conclude by offering a reinterpretation of nineteenth-century penal relations in which
it is proposed that state involvement was both more restricted and
operated upon a significantly different basis than it is commonly
supposed. It will be argued that the nature of state involvement was
overwhelmingly administrative rather than 'political', and that this
poses major problems for these explanations.

Sociological theory, the state and penality
There exists a close interconnection between the movement to situate
work in a theoretical framework, the identification of the state as a
medium or instance which governs the nature of penality, and perceptions of the possibilities of political practice. The relationship
between the last two is apparent and self-evident. If the state is
defined as the site of politics – be they class or otherwise – and there
exists the degree of connection and overlap between it and penality
described, then transformations in one raise the possibility of transformation in the other. In principle, this can be a two-way functional

relationship. Not only does it work from the generality of the state to the particularity of penal relations, but the reverse may also be true. Penality can be perceived as a point of entry into superordinate political forces and processes – a lever by which to prise open the nature of politics more generally.

As much of the contemporary work in penality is produced by those who claim a radical and progressive form of politics, the salience of this relationship is paramount. Penality becomes a strategic moment at which to intervene into class politics and, further, generates questions about the nature of control or discipline in a more socialist system of social arrangements. Moreover, as the most significant development within Marxism has involved a major revaluation of the relationship between economy and superstructure (Jessop, 1978; Young, 1980), thus forming the bedrock for the emergence of a Marxist theory of the state, it is only to be expected that the state has become a crucial locus of analysis. Penality, politics and the state are perceived to interconnect for reason of good political practice.

The relationship between theoretical elaboration and the state, however, is neither as clear-cut nor as apparently natural as the one just described. Indeed, the link between the construction of sociological theory and the stipulation of the state as a determinant of penality is contingent, even arbitrary. Apart from a nominalist public-law perspective, in which the formal constitutional network of the penal system is defined by law, it will be argued that there are no general grounds for asserting that the state should be a necessary factor in explaining penality. Moreover if this nominalist position is accepted, and the state enters the scene, this hardly provides sufficient warrant to consider the relationship a causal one. Yet this, with varying degrees of elaboration, is precisely the conceptual configuration adumbrated by many theorists. For example, Ignatieff consistently refers to the growth of the reformatory prison system as being causally tied to the activities of the emerging liberal, capitalist state (1978: xiii, 42, 54–5, 175 ff. etc.); Scull (1977a), accounts for the growth of decarceration by arguing for a combination of interests between powerful groups, especially professionals, who are perceived as agents of the state. To shift the focus to the twentieth century, such commentators as Cohen and Mathiesen (see Chapters 5 and 6) either explicitly refer to the state or imply its existence as an assumed force. Thus, there seems to be a unanimity (with the possible exception of Foucault, 1977a) amongst those explanations most commonly referred to by penal analysis, that the state is an essential and unavoidable part of any explanation of penality.

What are the grounds upon which these assertions are made? The empirical evidence to support these contentions is not, as we shall endeavour to demonstrate later, as unequivocal as it is commonly supposed. To treat changes in nineteenth-century penality as though they were dependent upon state action is, upon empirical consideration, a gross over-simplification. Not only did many of the sanctions or forms of control not emanate from direct state action (for example, police court missionaries and many of the charitably based forms of care), but the expansion of imprisonment (that most state-like of all punishments) was due more to the use of it by local magistrates – who were often in contest with the central government – than it was to a systematic plan by the capitalist state (cf. Minson 1980a).[1]

If these assertions do not have a secure empirical foundation, their origins must be sought elsewhere. It is here that the practice of situating explanations on a prior theoretical framework is of importance, because it is within it that the origins of these assertions are located. The stipulation of the state as a determinant of penality is an effect of this theoretical practice, the conception of theory with which it works and the role that theory is perceived to perform.

One of the consequences of this desire to engage in theoretical elaboration is to encourage a proclivity to treat theory as though it were a self-contained, hermetically sealed entity. Theory is treated as if it were an epistemological exercise in its own right. Rather than being defined as a set of related empirical propositions describing the connections between events, theory is perceived of as a series of concepts which determine the nature and status of the objects to be analysed; as one recent commentator put it, theories create their own 'objects of knowledge' (Hirst, 1975b). This contention is meant to convey more than the often asserted conventionalist case that facts are 'theory dependent'. For a conventionalist, theories serve as conceptual nets or filters which organise our knowledge of an ontologically separate reality. However, the argument propounded above presents a far more radical epistemological thesis. This thesis denies for all practical purposes the existence of an independent reality. Rather, our knowledge of reality is a creation of the structures of knowledge with which we work; it depends upon them for its ontological status. Thus we do not have 'facts' of an independent universe, but facts of one constructed in knowledge itself. Hence an 'object of knowledge' is a theoretical construction that need not have any relationship other than the one internal to the particular theory in question. Moreover, combined with this, and partly as a derivative of it, theory is conceived of also in an essentially formalist and holist fashion; theory is deployed as the medium through which specific social facts can be connected to the totality.

To explain theoretically thus amounts to demonstrating the connections between one holistic, conceptual proposition and another.

And, as it operates with the notion of theory outlined above, this, of necessity, becomes a procedure conducted purely upon grounds created by the framework of knowledge itself. Sociological explanation, in consequence, becomes an exercise in seeking coherence and internal harmony. A 'good' explanation is one in which a cosy, even aesthetically pleasing, relationship is established between that which is to be explained and the already existing conceptual structure.

The state fits into this partly because of its coherent conceptual nature and partly upon descriptive grounds. I will take the latter first. As has been conceded, there are nominalist and descriptive grounds for arguing for the centrality of the state in an explanation of penality. In a literal, legal sense, the penal system is defined institutionally by the state through the agencies of law, convention and rules. However, the transposition of this descriptive relationship into an explanatory one is an entirely different matter. The predilection of sociologists to do this arises from their use of the conception of theory described. As theory is perceived in an epistemological sense, empirical or descriptive relationships will tend to be transposed into conceptual and theoretically explanatory ones.

This practice is the obverse of the fallacy of misplaced concreteness. Although this fallacy involves treating theoretical or conceptual arguments or analogies as though they were concrete and real, the processes described above involve the opposite: empirical, descriptive relationships become treated as conceptual ones. There is an apparent theoretical and conceptual inflation at work.

One objection to this analysis would be to contend that in one way of viewing explanations, a description does have explanatory status. Without arguing for the merits of this viewpoint, the objection misses the point. The conception of theory used by contemporary sociologists rules out this possibility; to explain necessarily means more than the provision of description. The conceptual inflation follows on from this, and because of it the state is given an explanatory status above and beyond its more limited empirical import.

The state achieves centrality also because of its inherent conceptual nature. Typically, when theories of the state are used, they portray it as a unifying instance within the social formation. The state is perceived as functioning, for example, to 'balance out' competing interest groups or as reproducing the conditions of capitalistic expansion. Deployed in this manner the state appears as a holistic concept which fits easily and harmoniously into the structure of sociological theory. Even a theory such as that of Poulantzas (1973), which offers a more complex rendition of the state as a series of possibly discrete institutions and interests, still commits itself to this holism. For Poulantzas, the state is functionally central to the capitalist formation as it orchestrates the conditions of existence and expansion of capital. In a profound sense, the state is described as fundamental to the very nature of capitalism, as it guarantees the conditions on which the capitalist economy operates. For Poulantzas, it is the state which unifies and lends coherence to capitalism. Thus, although Poulantzas's actual notion of the state may portray it as being internally differentiated, this complexity is underpinned by a holistic conception of its functions: the state remains the principle by which the totality is maintained.

The state is encapsulated in contemporary sociological explanations of penality by two inter-related movements. One movement presents a conceptual homology between the idea of theorising and the idea of the state, and the other movement cements this by virtue of the political propensities of radical work. Consequently, the state appears as a natural, convenient and powerful explanatory tool. However, what is problematic about this encapsulation is that it takes place more or less entirely within the realm of abstracted theory. Conclusions are reached a priori of any investigations of the specific nature of penality. It is as though pre-existing ideas of how the state should inter-relate with penality are imploded[2] on to the possibilities of its occurrence and reality.

This procedure carries with it serious and deleterious consequences. In particular, it leads explanations of penality into assuming that the nature and pattern of the relationships between the state and penality follow certain prescribed courses. Usually these are established by a pre-emptive comparison or analogy between the state relationship relevant to an already researched area – typically of an economic or conventionally political sort – and penality. Put another way, this procedure leads explanations into presuming how the generality of state relationships intermesh with the particularities of penal ones (for example, Lea, 1979). The possibilities of uniqueness or discreteness are ruled out before the investigation begins; the explanations presume that which they ought to explain.

A similar presumption is made concerning the nature and direction of causality between the penal and the political. This second presumption follows on from the first. If the relationship between the general and the particular is assumed, then by extension, although not of necessity, so too will be the direction and, in some cases, the nature of causality. The penal will be perceived as a consequence or a reflex of political, state-located action. Such a presumption, again, rules out the possibility of other types of political relationships existing between the penal and other agencies, and, as it was argued earlier, this is a crucial consideration in the context of the nineteenth century. Penal relations were not always the expression of state relations, their administration and implementation sometimes being founded in 'private' bodies who were in contest with the state precisely over the penal issue.

On occasion, the inflexibility introduced by these presumptions surfaces as a series of tensions or even inconsistencies in particular explanations. For example, although Ignatieff (1978) wishes to contend that the prison can be explained by pointing to the activities of the 'powerful' classes and the state, he also provides evidence to counter this thesis. In discussing 'The politics of prison reform in the Peterloo era', Ignatieff argues both that all members of the bourgeois were, 'of necessity, drawn into the tactics and strategy of class rule in a time of conflict' (p. 163) and that central government responded in a systematic way to this, yet he contends also that some members of this very class, the magistracy, were able to resist government direction and find exemption from central controls (p. 168). Here, not only is evidence presented to suggest that there was not a homogeneous class response, but also that penal administration worked successfully outwith the state (for example, early local prisons). This is not simply a question of insensitivity to empirical detail and complexity. The evidence offered by Ignatieff points to the possibility of quite different relationships of power between the penal system and the state: the evidence will not bear the imposition of the strong state thesis entailed in recent sociological accounts.

The consequence of this form of theorising thus is to impose upon explanation a series of conceptual and empirical closures which limit the interpretations it is possible to offer before investigation actually commences. The objection to this is not that these closures exist – such a consequence seems inherent in the very notion of explanation – but that they arise from a procedure conducted purely within abstracted theory. It is as if penal history exists quite separate from these theoretical elaborations, quietly and meekly waiting to be appropriated by them. As a result, any idea of an equivalent relationship between the theoretical and the concrete is put under severe constraint, if not dismissed altogether; they become quite separate, even distant, stages in the explanatory process. This is methodologically suspect and can lead only to the impoverishment of the discipline. Explanatorily, it ultimately creates a stultified discipline unable to push beyond the limit set by these closures; politically, it enforces a similar limitation upon the range of actions imaginable.

A further notable ramification of these closures is a tendency to introduce a latent functionalism into the explanation. Arising from the explicit holism of these accounts, this functionalism can be discerned in the portrayal of the social formation as a unity of institutions or structures which, welded together, form a totality.

Moreover, typically, these institutions or structures are differentiated into a hierarchy of sub- or superordinate, with the state or some notion of economy at the centre of the stage. Parallel to this differentiated hierarchy is one of functional dependency. Those structures given a place at the bottom of the hierarchy – like the penal system – are perceived to be functionally dependent on those at the top.

Conceived of as a functional entity, penal relations become described as possessing overtly unified and coherent characteristics. This latent functionalism tends to portray penal relations as having a necessary principle of unity and order within 'the subsystem'. Again, this conclusion is reached independent of any investigation of the nature of penal relations in specific historical conditions. Penal relations are simply assumed to exhibit an internal unity to parallel the external functional dependency they are purported to have with the superordinate institutional structure of the state. However, why should it be assumed that penal relations are systematic, rather than incoherent or discontinuous? Yet it is just such an assumption that commonly underpins histories and explanations of penal relations.

This assumption gives rise to a further inter-related problem. As penal relations are perceived to possess an inherent criterion of order, explanations of change are inevitably predisposed towards describing them as being dominated by one institutional form or ideology at particular points in time. Thus, penal relations are typically portrayed as moving from periods dominated by deterrence to periods dominated by reform: that, for example, we have moved from a time at which the prison, based upon deterrence, constituted *the* form of punishment, through a period dominated by correctionalism, and latterly we are supposed to be moving into a time characterised by community control and hidden discipline (see Chapters 5–7). As broad schematic histories, these are not totally incorrect. However, in their desire to find one principle by which to render penal relations as a whole, these accounts are, to say the least, partial. As Rodman (1968) and Tomlinson (1981) have endeavoured to demonstrate, penal history is not linear or sequential. Often competing ideologies coexist, admittedly with one in dominance, but others lurk behind it as important ideological resources available for use. 'Deterrence' and 'reform', as ideological signs and justifications for penal relations, have cohabited since Bentham, if not before. Moreover, the assumption, often deeply embedded in many accounts, that the prison constitutes the institutional norm (for example, Rusche and Kirchheimer, 1939) to which most other sanctions are alternatives, is a gross exaggeration. In the period 1780–1850, during which the prison evolved as the supposedly ideologically normal mode of penality, more individuals were transported, executed, fined or simply let off than were imprisoned (for offences and crimes). This is not an insignificant observation and it suggests the need to evolve a concept of penality capable of recording this complexity.

The functionalist desire to seek for harmony and singular, internal principles of order is perhaps best exemplified by the more or less exclusive concentration upon the prison as the normal and central means of penality. This concentration is both unwarranted and lacks systematic evidence to support it. First, the prison has never been the singular, and rarely, the most common penal sanction. Deprivation of resources, such as the fine and compensation, or physical sanctions, such as execution and corporal punishment, have constituted historically the statistically most recurrent types of penality. Second, there appears to be a confusion or conflation at the heart of this thesis. Theorists typically conflate the use of the prison with the more general principle of deprivation or qualification of liberty. Prison is not, nor has it been, the only way of depriving or limiting people's right to liberty. Transportation and banishment were both at various times more common than imprisonment. As Foucault (1977a) rightly argues, a prior condition to the emergence of the prison is the generality of the presumption that individuals both possess a right to freedom and that deprivation of it constitutes a penal sanction. As he also demonstrates, the prison was not considered to be the only or necessarily the best way of depriving people of their liberty by those who wished to see the latter as typifying punishment. However, the majority of contemporary accounts of penality seem bereft of these considerations. Not only do they seem blind to the full implications of the historical consciousness that they otherwise endorse as an essential aspect of explanation, but they systematically reiterate untested and untried propositions.

The centrality of the state, the holism and functionalism of these accounts, thus emanates from a particular theoretical practice within sociology. It produces explanations which not so much lack concrete support, as make this redundant. The consequences of this have been described above; it encourages explanations which are unable to account for the complexity of penal relations and which operate by a series of closures that forestall the possibility of considering alternative explanations.

Penal history, the state and penal relations

So far I have endeavoured to demonstrate that there are only weak grounds for claiming a centrality for the state in explanations of penal relations. This argument should not be taken, however, to imply that a consideration of the state is entirely irrelevant to an account of penality. Rather, I have put forward a more limited thesis, that a certain type of argument lacks sufficient grounds for reaching its conclusions concerning the state. In doing this, of necessity, certain statements which implied a particular relationship between the state and penality were mooted, but not developed. This section will take up this theme. Its object will be, in reviewing empirical and concrete evidence, to arrive at some conception of the involvement of the state in penal affairs in the nineteenth century.

There are four broad, interconnected developments concerning the relationship between the nineteenth-century state and penal relations. These are:

(1) the debate focusing upon the centralisation of local prisons by central government culminating in the 1877 Prison Act;
(2) a closely allied argument surrounding the emergence of a centralised bureaucracy – the Home Office – as the administrative agency responsible for the penal system;
(3) the incorporation of many of the private, charitably based agencies which operated in the penal system (police court missionaries, after-care, reformatory schools) into the bureaucratic system;
(4) the emergence of an ideology of reform and rehabilitation which seemingly originates from within the penal bureaucracy and certainly was dependent for its implementation upon bureaucratic initiative.

Taken together these four developments seem to supply strong evidence indeed for a major involvement of the state in penal affairs. They describe a process starting in the early decades of the nineteenth century with the establishment of a central or convict prison service, then spreading through controls by government which aimed to rationalise local prisons, and reaching fruition in the late nineteenth century with the emergence of the Prison Commission (1877), the growth of the Home Office itself and the increasingly purely bureaucratic initiatives to either hinder or foster more penal legislation. The 'incorporation' of a number of penal practices located in private charities – such as in the 1907 Probation Act, the reorganisation of after-care in the 1860s and then in 1911 and 1918 to give partial state involvement – also seems to provide further and greater support for this thesis. Both traditional and more recent histories of the penal system appear to advocate this very idea. Fox (1952), for example, perceives nineteenth-century penal history to be characterised by the growth of humanitarianism and the ever-increasing involvement of government, combining to produce a progressive and rational penal policy. Similarly, Ignatieff (1978), Scull (1977a) and Young (1980) maintain a not dissimilar thesis, with the crucial difference that humanitarianism is reinterpreted as being perfectly consistent with ruling-class ideology, and the state's involvement is conceived of as a partial response to class interests and a generally changed form of economic intervention. Indeed, in an earlier article (1980), I argued that the growth of an ideology of reform and rehabilitation was intimately tied up with the state's need to justify a new theory of political legitimation espousing intervention as a response to the emergence of monopoly capitalism. Rehabilitation was portrayed as serving important ideological functions. By originating in an area like crime, where there was increasing common agreement that positive steps were needed, the principle of intervention was more easily justified than if it occurred in other more central parts of the social system. In this sense, then, rehabilitation was construed as a crucial step in legitimating a basic shift from what Neuman (1964) has called negative freedom (lack of state intervention) to positive freedom (increased and accepted state intervention).

Such an apparent unanimity over events, spanning such a considerable period, and between such different accounts, must be rare. This unanimity, however, is deceptive, not least because of some important internal differences in emphasis and interpretation. It is deceptive most significantly, however, because, although there was obviously increased state involvement in penal affairs, the general interpretation of this as being founded within some explicit political/economic intention is highly contestable. It is one thing to use the evidence reviewed to describe increased state involvement; it is quite another to explain the nature of this involvement by it. That most contemporary sociologists do this is discernible from even the most cursory knowledge of their texts. Scull, for example, argues this case strongly (1977a: 31–3), as does Ignatieff (1978), and it is explicit also in the brief account of my own earlier work, given above.

However, if this thesis is maintained strongly, then considerable problems arise. In part, these problems were referred to in the previous section. The evidence for it is limited more or less only to the *general* developments reviewed and cannot accommodate a more detailed examination of the subject-matter. For example, the centralisation of the local prisons was resisted with great vigour, and with some considerable success, by local people, especially magistrates. Its final success depended not upon there being some urgent and powerful governmental action, but more importantly because throughout the 1860s and 1870s local rates were then, as now, a crucial *local* issue. The campaign to resist central government control faded as local magistrates and politicians retreated under pressure from the gentry to relieve the rate burden by accepting increased exchequer grants which ultimately entailed centralisation (Webb and Webb, 1929). The actual passage of the 1877 Act through Parliament thus took place with little resistance, and was introduced and justified upon grounds of rationalisation and economy, not in terms of political principle. Prisons were centralised, therefore, not because the state wished to defeat local middle-class resistance nor because of a general strategy aimed at controlling the dissident. Its justification was administrative and mundane.

The local resistance to centralisation was not limited to the case of the prisons. It existed also in the activities of the local moral and social reform groups which were involved in work within the penal system. The over-riding presumption of these groups was that good charity was voluntary. Moral reformation was only possible if the individuals involved were present of their own volition. The state could be involved, if at all, only on Christian principles and certainly not on grounds of political expediency. As one William Shoen argued, if law ever conflicted with 'the Law of Conscience', national downfall would result; or as Mrs Butler put it, 'Rulers require from time to time to be rebaptized in first principles, and in that renewal to get rid of their theories of expediency, and state necessities, their slavery to precedent, and to deadly routine' (quoted in Harrison, 1974: 315).

In the penal sphere this resulted in a compromise typical of the nineteenth century. The state was to be involved in charitable reform, only if the fundamental organisation remained independent. Thus, after-care, reformatory schools and probation all remained in the control of charitable agencies with the central government providing funds. In the example of probation, it was not until a national probation service was founded that the private basis of this form of control disappeared. This was finally achieved in the 1930s, not in the 1800s, and again met with resistance, this time futile but still there. (For instance, evidence given to the House of Commons Committee on the 1924 Administration of Criminal Justice Act indicates strongly that the police court missionary – the early probation officer – was still very much alive.)

Generally, state intervention and involvement were frowned upon. They were perceived by many as illiberal and un-English. No government could make them an explicit political issue without risking defeat. Even the external imperial expansion of the state was opposed, as is evident in Gladstone's equivocal attitude towards it. Actual involvement thus was possible only if a non-political justification could be given.

That historical actors proffer non-political justifications does not, of course, rule out the possibility of ulterior motives that are explicitly political. However, these justifications did form the context of social actions; they imply a specific form of social organisation with its own contingencies and requirements, and therefore are of paramount importance to an understanding of nineteenth-century penal relations.

A description of the form of social organisation suggested by this analysis is best conveyed by the notions of administration and bureaucracy. Above all else, nineteenth-century penal relations were about the emergence of a culturally and historically specific form of administration. The hallmark of this cultural form was an adherence to a pragmatism which guided the principles of action. Penal policy evolved through the application of this pragmatism to sets of specific problems as they arose. The idea of a general policy was an anathema to policy-makers and implementers. Rather, a series of discrete policies evolved and were grafted on to already existing institutions and practices, with sometimes little regard of the consequences. For example, as Tomlinson (1981) has argued, penal servitude evolved not as a homogeneous policy initiative, but through a sequence of sometimes incompatible responses to the problems of prison discipline, moral panics about crime, the structure and availability of different sorts of prison architecture and the demands of prisoners. It provided different types of regime and discipline for the same category of prisoners at different times, and it was not until this inconsistency stimulated concern over prison discipline that it was resolved.

Again, throughout the nineteenth century there were various attempts to introduce systems of classification for prisoners. These emerged, first, in the early decades of the century, especially under the dominance of the idea of reform through cellular isolation and contemplation; they disappeared by the mid-century during the heyday of less-eligibility and deterrence; and reappeared after the Du Cane period through the report of the Gladstone Committee in 1895. Theoretically, all those systems of classification were evolved to meet the 'needs' of different types of prisoner so that some potential for reform could be offered. However, the implementation of these systems was compromised by its being yoked to the more mundane demands of prison discipline. A system of privileges or marks emerged which were awarded, not if the prisoner showed signs of reform, but upon the evidence of good behaviour. Reform and discipline were collapsed to mean the same thing. Thus the emphasis upon reform remained at the level of representation or symbol, whereas the details of the classification systems were made compatible with the demands of the administrative system.

Further evidence of the importance of administration to penal relations is supplied by Bochel's (1976) analysis of probation. She provides a compelling and detailed demonstration of how demands for the probation service emerged from internal initiatives within the

Home Office. The appointment of Gladstone as Home Secretary and the existence of civil servants such as C. E. Troup, who were broadly in favour of probation, were necessary preconditions to the introduction of the 1907 Act. Again, the establishment of the National Association of Probation Officers (NAPO) was an initiative from the Home Office and not from the service itself.

The relationship between the actual administrative agencies and the ideological representation of penal relations was and is complex. As the discussion of classification systems suggests, the two often worked on apparently different principles. Generally, it is possible to draw a distinction between penality as a form of representation and as a form of administration. Sometimes the two worked hand in hand – as in Du Cane's regime as Prison Commissioner; more often they appear to be apart. However, before one concludes that there is an irredeemable gap between the two, a number of qualifications should be made.

First, as it was contended earlier, at any point in time penal relations are rarely expressed in terms of a singular ideology. Rather, there normally exist a number of representations that can be used to describe the actual state of penal relations. It is necessary for the penal bureaucracy to display these different ideological forms and justifications to maintain its sense of administrative competence and also to offer a variety of legitimations for penal practices. Consequently, normally ideological representations are stratified according to the demands placed upon them; according to the priority placed upon one particular justification against another. Why these priorities shift is a complex question that can only be answered in concrete terms.

One result of this stratification of ideologies and representations is that it becomes impossible to describe any one period as being dominated by one form of them to the exclusion of all others. For example, even in the period when rehabilitation received its fullest and widest support (1948–69), the prevalent tone of dispositions – as demonstrated by sentencing practice, prison discipline, etc. – was still legalistic and administrative. Again, even in Du Cane's regime the idea of reform never absolutely disappeared. It was suppressed and downgraded, but for Du Cane the eradication of crime by changing the offender was still a possible object of imprisonment. At the level of ideology and representation, then, penal relations express a stratification and complexity that parallels their administrative and organisational form. Moreover, this ideological level has a material existence both in its precise form of expression and in the ramifications it has for the concrete implementation of penal measures.

The involvement of the state in nineteenth-century penal affairs thus was on administrative grounds. Politics, in the sense of class relationships, remained foreign to the actual grounds of intervention. This, of course, does not deny that administration itself is political, but it does warn against a form of explanation in which consequences are mistaken for intentions. A general interpretation of penal history consistent with the arguments put forward would view it as one in which administration and bureaucracy develop and provide the context in which penal relations are expressed. Thus, for example, the expropriation of both local prisons and private charities by government can be perceived in Weberian terms as an enforced separation between the ownership and control of the means of administration. This is a necessary and prior condition to be met before bureaucracy, in the technical Weberian sense, can emerge. This separation is essential because on it are founded the development of the other characteristics of bureaucracy, such as a hierarchy of authority, a 'professional' staff and regularity of administration (in the narrower sense). Whilst the administration of sanctions remained in private hands, none of these conditions could be met. Furthermore, the resistance and struggle to centralisation can be conceived as material conditions which both hindered and encouraged this separation to take place.

The view of penal relations that emerges from this analysis is one which is both more complex and, in some ways, less exciting than that offered by those theses which portray a political centrality for the state. It conceives of the penal system as an internally differentiated system, working upon principles of administration and bounded by a bureaucracy. Class relations and economic interests may work through these forms, but rarely, if ever, are they the cause of some change in them. Because of its bureaucratic nature, the penal system is surprisingly resistant to change; both ideologically and administratively, it can neutralise and diffuse demands for changes in it. The stratification of ideology and the various forms of representation expressed are crucial to this process of diffusion.

Conclusion

There are a number of theoretical and political implications that should be drawn out. Theoretically, the overwhelming conclusion must be a call for a more sensitive and complex form of analysis that is capable of recording the nature of penal relations as they have been described in this essay. One of the crucial issues here, of course, would involve a further elaboration of what is entailed in the concept of the state. Although it has been used in a rather straightforward, even cavalier fashion in this work, it is not a simple conception. Perhaps the example of Poulantzas's work should be an object lesson. As he developed it, the actual unity of the state becomes increasingly dispersed so that in *State, Power, Socialism* (1978) it has only a rather haunting presence; class seems to re-emerge as the cardinal concept.

Moreover, it must be remembered that this dispersion took place under the impact of Foucault's work, which seems to dispose of any concept of the state whatsoever. Instead, it is replaced by a notion of power which appears to achieve the Aristotelian status of a prime mover or final cause.

Politically, there are a number of considerations that flow from the essay. Its emphasis upon organisation (as a more general category than administration) aligns it, I suppose, with some form of anarchism. The implication of the analysis is to focus attention upon organisation as a critical condition of political practice. If the framework of penal politics inheres in administration, then it is to this force that we should turn to seek change. The examples of systems of popular justice suggest that there is some credibility in this conclusion. The changes in the Chinese system of justice since the death of Mao, the expansion of the bureaucratic system and the curtailment of the popular system lend support to the argument. Organisation is imperative to successful political practice.

Finally, the challenge posed to these theses which claim a centrality for the prison raises some important issues. Most of the theoretical and practical politics of the radical movement are aimed at transforming the prison. (Even debates upon decarceration take their starting-point from this debate, as it is the prison which is portrayed as central to this process.) However, if deprivation of resources or different ways of depriving or limiting people's liberty are actually more common than the prison as sanctions, then there are good grounds for suggesting a reorientation of policies to accommodate this.

Notes

1   It could be objected at this point that the various texts mentioned simply work with an inadequate theory of the capitalist state, and that a more sophisticated version (such as that outlined in the introduction to this article) can accommodate this observation. For example, local magistrates can be conceived of as part of the state, but also as working with the independence envisaged by, say, a notion of relative political autonomy. It is, of course, true that local magistrates were appointed, ultimately, by the state and that they were given the task of enforcing state law. However, to jump from this observation to the conclusion that *therefore* (no matter what their local political activity may have been) they were state actors or agents is unwarranted. It is unwarranted, first, because it is a mistake to presume that a certain social status becomes the dominant determinant of political action; it is impossible to understand nineteenth-century history unless one appreciates the significant conflict between local bourgeois and the central state. This conflict was not merely marginal or without effect. It was a crucial determinant of the pattern and distribution of power. Second, these observations do pose what must be, at the least, a problem for the conception of the relationships between social classes and the state with which the explanations referred to in the essay work. How far can these theories extend the idea of an ultimately homologous relationship between state and class in the light of this, and other, evidence?
2   The notion of implosion is taken from work on the nature of the self, not, as my co-editor has erroneously maintained, from TV repair manuals.

5 Social-Control Talk: Telling Stories about Correctional Change
Stanley Cohen

This is a paper about stories, words and talk: what do the people who run the social-control system say about what they are doing? Of course, these are not just ordinary 'people', but politicians, reformers, social workers, psychiatrists, custodians, researchers, official committee members, professionals and experts of all sorts. And they may not be 'running' or 'doing' very much at all. Most of their words are produced to describe, explain, justify, rationalise, condone, apologise for, criticise, theorise about or otherwise interpret things which have been done, are being done or will be done by others. And all these words might bear only the most oblique relationship to what is actually happening in the cells, buildings, corridors, offices and encounters of the social-control apparatus.

This vexed question about the relationship between words and action is obviously not just a problem for students of social control. It appears in any interesting psychological inquiry about an individual human being or any interesting sociological inquiry about a whole society. This is what is meant in the debates, respectively, about 'motive' and 'ideology'. What is perennially at issue is how surface reasons can differ from 'real' reasons, or how people can say one thing, yet be doing something which appears radically different. Perhaps such gaps between appearance and reality, or between words and action, exist because people cannot ever comprehend the real reasons for their actions. Alternatively, they may understand these reasons only too well, but use words to disguise or mystify their real intentions. Or perhaps the stated verbal reasons are indeed the real ones, but because of the obdurate nature of the world, things somehow turn out differently.

We will be returning later to such different theories about words and actions, intentions and consequences, but first we must define the subject-matter of social-control talk. The term 'social control' has lately become a Mickey Mouse concept, used to include all social processes ranging from infant socialisation to public execution, all social policies whether called health, education or welfare. This vagueness in historical studies of social control has already been commented on (Stedman-Jones, 1977), as well as the problems in seeing all state social policy as social control (Higgins, 1980). In the absence of a more satisfactory term, however, I will continue to use 'social control' to refer to something narrower and more specific than the standard sociological and anthropological concept, yet something wider and more general than the formal legal apparatus for the control of crime. This in-between territory belongs to all organised responses to crime, delinquency and allied forms of deviance – whether sponsored directly by the state or by institutions such as social work and psychiatry, and whether designated as treatment, prevention, punishment or whatever.

This is the conception of social control which I adopt in the larger project from which this paper derives. Here, I am concerned with a more restricted part of the topic: the working ideologies which inform current changes and apparent future directions in the control of crime and delinquency. The American textbook notion of 'correctional change' covers this subject-matter well enough; one useful recent version refers to:

> (1) A transformation of the structural arrangements employed to deal with convicted offenders (for example, the establishment of the penitentiary system); (2) a change in the severity of punishment dispensed to offenders (for example, an increase in the average length of time offenders spend in confinement); (3) a change in either the numbers of the proportion of convicted offenders dealt with by various components of the correctional system (for example, an increase in prison population or assignment of an increasing number of convicted offenders to pre-trial diversion programmes); and (4) a change in the prevailing ideologies employed to 'explain' or make sense of offenders and their involvement in criminology. (Shover, 1980: 36)

Such definitions, however, pick up too many minor and ephemeral fluctuations. There is general agreement that, behind such fluctuations, two master correctional changes in western industrialised societies can be detected. The first, which took place between the end of the eighteenth and the beginning of the nineteenth centuries, laid the foundations of all subsequent deviancy-control systems. The second, which is supposed to be happening now, is thought to represent a questioning and a partial reversal of that earlier transformation.

The original change was marked by the following key elements: (1) the decline of punishment involving the public infliction of physical pain – the mind replaces the body as the object of penal repression; (2) the development of a centralised state apparatus for the control and punishment of crime and delinquency and the care or cure of other types of deviants; (3) the increasing differentiation of these groups into separate types, each with its own body of scientific knowledge and eventually accredited experts and professionals; (4) the increased segregation of deviants in asylums, penitentiaries and other closed purpose-built institutions: the prison emerges as the dominant instrument of behaviour modification and as the favoured form of punishment.

The recent revisionist historians of this transition are all agreed on the reality and clarity of these momentous changes (Rothman, 1971; Foucault, 1977a; Scull, 1977a, ch. 2; Ignatieff, 1978). The point where there is disagreement, is just *why* these changes occurred. The second master correctional change (the subject of this paper) is considerably more opaque. The very essence of the transformation – just *what* is happening – is open to dispute as well as its supposed causes. For some of us (Scull, 1977a; Cohen, 1979b; Mathiesen, Chapter 6 of this volume), there have indeed been real changes – the increasing extension, widening, dispersal and invisibility of the social-control apparatus – but these have been continuous, rather than discontinuous, with the original nineteenth-century transformation. Moreover, these changes run in almost every respect diametrically opposite to the ideological justifications – the words – from which they are supposed to be derived.

If we listen just to the words, today's social-control talk tells us something quite profound: no less than a reversal of the direction taken by the system in the late eighteenth century. A great destructuring and abolitionist impulse seems to be at work. The move from body to mind (the first of those original four changes) is not alleged to have been reversed, but each of the other three has been the object of well-defined destructuring movements – movements with slogans of deep resonance for today's apostles of correctional change. First, under such slogans as 'decentralisation', 'diversion', 'deformalisation' and 'decriminalisation', there appears the notion of dismantling or bypassing the central state apparatus; then under 'delegalisation', 'deprofessionalisation' or 'demedicalisation', a widespread distrust of the monopoly and presumptions of experts; and finally, under 'decarceration', 'deinstitutionalisation' and 'community control', a move against the dominance of the traditional closed custodial institution.

So patently are these slogans at odds with the reality of contemporary crime control, that it is hardly surprising to find them already subject to much sociological debunking and demythologising. But such exercises are really a little more complicated than first appearances would suggest. For one thing, the task of accounting for the gap between rhetoric and reality still remains. So does the problem of making sense of the rhetoric and of explaining the real changes which have occurred. And there is a curious ambivalence in all this debunking. Those of us who have participated in the exercise seem to be saying simultaneously that the desired changes we have always fought for (such as prison abolition, weakening professional power, informalism) are not after all as desirable as we thought; but also that these changes have not been taking place anyway.

A first step towards confronting these complications might be to listen a bit more carefully to current social-control tales than the notion of 'demythologising' implies. What I propose to do is to analyse the internal logic, background appeal and obvious paradoxes of three such representative tales. First, though, I will look backwards to the first transformation, for sociological scepticism about current change very much draws on the revisionist rewritings of this history.

Some historical tales

The justification for beginning with the past is not just the simple empirical one that current changes must be understood in terms of the system's original foundations. Equally important are the conceptual analogies with the present, thrown up by the extraordinarily interesting current debates about eighteenth and nineteenth-century structures of punishment and justice. For these are not just competing versions of what may or may not have happened in history, but are informed by fundamentally different views about the nature of ideology and hence quite different ways of making sense of current correctional changes. Because the lines of these historical debates have been drawn so sharply, we can use them as some sort of template on which to mark current ideologies of control.

Three putative models of correctional change emerge from the historical debate. These I will caricature as 'uneven progress', 'benevolence gone wrong' and 'mystification'.

Uneven progress

The conventional view of correctional change in general, and prison history in particular, presents all change as a record of progress. The birth of the prison in the late eighteenth century, as well as concurrent and subsequent changes, is seen in terms of a victory of humanitarianism over barbarity, of scientific knowledge over prejudice and irrationality. Early forms of punishment, based on vengeance, cruelty and ignorance give way to informed, professional and expert intervention.

The vision is not altogether complacent. The system is seen as practically and even morally imperfect. There are abuses such as overcrowding in prisons, police brutality and other remnants of irrationality, but in the course of time, with goodwill and enough resources (more money, better trained staff, newer buildings) the system is capable of being humanised by good intentions and made more efficient by the application of scientific principles. Failures, even tragedies, are interpreted in terms of sad tales about successive generations of dedicated administrators and reformers being frustrated by poor co-ordination or problems of communication (McKelvey, 1977: i). Intentions are radically separated from outcome. It is not the system's professed aims which are at fault, but their imperfect realisation. The solution is 'more of the same'.

A modern version of Enlightenment beliefs in progress, this vision represents the mainstream of penal-reform rhetoric. Its believers are the genuine heirs of the nineteenth-century reform tradition.

Benevolence gone wrong

The second model (which might also be called the 'we blew it' version of history) is a more recent, more complicated and more interesting heir to this tradition. Roughly from the mid-1960s onwards, a sour voice of disillusionment, disenchantment and cynicism – at first hesitant, now strident – appeared within the liberal reform camp. The message was that the reform vision itself is potentially suspect. The record is not just one of good intentions going wrong now and then, but of continual and disastrous failure. The gap between rhetoric and reality is so large, that it can only be understood by crucial flaws in the rhetoric itself and by problems in reality which are not merely technical ones.

Good intentions must still be taken seriously, but an appreciation of their historical origins, the political interests behind them, their internal paradoxes and the nature of their appeal shows that the reform vision was far more complicated than terms such as 'reform', 'progress', 'doing good', 'benevolence' and 'humanitarianism' imply. An appreciation of how reforms are implemented shows that the original design can be systematically – not incidentally – undermined by managerial and other pragmatic goals. In the terms used by Rothman, the most important and convincing exponent of this model, the continual tension is between 'conscience' and 'convenience'. This is the model he uses for analysing the original establishment of the prison and asylum in post-Jacksonian America (Rothman, 1971), the later setting up of probation and other alternatives during the 'Progressive Era' (Rothman, 1980), and much current social welfare and control policy in general (Rothman, 1978).

Informed by a particular ideology about the desirable limits of state intervention and by the same intellectual currents as labelling theory's ironical view about social institutions, the lesson extracted from history is that benevolence itself must be distrusted. A guide to future policy might be 'do less harm', rather than 'do more good' – or anyway 'do less altogether', rather than 'do more of the same'. But if the reform enterprise is to be distrusted, it is certainly not to be dismissed as being foolhardy or deceptive. No inevitable historical forces determine correctional change: 'Choices were made, decisions reached; and to appreciate the dynamic is to be able to recognise the opportunity to affect it' (Rothman, 1980: 11). There is an implicit identification between the analyst and the historical reformers being analysed – hence *'we* blew it'. A new type of liberalism, unencumbered by the naive optimism of its historical predecessors, still allows room for manoeuvre.

Mystification

The third and most radical model may be called the 'it's all a con' view of correctional change. Its departure point is the question of the supposed 'failure' of the reformed nineteenth-century prison. In the stream of revisionist history gathering momentum over the past few years, the explicit argument is that the prison was not a failure, but a success (Ignatieff, 1978).

Drawing upon Marxist theories of history and ideology, this model assigns a quite different significance to the matter of state intent. The problem is neither one of uneven realisation of the reform vision, nor of a tragic cycle of failure arising from the historical tension between 'conscience' and 'convenience'. In this view, everything has occurred as ordained by the needs of the capitalist social order. Intentions and ideologies cannot change the story much. Stated intentions are assumed a priori to conceal the real interests and motives behind the system. They constitute a façade to make acceptable the exercise of otherwise unacceptable power, domination or class interests which, in turn, are the product of particular politico-economic imperatives. Ideology is important only in so far as it succeeds at passing off as fair, natural, acceptable or even just a system which is basically coercive. Unlike either of the first two models, the analyst can have little in common with the reformer or manager. Those who run the system are either knaves who are deliberately hiding their true intentions, or else fools who are sheltered from full knowledge by the vantage point of their class interests. Only the outside (Marxist) observer, uncontaminated by false consciousness, can really know what is going on.

This model appears in a number of somewhat different versions. The first is actually quite close to Rothman's in its close scrutiny of stated intentions. Thus Ignatieff (1978) acknowledges the reformers' motives to be very complex. Driven by a perceived disintegration of society as they knew and valued it, they yearned for a return to what they imagined to be a more stable, orderly and coherent society. They acted out of political self-interest, but also religious belief and a sense of guilt: an understanding that the wealthy had some responsibility for crime. These motives are, of course, very similar to those attributed by Rothman to his reformers, but the changes are conceived more directly as the product of economic and material interests – and, moreover, as being successful.

A second, tougher, version of the story shades into this, but stresses more starkly the eventual irrelevance, or at least derivative status, of stated intention. The control system continued to replicate and perpetuate the forms needed to serve its original purpose: ensuring the survival of the capitalist social order. The only real changes are those required by the evolving exigencies of capitalism: changes in the mode of production, fiscal crises, phases of unemployment, the requirements of capital. The theory of change is unambiguously materialist: knowledge, theory and ideology are generated as instruments to serve ruling-class interests (for various versions, see Rusche and Kirchheimer, 1939; Scull, 1977a; Spitzer, 1979a and 1979b; Melossi and Pavarini, 1981).

In a third version (Foucault, 1977a and 1980d), and to my mind the most complex and useful, power and knowledge are inseparable. Humanism, good intentions, professional knowledge and reform rhetoric are neither in the idealist sense the producers of change, nor in the materialist sense the mere product of changes in the political economy. They are inevitably linked in a 'power–knowledge spiral': 'We should not be content to say that power has a need for such-and-such a discovery, such-and-such a form of knowledge, but we should add that the exercise of power itself creates and causes to emerge new objects of knowledge and accumulates new bodies of information' (Foucault, 1980d: 51; see Smart, Chapter 3 of this volume).

I will use something of this view later. Let me just make a final contrast between idealist and materialist views about crime-control talk by drawing an analogy from the field of literary criticism. In the liberal humanist tradition, the text is a matter of interpretation in which the author's intentions and motives are taken seriously. The question is: what does it mean? The new criticism – Marxist and/or structuralist inspired – approaches the 'text' in a quite different fashion. A 'reading' has little to do with matters of surface meaning and interpretation, and even less to do with the author's stated intent. It is a matter of decoding, demystification, unmasking. There is always a deeper reality behind the texts surface appearance.

This is hardly the place to arbitrate between these great metatheories of human history. For, as I have said, the more parochial debate about how to interpret correctional change derives from just such grand differences – rival theories of social change, epistemology, sociology of knowledge, materialist versus idealist versions of history. Let me merely extract from this debate a few points which might help us make sense of current control talk.

What must first be said is that the 'distrust of benevolence' model has great potential in understanding correctional change. To the extent that we can simultaneously take intentions seriously and also grasp their structural context, we can indeed detect and be warned against good intentions going wrong. Critics have done less than justice to Rothman's histories by taking his view of intentions as being a simple-minded one. Such critics might be more justified in pointing to the incompleteness of the model's account of the structural conditions under which the original transformation took place, and to its implicit identification with the reform enterprise itself. As reviewers of Rothman's most recent book claim, his own criticism of Progressive penology is launched from a point of view well within the Progressive consensus: he is 'a Progressive in spite of himself' (Davis, 1980; Lasch, 1980b; Scull, 1981). The demonstration that custodial, pragmatic and managerial goals ('convenience') have undermined treatment, reform and rehabilitation ('conscience') might leave other questions unexamined. For Lasch (1980b: 30): 'Only by transforming the terms of the debate can we explain why an institution that has consistently failed and whose failure has been criticised in the same words from the very beginning of its history, has nevertheless survived essentially unchanged for more than a century and a half.'

To these critics, Rothman's model is fixated with ideas: 'Ideas remain free-floating and change remains the product of the "power of the rhetoric" the reformers invent' (Scull, 1981: 308). Their complaint – not always, I think, a fair one – repeats Marx's famous warning against taking words too seriously: 'Whilst in ordinary life every shopkeeper is very well able to distinguish between what someone professes to be and what he really is, our historians have not yet won this trivial insight. They take every epoch at its word and believe that everything it says and imagines about itself is true' (Marx and Engels, 1970: 67).

But to let the matter rest here and to 'transform the terms of the debate' into a simple materialism would also be mistaken. To reduce ideology to epiphenomenal status, a mere mirage, or to dismiss stated intent as an index of confusion, delusion, partiality, class interest or whatever is to ignore why institutions like the prison were seen as solutions to lived-through problems. It would be to underestimate what Berlin refers to as 'the terrible power over human lives of ideological abstractions' (1978: 193). Ideas, of course, do not exist in some numinous realm of their own, abstracted from political and material interests, but they do vary over time and one must argue seriously about why they take particular and successive forms. Even independent of any supposed influence they might have, even if they are wholly spurious, they are still of sociological interest. The structure might indeed only 'allow' certain ideas to dominate at any one time, but once this facilitation occurs, the ideas take on something of a life of their own – a life which generates its own social facts. Not often do these facts take the form of conscious and intentional falsification and distortion.

Knowledge is its own form of power – whether or not the knowledge is self-deceptive. In the hands of the state intelligentsia, ideas obviously serve purposes other than those stated or accessible. But they must still be seen as lived-through solutions to certain moral demands. And as Berlin suggests, our judgements of these solutions – past or present – cannot be made simply in terms of an a priori epistemology nor even by an appeal to how things actually turned out, but in terms of dilemmas and contradictions actually seen and theorised at the time. Even if apologists for the system are *only* apologists, they cannot be consigned to represent abstract historical forces.

In practice, just as few liberal historians of social control 'take every epoch at its word', so do most Marxist alternatives pay attention to these words. And although the fundamental division between these positions remains, they might both want to ground the study of social-control talk in terms of its actual working functions. This is a less grand way of stating Foucault's view that control ideologies or theories are forms of knowledge which are wholly utilitarian: they serve as 'alibis' for certain measures.

What I propose to do now is to discuss three exemplary themes from the type of social-control talk which has been heard – mainly in Britain and North America – over the last two decades. In each case I give a fairly literal summary of the story, then consider its appeal and, finally, its ramifications, anomalies and paradoxes. My first two examples – 'community' and 'minimal statism' – appeal to a partly mythical past and signal falsely a future which has not come. The third example – 'new behaviourism' – signals a partial, but real, change which has not been registered fully.

Community
All of today's destructuring ideologies (decarceration, diversion, decentralisation) and their implied or actual preferences (substantive justice, informalism, community control) are sustained by and owe their public appeal to the rhetoric of community. It would be difficult

to exaggerate how this ideology – or, more accurately, this single word – has come to dominate western crime-control discourse in the last few decades.

What 'community control' (or 'treatment' or 'alternatives' or 'placement' or 'correction') actually means is difficult to know. The surface ideal is clear enough: to replace, wherever possible, the individualistic mode of intervention symbolised by cellular confinement behind the walls of the classic penitentiary. This replacement is described, theorised about or idealised primarily in negative or abolitionist terms. Community control is not individualistic, not segregative, not behind walls, not in a specially created institution. In the hagiology and demonology of crime-control talk, the contrast is between the good community – open, benevolent, accepting – and the bad institution – damaging, rejecting, stigmatising.

The surface – and just below the surface – reasons for the successful appeal of this ideology from the mid-1960s onwards, have already been described in detail elsewhere (Greenberg, 1975; Scull, 1977a and this volume; Cohen, 1979b). It is not difficult now to categorise these appeals: pragmatic arguments about the system not working; humanitarian and civil-liberties critiques; labelling and stigma theory; cost-benefit and fiscal-crises pressures. The positive message from these various sources was that methods outside the institution would be more effective, more humane, less stigmatising and cheaper. The community was self-evidently good or at least could not be worse than the institution.

There was another element in the appeal which has received much less notice and which gives an important clue to the shape taken by community control. The causes of deviance, so the theory runs, lie in the community, especially in the form of weak or defective social control exercised by the family, school, religion, neighbourhood and other such institutions. The state therefore has to compensate by creating new external controls (see Chapter 6). The founders of the nineteenth-century asylum had similarly and correctly diagnosed the causes of deviance in community breakdown (anomie, disorganisation), but had incorrectly located the solution in a simulated, artificial setting. The compensatory controls which the state now has to create are 'external' only in the sense that they could hardly emerge organically from the very institutions which have caused the problem. They would have to be 'internal', though by being physically located back in the community.

To trace the ideological anomalies in this story, we might start with the word 'community' itself. This is not only a word rich in symbolic power, but it lacks any negative connotations. This is true of its everyday usage, its political appeal to left and right, and also – more remarkably – of its social-scientific connotations.

Much of this symbolic power derives from a powerful sense of nostalgia, which is, as we know, a rather more complicated phenomenon than first appears (Davis, 1979). The form it takes in crime-control ideology is a look backwards to a real or imagined past community as providing the ideal and desirable form of social control. This impulse is reactionary and conservative – not in the literal political sense, but in always locating the desired state of affairs in a past which has now been eclipsed by something undesirable. As in all forms of nostalgia, the past might not really have existed. But its mythical qualities are profound. The iconography is that of the small rural village in pre-industrial society in contrast to the abstract, bureaucratic, impersonal city of the contemporary technological state.

This iconography is, of course, as old as sociology itself. Conventional histories of the sociological tradition have regarded community not only as 'the most fundamental and far-reaching' of sociological ideas, but have also seen the 'rediscovery of community' as 'unquestionably the most distinctive development in nineteenth century social thought' (Nisbet, 1962 and 1966: 44–96).[1] Community continued in classical theory both as fact and value (Plant, 1974): not just a concept but a quest, not just a classificatory term to designate how life is led in a particular geographical or social space, but how life should be led.

This idealisation of community was already apparent in the late eighteenth century, the point when contemporary deviance-control systems took their shape. The original inspiration might have been something like the Greek *polis*, the homogeneous participatory democracy of Periclean Athens. Both conservative and radical critics of industrialism were to draw on this ideal: to the conservative, the image was of a lost stability, hierarchy, sense of order; to the radical, the image was participation, devolution of power, emotional involvement. Even when this polarisation became more complicated in sociological theory proper, its traces remained.

In community lay everything the opposite of alienation, estrangement, rootlessness, loss of attachment, disintegration of the social bond. These were the products of the city, of mass society, of technology, of industrialism. As one observer notes, 'Community is often defined in much the same way as God was in medieval Jewish theology – that is to say by the *via negativa* that is, saying what God is not rather than describing his particular attributes' (Plant, 1974: 47–8). But there was also a positive picture available – not so much Periclean Athens, but the small rural village, whose traces still existed in living memory (or at least in the pages of the *National Geographic*). Here, there could be a sense of belonging, shared values and rules, commitment to the group, mutual aid, intimacy, stability.

Such a rich iconography depended on an equally rich image of urban confusion and degradation. The intellectual distaste for the city was to combine in American sociology with the classical European tradition to create a particularly powerful influence on social-control theory. This was what Mills called 'the professional ideology of social pathologists': a view of social problems in which 'all the world should be an enlarged Christian democratic version of a rural village' (Mills, 1943).

By the 1960s, of course, this vision had been largely disowned in sociology itself. The ascendancy of abstract structural functionalist theory and then the fragmentation of the sociological enterprise, caused by interactionism, phenomenology, Marxism and feminism, all replaced that naive moralism with more complicated theories and values. Social workers, criminologists and other 'social pathologists' might indeed have continued being influenced by the older, more 'primitive' nostalgia, but the theorists around them were responding to more sophisticated chords.

Sophisticated, but not radically different in their underlying vision of the good society. For the 1960s witnessed yet another renewal of the quest for community. The diffusion throughout the educated middle class of bohemian, underground, radical and counter-cultural values took the form of a great destructuring impulse. Traditional forms of authority were questioned and utopian alternatives were evoked from a lost past or from societies as yet untainted by industrialism. This demodernisation movement sanctioned the powerful emotional appeals behind communes, people's parks, 'free' or 'community' schools, hospitals, clinics, universities.

In social-control talk, this destructuring impulse took the form of what Beck (1979) calls an 'anti-institutional sentimentality'. Anarchist and other such ideologically consistent critiques were lifted, and vulgarised by otherwise unsympathetic people. Sentimental anarchist ideas – bureaucracies are impersonal, the state is evil, small is beautiful – could be relied upon to win support for any policy which appeared to create free, collective living space, liberated zones where you could do your own thing apart from the state.

The appeal of deinstitutionalisation, Beck argues, lay in invoking this ideal not on behalf of the self,[2] but some other oppressed or disadvantaged group, especially those behind the walls of the closed institution (Beck, 1979: 5). For many middle-class radicals, the message from the counter-cultural heroes of the time – Illich, Kesey, Marcuse, Laing, Szasz, Goffman – was that the benign terminology and pretensions of all these places (helping, nurturing, healing) was a fraud and had to be exposed. These places could only be brutalising and degrading. Beck is aware, of course, that the appeal of these sentiments depended on certain objective changes: the institutions were under strain from overcrowding, administrative difficulties, fiscal pressures, periodic scandals. Just as anarchist sentimentality could be genuinely subscribed to by liberals and radicals, so it could be used as an alibi by the new cadre of foundation directors, managerial consultants and professionals at the forefront of correctional change. But we must be careful of being too cynical about motives and of underestimating the deep resonances of the image: not just tearing down the walls, but also re-creating the community for those let free and those not yet locked away.

The place where a dose of cynicism might be required is in comprehending the results: not why the reality is so unlike the vision, but how could anyone expect it to be at all like it. I will suggest four overlapping lines of inquiry.

(1) The first line of inquiry is the idealistic flaw of trying to base a social-control ideology on a vision derived from another society. Leaving aside the fact that these visions (the pre-industrial rural village, the tribal or folk society) are often historical and anthropological nonsense, even the authentic or ideal typical features of the vision cannot simply be re-created mimetically – like exhibits in a folklore museum. The overall societal conditions which made 'community control' possible – fixed hierarchies, the pervasiveness of ritual and traditional – are simply absent in industrial society.[3]

(2) We must note particularly that the essence of community, when it appeared as an ideal in classical political philosophy, was of something apart from the state. The eighteenth and nineteenth-century defenders of the community ideal saw well enough how the modern industrial state was antithetical to community life. The quest for true community would have to take place on a voluntary basis, it would be a retreat from the all-embracing state.

But the most obvious and incontrovertible feature of current correctional policies is that they are the creatures of the state: they are sponsored, financed, rationalised, staffed and evaluated by state-employed personnel. There are indeed 'community workers' – but they are usually people employed to tell other people that they do, after all, have a community. The notion that the very same interests and forces which destroyed the traditional community (bureaucracy, professionalisation, centralisation, rationalisation) can now be used to reverse the process is bizarre. Under the guise of destructuring, the movement is really one of colonisation: from the established 'closed' institutional domains to new territories in the 'open' institutions of society.

None of this is new, surprising or particularly subtle. It is difficult to think of the historical evolution of social control in terms other than a decline in private space and an increase in public regulation. It is not that institutions like the family, eduation and the community lost their social-control functions – the metaphor of 'emptying' – but that state agencies entered their space (Foucault, 1977a; Lasch, 1977 and 1980a; Donzelot, 1980).

(3) In other words, the destructuring and abolitionist elements in community ideology are largely illusory. The gates are not being altogether opened and the community agencies are enlarging their reach by processing new populations. Deinstitutionalisation hardly affects the original problem of how to control deviant populations. As Beck reminds us, these are populations already certified inadmissible for one or other reason (unwillingness, incompetence, disability, moral blemish) to the world of work. They are marginal, residual, embarrassing groups; the development of alternative control strategies neither eliminates these populations nor the processes whereby they were initially identified and classified (Beck, 1979: 7–8).

(4) Moreover, although they may perhaps be 'in' the community, these new institutional arrangements can hardly be described as providing compensatory communities in any recognisable sense. For many offenders, of course, such compensation is hardly needed; they were perfectly well integrated into communities before their offences. For many more offenders, though, there is simply no community to which they can return: 'The fact that they have fallen among state officials is eloquent testimony to the lack of social, political and economic resources that support the kind of household and community life that protects the individual from the hard edge of the state' (Beck, 1979: 9).

Few of the new programmes even begin to provide such resources. Deviants are transferred from the case-load of one agency to another, or on to public welfare rolls or into the private sector. They find themselves physically in the wastelands of the inner city and in communities quite unable to look after them or tolerate their behaviour (Scull 1977a and this volume). Furthermore, the type of help they actually receive, though justified (as we shall see) in terms of 'reintegration' rather than 'rehabilitation', often looks suspiciously like the old one-to-one treatment encounters. Although the notion of 'internal' individual pathology appears to have been discredited, the offender is still someone with a defect to be corrected: not his psyche, but his ties to the external social world, his social and vocational skills, his role competence, his presentation of self.

Minimal statism

The segregative mode of control, signalled by the 'Great Incarcerations' of the early nineteenth century, was the object of reform and criticism from its very inception. In a sense, there have always been 'alternatives' – conceptual and actual – to the prison and asylum. But the master correctional change in which the victory of the asylum was embedded, the development of a centralised-state monopoly for the control of crime and delinquency, has only recently been explicitly questioned. In the last few decades, and in response to the same ideological currents which inform current talk about community, a new story is being told which blames the failure of crime control on an over-zealous extension of state power. The post-welfare, liberal democratic state, we are told, has over-reached itself. It must pull back or withdraw from selected areas of deviancy control.

This movement has appeared in many diverse (and sometimes disguised) forms. The notion of 'delegalisation' alone (Abel, 1979) covers major substantive changes (such as the decriminalisation of crimes without victims and radical non-intervention) and even more momentous formal changes: decentralisation, deformalisation, removal of professional power, diversion outside the system. But even more diverse than these forms are the extraordinary collections of ideological bedfellows grouped around the minimal state slogan. I have space merely to list some and comment briefly on others.

Pragmatism

Parallel to the 'nothing works' critique of prison and rehabilitation, the whole centralised-state apparatus has been attacked on pragmatic grounds. The system is inefficient, clogged up with minor cases, incapable of using discretion rationally. Justice is being discredited. The answer is new forms of control somehow 'outside' the law.

Disillusioned liberalism

The historical model of the 'distrust of benevolence' both draws upon and amplifies a particular ideology about the desirable limits of state intervention. We must be wary of good intentions; organised benevolence might do more harm than good; the zeal of liberal reformers and moral entrepreneurs of all sorts must be curbed; the welfare state must pull back. But aside from these specific morals drawn from the history of deviancy control, there is a much wider ideological current here: the mood of revisionism, self-doubt and retrenchment about the basic premises of the liberal tradition. Its shifting perspectives on crime and punishment can be used to illustrate the shattering of the post-war American liberal consensus that programmes for a better society can be devised (Bayer, 1981). The vigorous and self-confident strain in liberalism, which dismissed conservative and pessimistic formulations as backward or stupid, has given way to an altogether more uncertain and pessimistic mood about crime and punishment, about changing people or the world.

Neo-conservatism

With this pessimism, a strain in liberal thought now increasingly resembles the conservatism to which it was originally opposed. From the Second World War onwards, most capitalist societies took for granted a Keynesian state interventionism in the economy. The socialisation of production was associated with a belief in reformism, amelioration and benevolent state intervention which even most conservatives shared. During the 1970s, though, this tendency came under severe attack by a loose consensus labelled 'neo-conservatism' or the 'new Right'. The drift to the right evidenced by the 1979 British and 1980 American elections was taken to reflect populist support both for 'law and order' and for welfare-state retrenchment. Neo-conservatives played on both these strains, with the more traditional, 'genuine' conservative crime-control ideologues attacking liberal solutions as played out and hopelessly optimistic. This was the tone of the 'new realists' of crime control (Platt and Takagi, 1977).

Anti-professionalism

At the level of ideas, at least, the 1960s marked the start of a radical questioning of professional monopolies and claims to expertise. Slogans such as 'deschooling', 'demedicalisation' and 'anti-psychiatry' moved from the counter-culture and the universities into the rhetoric of the very state professionals being attacked. Moreover, at the soft edge of the system, groups like social workers had their moral licence to be doing good severely questioned and found themselves charged with being policemen in disguise.

Sentimental anarchism

The same sentimental anarchism that was invoked against the closed institution was extended more generally to other forms of state interventionism. A popularisation (and usually distortion) of such philosophical writings as those of Rawls and Nozick found its way into both left and right versions of libertarianism. The state must limit itself.

Given the diversity of these inputs, it must clearly be expected that all sorts of paradoxes, contradictions and anomalies appear in the ideology of minimal statism. Indeed, even if we stayed at the surface level of all these 'texts' – without venturing into the political economy – we should be not at all surprised to find that current correctional change is occurring in precisely the opposite direction to the story. We are seeing an increase rather than a decrease in the level and degree of state intervention, an increase rather than a decrease in professional and bureaucratic power. I will explore three different tensions within the minimal-state ideology which might, in themselves, contribute to these apparently paradoxical results.

First, there is the complicated nature of the terrain shared by neo-conservatives and disenchanted liberals. On one level, this reflects the real move over the twentieth century against the enlightenment faith in reason and progress. Utopias become displaced by dystopias: a sense that industrialism is played out, that the machine will devour us, that we must conserve and retract rather than expand. But a closer examination of neo-conservatism (Steinfels, 1979; Waltzer, 1980) shows not just a simple conservative impulse to retreat into the past out of a sense of crisis, apocalypse, imminent or actual loss. True, in the voices of Bell, Glazer, Kristol, Moynihan *et al.* (and their less articulate counterparts in Britain) one does detect a sense of crisis: the collapse of authority, the disintegration of community ties, the erosion of traditional values. True also, there is a simple conservative backlash against the undercurrent of 1960s radicalism. But in other respects, these intellectuals are not at all real conservatives. They take for granted most features of the interventionist state; they seldom propose a *laissez-faire* social policy to solve any legitimacy crisis; they eventually remain committed to the very political and economic arrangements which cause the transformation they so bewail.

The tension in modern liberalism is between freedom, individual rights, the pursuit of human happiness, on the one hand, and the requirements of community, traditional authority and morality, on the other. As Waltzer (1980) points out, the neo-conservative answer to the problem of fostering moral habits and communal ties that could check an unbridled individualism and hedonism is to shore up the 'non-political' attachments of society: church, family, school, welfare, neighbourhood. By another route we return to the state, having to compensate for weak social control. Whether this takes the form of heightening the visibility of the hard edge of the system (law and order) and/or decreasing the visibility of the soft edge, the end result can only be increased intervention. One need only pause for a minute to see that although in areas like mental illness the private sector might genuinely displace the state, this would be an impossible outcome in crime control. For the state to give up here would be to undercut its very claim to legitimacy (see Chapter 7).

If this is the neo-conservative answer, there is little in Waltzer's 'democratic socialist' alternative – politicising society from the grass roots upwards – to reverse this trend:

> politics can be opened up, rates of participation significantly increased, decision-making really shared, without a full scale attack on private life and liberal values, without a religious revival or a cultural revolution. What is necessary is an expansion of the public sphere. I don't mean by that the growing of state power – which will come anyway, for a strong state is the necessary and natural antidote to liberal disintegration – but a new politicising of the state, a devolution of state power into the hands of ordinary citizens. (Waltzer, 1980)

This mention of public and private leads on to the second of my two contradictions in minimal statism. In the classic political philosophies of western political democracies, the state is seen as creating and managing the public sphere. The emergence of the idea of civil society in the modern state strongly depends on a separation of politics from private and social life. The public and the private emerge as clear categories (Sennet, 1978). Intermediary agencies like the school are buffers to the private realm or mediators with it. This vision is usually contrasted with totalitarianism or fascism, where the ideological function of the state is to unify public and private. The nightmare of fascism (and of all science-fiction dystopias) is the total fusion of public and private: the child informing on his parents.

Whether the modern bourgeois state ever achieved a radical separation of public from private is another matter. Certainly, in the sphere of crime control, once the separations insisted upon in classical criminology broke down (act from actor, the rule of law as a 'protection' from the state), the public and private spheres began to overlap. Positivism merges act with actor: judgements about private life (family, personality, toilet training, even dreams) become part of the public sphere. Those who have followed Foucault's method – notably Donzelot (1980) in his analysis of the juvenile court – have shown vividly how social control in fact creates a separate realm which is neither public nor private – a hybrid domain. In Donzelot's metaphors, the family is 'encircled', 'suffocated' or 'invaded' by the juvenile court, social workers, psychiatrists. And with a different method, but a similar metaphor, this is what Lasch describes as the family 'besieged'. The bourgeois family of liberal capitalism – a privatised refuge from the harsh economy – becomes increasingly subject to professional judgement and surveillance (Lasch, 1977 and 1980a).

The image of these same state professionals, experts, bureaucrats and managers rallying around the libertarian, non-interventionist flag strains credulity. And the possibility that they will support policies which will result in anything other than more work, prestige and power for people like themselves is even more incredible. The same result might also stem from the more genuinely radical pressure in the 1960s to legislate or otherwise control previously unpatrolled areas of private and social life. Some radical feminists, for example, are beginning to warn that the unintended consequence of increased state regulation and surveillance of private and domestic life is to substitute one patriarchal authority for another (Stang and Snare, 1978).

Thus, although much of the critique of benevolent state intervention – the 'state as parent' (Gaylin *et al.*, 1978) – was genuine enough, it was curiously beside the point. There is no need for the state to act as parent and teacher, if parent and teacher can be made to act as state.

My third and final example of the problems in the minimal-state story is more concrete. When they are being less grandiose, the new movements present their objective not as a total destructuring of the apparatus, but as a dismantling of the soft bits which have attached themselves like leeches to the core. If one could only dislodge these soft bits (status offences, crimes without victims, minor disputes and conflicts), then the apparatus could concentrate on the real hard stuff of dangerous crime. This dislodging is the main guiding principle of movements towards diversion, delegalisation, extra-judicial dispute processing and so on.

This is a logically consistent argument and follows from the bifurcation policy now dominant in most western crime-control systems: the soft offenders are to be removed from the system, the hard core are to be the target for the full (and now concentrated) weight of the state. The fundamental flaw in this model, though, is that the dislodged soft bits are hardly being left to move in a free-floating voluntaristic realm, far away from the scrutiny of the state. The new agencies responsible for the dislodged bits, first, are dependent on the selection procedures, discretion, patronage and back-up authority of the core parts of the system; secondly, they create new managerial and professional groups with their own vested interests; thirdly, they sweep into their orbit not simply the cast-offs from the old system, but new populations who might otherwise never have found themselves in contact with the official system at all. These processes might apply not just to crime control, but the whole ideology of informalism (Abel, 1981).

New behaviourism

By the end of the eighteenth century, the move from Body to Mind was well under way. The 'social' had been constituted as a special domain in which people could be scrutinised, supervised and changed. This transformation incorporated and facilitated the victory of positivism: as the mind rather than the body became the object of penal repression, so the actor rather than the act became the object of criminological attention. Those developments, seen as specific products of the twentieth century – rehabilitation, the treatment ideal, the 'therapeutic state', the medical model, the whole baggage of Progressive penology – are all fully continuous and consistent with that original transformation.

In the last few decades, though, the story becomes a little more complicated than either the 'Progressive' defenders of this heritage or its 'radical' critics allow. Rather than talk being more dramatic than actual change, there have been changes too complex for the talk to register. The move towards mind has been seen as a unilinear process. Much post-war intellectual commentary – for different reasons, from liberal/humanist, radical/socialist and conservative directions – saw grave dangers in the psychiatrisation of social control. The nightmare was total thought control. Constructed from the instant pop iconography of *Brave New World*, *Nineteen Eighty-Four*, *Clockwork Orange*, the elements in the scenario could be purchased in every intellectual supermarket over the last few decades: electronic surveillance, data banks, informers and agents, drugs and psychosurgery. We have learnt to fear that our innermost private thoughts will be open to scrutiny and will be made to conform to the political dictates of the state.

Orwell's vision captured all these elements. Big Brother is watching you through the telescreen which receives and transmits. There is no way of knowing whether you are being watched. The Thought Police are in total control. Not only can they penetrate beyond behaviour to thought, but 'thought crime' is 'the essential crime that contained all others in itself'. The State is well on the way to mastering the secret of finding out what another human being is thinking. The great aim of the Party is to extinguish the possibility of independent thought, to achieve not just external compliance but uniformity of inner thought. There is that famous chilling moment in Winston's interrogation when he is informed that a simple punishment is not the point. Neither passive obedience, nor even abject submission is enough: he must be made to think in a particular way. As O'Brien tells him: 'We are not interested in those stupid crimes that you have committed. The Party is not interested in the overt act: the thought is all we care about' (Orwell, 1949: 254).

This is not the place to contemplate our proximity to 1984. What is worth pointing out here, though, is that the facile way in which many intellectuals have incorporated this vision into their private nightmares derives from their own contact (or fear of contact) with the political edge of the machine. Telephone tapping, informers, censorship of political journals and interference with academic freedom are not, after all, part of the everyday experience and concerns of the vast bulk of the population in western democracies. The daily business of the social-control machine does not consist of processing thoughts rather than overt acts. It is indeed 'stupid crimes' that matter and those who commit them – and always have – are not treated as traitors or thought-criminals.

With characteristic prescience, but in a part of his vision often forgotten, Orwell saw this. To control the proles – the 80 per cent of the population outside the Party and the Inner Party – the State did not really need Thought Police or telescreens. The proles could be segregated within ghettos 'the whole world-within-a-world of thieves, bandits, prostitutes, drug peddlars and racketeers of every description' (Orwell, 1949: 73), subjected like animals by a few simple rules. They had no political significance at all and left to themselves they could continue 'working, breeding and dying'. Their thoughts did not matter.

I do not want to argue that a split of precisely this type might be developing within western crime-control systems: deviant thoughts of the Party members being monitored and changed; deviant behaviour of the proles being punished or segregated away. Rather, we must look for some subtle manifestations of this split and also understand that in some respects, current correctional changes are moving in the direction of body rather than mind. Tales – sad or glad – about the inexorable victory of positivism are simply wrong.

Current versions of the body–mind/behaviour–thought/act–actor dichotomies are hardly novel. Indeed they were prefigured exactly by the early-nineteenth-century battle between different prison systems. The Philadelphia system, we remember, stressed change through internal spiritual insight and rebirth. The object of change was mind, thought, actor. In the twentieth century, this was the vision to be captured in the Freudian model of rehabilitation. The Auburn system, on the other hand, stressed change through external compliance. The object of change was body, behaviour, act. And in the twentieth century, this became the Skinnerian model of behaviour control. The system has always contained these two different visions, and my argument here is that although there are contradictory tendencies strengthening each, a crucial move at the core of the crime-control system is towards the behaviourist vision. Let me first deal with this change.

The most readily observable reaction against the rehabilitative ethic was within the prison system itself. Here, the 'nothing works' debate, the anti-treatment lobby, liberal retrenchment and the 'back to justice' emphasis on procedural safeguards all combined to allow for a gradual replacement of Freudian by behaviourist methods. Not that behaviour modification is any less a form of 'treatment', nor that it provides better safeguards to civil liberties. But the rejection of an 'inner states' model in favour of one stressing 'behaviour patterns' was more congruent both with internal (managerial) and external (ideological) demands. Compared to psychoanalytically derived models, behaviour modification is simply the better technology; it is uniquely suited to settings like the prison. You can observe behaviour in a way that you cannot observe insights; you do not have to rely on verbal skills or indeed any form of talk at all; the theory tells you how to modify the regime.

As we move outside the prison walls to other control settings and strategies, the appeal of the behaviourist paradigm remains. Rehabilitation was always attempting something quite extraordinarily difficult: to change attitudes or even the whole person. The ideology which informs community agencies, such as diversion centres, hostels or half-way houses, is much more modest and limited. The criminal is not asked to change, but to show an ability to maintain the overt demands of a conforming life. One evaluation of half-way houses, for example, describes a move from rehabilitation to 'reintegration' in which the programme's objective becomes redefined as 'no serious behavioural incidents' (Seiter *et al.*, 1977). This is a long way from insight or attitude change.

When extended to the whole criminal justice system, the current fashion for 'applied behavioural analysis' sanctions a new way of evaluating correctional changes. Behaviour is the problem – not words, motives, attitudes or personality: 'The focus of the approach is not on what people report they do, but on how they actually behave and the conditions under which that occurs' (Morris, 1980: 135). The target for attack is 'behaviours' in daily living: the offence pattern, but also social, vocational and learning skills. The weapon is an applied technology, with procedures consistently replicable by other similarly trained personnel.[4]

When attention is shifted from individual 'behavioural sequences' to the wider society, this does not take the form of traditional, liberal, social reforms in the education, employment or community structure. Intervention is directed more at the physical environment (Jeffrey, 1976). The talk is about the 'spatial' and 'temporal' aspects of crime, about systems, ecology, defensible space, environmental psychology, feedbacks, situations, target hardening, design, opportunities. Crime is something which can be 'designed out' (Clarke and Mayhew, 1980) by changing the planning and management of the physical environment.

Even the most sacrosanct of the discourses of positivist criminology, the search for the criminal personality, has been touched by the new behaviourism. Indeed, current versions of the search (for example, Yochelson and Samenow, 1976) are only credible in terms of a revival of interest in the behavioural ideas of social defence and dangerousness. Screening and surveillance depend on the identification of certain wrong behaviours which are then tied to particular people. The treatment to be directed at this hard core has little to do with traditional rehabilitative change through insight. The whole point of the exercise is to identify those intractable offenders who are beyond change. The 'renaissance of the concept of dangerousness' in contemporary penology (Bottoms, 1977) depends on the decline of the rehabilitative ideal, together with the acceptance of a policy of hard–soft bifurcation. Although the old treatment modalities are discredited, new experts are to be given more power to perform the crucial role of separating out the dangerous from the rest of the system and devising suitable technologies to contain their behaviour ('predictive restraint') or change it through 'last ditch' treatment modalities (drugs, electronic control, psychosurgery).

These, then, are some manifestations of what I term 'new behaviourism': mentalistic concepts such as mind, thought, intention and insight are edged out of the discourse. The success of the change depends, as I have said, not just on its appeal to managerial goals, but its potential fit with wider ideological currents. In that common zone of pessimism shared by embittered liberalism and neo-conservatism, ambitions are to be limited and scaled down. As Rothman (1971) showed originally, the belief that deviants could be changed was essential to the initial victory of the asylum and depended on a switch from the pessimistic Calvinist view of human nature to the optimistic Enlightenment view that the psyche could be changed. The decline in fatalistic world views such as innate depravity removed the conceptual obstacles to intervention. The helping professions received their licence from this faith in change, reform, treatment, perfectability. This licence has now been questioned by the new realism of contemporary corrections. Failure rather than success must be assumed:

> Heretofore, at the heart of the penal system or of parole and probation was a 'success' model: we could reform the deviant. As an alternative I believe that we could accomplish more by frankly adopting a 'failure' model by recognising our inability to achieve such heady and grandiose goals as eliminating crime and remaking offenders. Let us accept failure and pursue its implications. (Rothman, 1974: 647)

Not only does rehabilitation not work, but root causes – psychological or social – are too difficult to deal with altogether. In Wilson's influential attack on liberal social policy: 'Ultimate causes cannot be the object of policy efforts, precisely because being ultimate they cannot be changed' (Wilson, 1974).

The 'unjoyful message' in the attack on liberal treatment and social reform comes from 'confronting the uncomfortable possibility that human beings are not very easily changed after all' (Etzioni, 1972a). For those bringing this message, the lesson of the optimistic 1960s was that solving social problems by changing people is simply unproductive. Accept them as they are or modify their circumstances.

Here is where the new behaviourism appears: it offers the modest prospect of changing behaviours rather than people, of altering situations and physical environments rather than the social order. To be sure, the pure Skinnerian model was a highly ambitious one: a totally synchronised and predictable environment. But the realists of crime control will settle for a derivative pragmatic version, sharing with the original a refusal to accept consciousness as a variable. As long as people behave themselves, something will be achieved. The vision is quite happy to settle for sullen citizens performing their duties and not having any insights.

These directions are, of course, also congruent with the neo-classical, back-to-justice movement. The initial victory of positivism was to admit questions of mental states into the discourse about crime: action could be interpreted, motives imputed, complex debates allowed about responsibility and culpability. Positivism, although later to be criticised for its inhumane scientism, in fact allowed room for the human. The conservative neo-classical movement, now dominant, looks forward to a return to an undiluted behaviourism – a view obviously much more conducive to the just deserts, modified Kantian, social defence and deterrence models now being canvassed.

The conservative model – as one of its leading ideologues (Wilson, 1981) has recently made clear – does not rule out the idea of treatment as such. 'Amenables' must be sorted out from those who cannot be changed; treatment must be devised on the basis of research, which (supposedly) shows that the strictness of supervision of delinquents (and not the treatment programme) has the greatest effect on arrest rates. 'Treatment', in the sense of any planned intervention, then becomes the same as special deterrence: 'Behaviourally, it is not clear that a criminal can tell the difference between rehabilitation and special deterrence if each involves a comparable degree of restriction' (Wilson, 1981: 13). Thus, if eighteenth-century crime as infraction became reconstituted in the nineteenth century by the invention of the delinquent actor, we are now moving back to a revised version of crime as infraction, 'pure' illegality.

Behaviourism, realism, justice – these are some of the tendencies which run counter to the simple body-to-mind story. But there are contradictory tendencies as well. For one thing, the burial of the old treatment model is somewhat premature. To be sure, the new behaviourism is less ambitious, but the old paradigm of one person doing something to another person has hardly been altered. Reality therapy, behaviour modification, transactional analysis have all introduced new vocabularies, but much the same groups of experts are doing much the same business as usual. The basic rituals incorporated in the move to the mind – taking case histories, writing social-inquiry reports, constructing files, talking at case conferences – are still being enacted.

However, it is outside the hard core of the criminal justice system – either in the softer community and diversion agencies, or in the more or less voluntary counselling and therapy business – that the treatment-through-insight model remains intact. The mass-therapy movement of the 1960s shows no sign of being resisted. And here, the question of 'who you are' is certainly still more important than 'what you do': behaviour is not the stuff of discourse, but insight, identity, fulfilment, self-actualisation, growth. The post-Freudian health movement – that whole army of psychiatrists, clinical psychologists, social workers, counsellors, sensitivity group leaders, mystics, EST operators and recycled Dale Carnegie and encyclopaedia salesmen which gathered force over the 1960s – are now concentrating on healthy neurotics. The business is more lucrative, the clients are only too willing to 'refer' themselves and they are quite satisfied with talking and being talked to, massaged or stroked in other ways. Outside these enclaves of narcissism, the 'community' can be left to work out its own model – using behaviour modification, drugs, cybernetics, environmental planning – to deal with those old deviants who will not voluntarily submit themselves to change. The up-to-date version, then, of Orwell's division is thus: the middle class (the Party members) obtain neo-Freudian self-scrutiny; the old deviants (the proles) are contained in their defensible spaces or, if they offend, have their behaviour patterns altered through negative conditioning, drugs, environmental design or token economies. Each side has its own 'community of interests' (Newman, 1980).

We are, I believe, only at the most rudimentary stage of understanding the three-part relationship between causal models of deviance. technologies of control, and the form taken by the dominant social order. What might turn out to be an important shift, for example, in current control models, is the lack of interest in any causal theory. A feature of behaviourism is its insistence that causes are unimportant (Beit Hallahmi, 1976): the result is what matters and causal theories are either contradicted by the programme or quite irrelevant to it. For conservatives particularly, trying to figure out why people commit crimes is futile: the point is to design a system of deterrence which will work without knowing what factors would promote crime in the absence of deterrence.

Conclusion: telling stories about change

Community, minimal statism, behaviourism – these are three of the more common stories about social control which are being heard today. Having retold and interpreted them, what now can be said about our opening debate regarding words and reality, ideology and practice?

Remember those three contrasting positions: first, all is going more or less well and according to plan; secondly, there is a radical, but unintended gap between rhetoric and reality; thirdly, the words are mere camouflage, behind which another plan is unfolding. There is no denying the radical theoretical differences between these positions. But, in one sense, the debate is phoney because each side is obsessed with the same quixotic search for fit, congruence and consistency. Everything we know about the way social-control ideologies originate and function should warn us about the delusion of ever expecting a synchronisation of words with deeds. If one side is like the child who believes that fairy stories are actually true and those who tell them always good, the other side is like the adult who laboriously tries to prove that fairy stories are not really true and that those who tell them are always bad.

No doubt there are some tellers of social-control tales who are either well-intentioned fools or ill-intentioned knaves. Let us imagine someone running a community-control project who actually believes that everything he does is fostering values of personal intimacy, emotional depth, social cohesion or whatever – and simply cannot understand suggestions to the contrary. Or a private management consultant drafting a crime-control programme in which he cynically inserts the word 'community' on every second page. But the social world is not always like this, and my contact with these story-tellers conjures up a much more opaque set of images: the same people sometimes knowing what they are doing, sometimes not; believing in what they are doing, yet also being sceptical about the whole enterprise; succeeding in some ways, totally failing in others.

An informed sociology of social-control talk can afford neither to be deceived by appearances nor to be obsessed by debunking. The notion of demystification is based on an inadequate understanding of the contexts, sources and functions of control talk. The point is that abstract ideologies of the type we have analysed only make sense when grounded in the day-to-day operating philosophies of control agencies. They constitute working or practice languages. For the most part, the workers and managers – who are simultaneously the apostles and architects of the new order – cannot explain very well what they are doing or what is happening. Therefore they improvise a vocabulary – drawing on those abstractions – which invests and dignifies their daily organisational imperatives and contingencies with the status of a theory.

What we might ask, then, is less whether these theories are correct or not, or whether they came before or after the policy, but how they can be made to work. We must begin neither with a simple congruence (whose presence or absence then has to be demonstrated) between words and deeds, nor with the existence of abstract forces which will render any such congruence illusory. The best working strategy is to assume, for perfectly concrete sociological reasons, that most of the time there will be incongruence, lack of fit, contradictions, paradoxes.

There are a reasonable number of good theories which might help us here. We can range from Mao's conception of the contradictory nature of ideology to Becker's more simple assumption that officials who run institutions like schools, hospitals and prisons will always be lying and covering up because these places hardly ever perform in the way they are supposed to (Becker, 1967). Interactionist studies teach us how these officials organise their talk (denying failures, explaining failure which cannot be hidden, saying what they would really like to do); Marxist theories guide us to the external conditions under which such talk – however internally implausible – gains acceptability in a certain social order.

In both cases we will be dealing with the symbolic language of politics, which invariably tries to convey choice, change, progress, rational decisions (Edelman, 1964). Even if things stay much the same, social-control talk has to convey a dramatic picture of breakthroughs, departures, innovations, milestones, turning-points: continually changing strategies in the war against crime. Professionals, politicians, agencies, fund raisers, researchers and the mass media are all mounting a complex socio-drama for each other and their respective publics. This takes the form of shamanism (Etzioni, 1972b): a series of conjuring tricks in which agencies are shuffled; new names invented; incantations recited; commissions, committees, laws, programmes and campaigns announced. All this is to give the impression that social problems (crime, mental illness, pollution, alcoholism or whatever) are somehow not totally out of control. Promises and gestures can be made, anxieties can vanish away or be exorcised, people can be reassured or mesmer-ised. So magical is the power of the new languages of systems theory, applied behaviour analysis and psycho-babble, that they can convey (even to their users) an effect opposite to the truth.

It might be that we need a model of correctional change much 'looser' than any of those we have considered: not the simple idealist, nor the simple materialist, nor even Foucault's complex power–knowledge spiral. The complications we have observed seem to elude these frameworks: consequences so different from intentions; policies carried out for reasons opposite to their stated ideologies; the same ideologies supporting quite different policies; the same policy supported for quite different ideological reasons. Any possible correspondence between ideas and policies will become even harder to locate as the system announces its own 'end of ideology'. Previous phases of crime control also exhibited ideological inconsistencies (classicism allowed some determinism, positivism allowed punishment), but then there was at least a dominant set of ideas from which departures could be noticed. Now, anything goes and policies need have nothing to do with causal theories.

On the principle that metaphors and analogies are often more helpful than substantive models themselves, let me conclude with stories about a quite different type of social change. In his classic analysis of Kachin social structure, Leach (1970) presents a highly suggestive analysis of how mythology can be said to justify changes in the social structure. Structure is usually seen as being 'represented' in certain rituals, and myths are the verbal statements which accompany and sanction ritual action. But this neat complementarity, Leach argues, hardly ever exists. Indeed, in Kachin mythology, contradictions and inconsistencies are fundamental: they are more significant than the uniformities. Inconsistencies are not occasions to select one version as being more correct than another. Even the 'simple' Kachin society is more complex than this: particular structures can assume a variety of interpretations, different structures can be represented by the same symbols.

As Leach makes clear, the explanations given by certain members of society about how particular institutions actually function necessarily constitute a fiction. Moreover, these fictions are quite different from the language used by outside anthropological observers. Members do not use such scientific verbal tools: they become aware of structure only through performance of ritual acts and reciting tales of ritual implications. Leach shows empirically that actual crucial changes within particular communities are not all reflected in the stories these communities tell about themselves. Kachin mythology is not a simple kind of history: the same characters and symbols are used, but the tale differs according to who is telling it, and justifies the attitude adopted at the moment of the telling:

> Kachins recount their traditions on set occasions, to justify a quarrel, to validate a social custom, to accompany a religious performance. The storytelling therefore has a purpose; it serves to validate the status of the individual who hires a bard to tell the story, for among Kachins the telling of traditional tales is a professional occupation carried out by priests and bards of various grades . . . But if the status of one individual is validated, that almost always means that the status of someone else is denigrated. One might then almost infer from first principles that every traditional tale will occur in several different versions, each tending to uphold the claims of a different vested interest. (Leach, 1970: 265–6)

Analogously, we must study not just the content of social-control talk, but the particular set occasions (inquiries, reports, evaluations) for which it is produced and the interests of the professional priests and bards who do the telling. Further, we must expect the tales to be 'unrealistic'. As Leach (1970: 281) comments on one example: 'At the back of the ritual, there stood not the political structure of a real state, but the "as if" structure of an ideal state.' When pushed, participants themselves will understand quite well that they are not talking about an actual society. Nobody running a community dispute-mediation centre in New York actually believes that this re-creates the conditions of a Tanzanian village court any more than 'house-parents' in a 'community home' believe that they are living in a family with their own children. And criminologists who mount research projects to determine whether an agency is in the community or not in the community are busy with theology, not science.

But this 'as if' quality of control talk (which renders it so vague, ambiguous or contradictory) derives from the ideal rather than the idealistic nature of ritual.

> Ritual and mythology 'represents' an ideal version of the social structure. It is a model of how people suppose their society to be organised, but it is not necessarily the goal to which they strive. It is a simplified description of what is, not a fantasy of what might be. (Leach, 1970: 286–7)

This means that the mythology of crime-control talk – even at its most fantastic and utopian moments – is very much grounded in the real world. The next stage is to study one part of this world: the 'new class' of salaried mental workers. We must look at the tellers – their distinctive structural position, vested interests, preferred language – and not the tales.

Notes

1 Nisbet (1962) interestingly quotes Marx as the only dissenting voice among the founding fathers who warned against the romanticism of the community ideal. Writing in 1853 about the village community in India, Marx (while deploring the 'sickening loss' of the traditional community as a consequence of English colonialism) noted also: 'we must not forget that these idyllic village communities, inoffensive though they must appear, had always been the solid foundation of Oriental despotism, that they restrained the human mind within the smallest possible compass, making it the unwitting tool of superstition, enslaving it beneath traditional rules, depriving it of all grandeur and historical energies'. Despite this warning, though, it does not seem to me that many contemporary heirs to the Marxist traditions have really questioned the idealisation of community. For a notable exception, see Sennet *et al*. (1977).
2 On such attempts to establish free enclaves of the self, see Cohen and Taylor (1977).
3 I deal elsewhere (Cohen, 1981) with the problems of transferring crime-control models back and forth between industrialised and developing societies.
4 Some recent reviews include Burchard and Harig (1976), Richard (1977) and Stumphauzer (1979).

6 The Future of Control Systems – the Case of Norway[1]
Thomas Mathiesen

On 26 May 1978, White Paper No. 104 On Criminal Policy – the 'Criminal Policy Paper' – was issued by the Norwegian Cabinet. A paper which had been commenced several years earlier had thereby finally been made public. In advance, the public debate concerning the long-awaited 'Criminal Policy Paper' had been comprehensive: in the course of a year and a half – from November 1976 to the publication of the paper – 1,300 smaller or larger articles on the 'Criminal Policy Paper' or closely related topics had been published in the Norwegian press. And from 18 February to 18 April 1978 – two months of continuous debate just before the publication – the four large Oslo newspapers alone produced 150 metres of newspaper columns on the topic. Rarely has a White Paper been so thoroughly debated *before* its publication.[2]

Some 137 years earlier – in 1841 – another recommendation was published concerning the criminal policy of Norway. This was the 'Account of the State of Norway's Punitive Institutions and Care of Prisoners as well as Opinion and Recommendation concerning a Reform in Both, according to the Pattern of Foreign States', which was published that year in Christiania (the former name of Oslo). A long debate also took place before the publication of that report.

For a long time, widespread discontent had existed in political and professional circles concerning the state of affairs in the prisons and correctional houses of the time. The number of prisoners had been rising – in absolute numbers and per capita – during all of the first part of the nineteenth century, and even if the rise had been related to the great shift in legislation – from corporal punishment to incarceration – which Michel Foucault describes in *Discipline and Punish*, it must have appeared ominous to the people of the time. The fact that the figures peaked around the middle of the century (in 1843, to be exact), and that they slowly but steadily declined again in absolute figures as well as per capita as the year 1900 approached (after which they stabilised and remained more or less stable up to our own time), could not be known at that time.[3] Something had to be done, and something was in fact in the making. As early as around 1820, a medical doctor – and later professor – by the name of Fredrik Holst went abroad to study what was being done there with criminals. In 1823 he published a book, bearing the title 'Reflections on the Newer British Prisons, especially with regard to the Necessity of an Improvement in Prison Care in Norway'. Holst was concerned with the unsavoury circumstances of the prisoners. He presented the prisons and the correctional houses as inhuman institutions. And he was deeply concerned with the fact that the institutions did not contribute to the general improvement of the prisoners. He advocated the notion of the penitentiary: the inmates were to serve their sentences in complete isolation – in silence and religious contemplation – whereby they would turn to better thoughts. Holst was made a member of the Commission on Punitive Institutions, which was established in 1837.

The Commission worked for about four years – about as long as the Ministry of Justice took to prepare the 'Criminal Policy Paper' of our own time. In July 1841 the 'Opinion and Recommendation', totalling 707 pages, appeared, printed in black letter types. The 'Opinion and Recommendation' contained a devastating critique of the punitive institutions of the time. The institutions were found to be completely unsuited to their task: the administration was poor, the officers were too few and too poorly paid, the buildings were miserable, there was unrestricted intercourse between the prisoners day and night, and – not least – discipline was virtually non-existent. The closing down of all of the old punitive institutions, both in the fortresses and in the correctional houses, was most urgently recommended, and the construction of seven new prisons built according to the principles adopted in Philadelphia, with a total capacity of 2,100 prisoners, was requested. These prisons, it was maintained, should be built in the course of a 20-year period. A prison for men in Christiania should be the first institution. It was estimated that the building programme would cost altogether over 1.5 million Rix-Dollars (a coin used until 1873 and worth about one American dollar), but according to the Commission it would be a good investment.

The Ministry of Justice declared its agreement in all essentials with the Commission, and agreed that a start should be made with a prison for males in Christiania, able to house 500 prisoners. The Committee on Criminal Matters in Parliament also agreed, but maintained that the construction period should be stretched to 25 years, and that a smaller prison should be the first institution. The Committee recommended an appropriation for a prison for women, housing 240 inmates, in Christiania. In 1842 the appropriation was made by

Parliament, construction started in 1844, and on 5 May 1851 *Botsfengslet* received its first prisoner.

As we know today, Botsfengslet became a prison for men, and remained the only new Philadelphia prison in Norway – the rest of the construction programme was not carried out. There were probably several reasons for this – including the above-mentioned peaking of the prison figures, and the fact that the economic burden of the construction programme was great. But during the 1850s and 1860s, as many as 56 smaller 'cell prisons' (district prisons) were established throughout the country, giving room for a total of about 800 prisoners.

The basic principles of prison reform during the first part of the nineteenth century have been described and debated elsewhere.[4] So have the economic and societal background explaining why reform came when it did.[5] Here I only repeat that it was reform with European dimensions. In Norway we borrowed the ideas from, among other places, England, and we were a little behind in time, but not much. I also briefly repeat that the most basic principle of the new programme emphasised religious discipline: the prisoners were to repent – in isolation and silence – and thereby turn to better thoughts – improve. The whole architecture of the new prisons revolved around this principle.[6]. The principle received overwhelming support at the time, for example, in the above-mentioned 'Opinion and Recommendation' of the Norwegian Commission on Punitive Institutions. A single political figure in Norway – MP, Ludvig Kr. Daa – criticised this Norwegian penitentiary reform, with its emphasis on isolation, for what it was: a brutal and gruesome method of punishment, also 'for its time'. He maintained that the Commission on Punitive Institutions had refrained from reporting results which did not speak in favour of the principle of isolation. However, Daa did not win support for his view and remained alone.[7]

Let me now point out one aspect of the basic principle of this nineteenth-century reform which is often overlooked, but which I believe is crucial: the basic principle of the reform was distinctively *individualistic*. By this, I mean that the disciplining, through the criminal justice system, of that part of the working class which was registered as criminal took place *as a disciplining of individuals*; a disciplining of the law-breakers 'one by one'. The individualistic nature of the disciplining was so pronounced that total isolation of the individual prisoner was, to repeat, regarded as being the very foundation of the system.

I emphasise that the individualistic principle, also known earlier but systematised through the great mid-nineteenth-century reform, constituted the main basis for penal practice throughout that century and into our own. The external form certainly changed: while *the notion of religious repentance* prevailed during the breakthrough of the prison reform, *the notion of treatment* prevailed during the first part of the twentieth century, *the notion of work* (with modern industrial prisons like the Norwegian Ullersmo and the Swedish Kumla) prevailed from 1960 on, and *the notion of schooling* prevailed (at least in Norway) during the 1970s. An analysis of the shifts between these ideological justifications would be interesting, but must wait till some other time.[8] Here the point is that the individualistic principle has been central, regardless of concrete ideological form;[9] the disciplining of those of the working class who have been registered as law-breakers has all the time primarily taken place as a disciplining of them individually.

What can be said about the background of the individualistic criminal policy? The question is obviously complex. Let me point to one set of circumstances which I believe has had significance.

The individualism contained in penal policy has been a part of a basic individual-liberal mode of thought which has prevailed in a general sense far into the present century. Generally speaking, an individual-liberal interpretation of human behaviour may be maintained as long as the behaviour of the individual appears rational in relation to the external conditions which constitute the framework of the behaviour. This also holds for an individualistic interpretation of crime: individualism in penal policy is a principle which may be maintained as long as people's criminal acts may be explained as *in themselves understandable – however unacceptable – individual reactions to the environment*.

For a long time it has been possible to interpret crime this way. The question of whether the various individualistically oriented theories of crime have been wrong or not is not the issue here. The point is that the basic individualistic precondition contained in all the theories has appeared reasonable against the general background that the object of the crime – usually private material property in one form or another – *has appeared as an object which the offender would understandably want*.

More explicitly, it is obvious that the thefts of the last century – at that time, as now, constituting the main bulk of registered crime – were to a significant degree crimes of need. And if they were not understood as such, they were at least seen as understandable, materially oriented acts. The same conception has been able to prevail far into the present century. Against this background it has been the 'obvious' thing to maintain an individually oriented criminal policy: it has been the obvious thing to react primarily to – and to try to discipline – the individual who has stolen.

Another possibility was theoretically present: the authorities of the time might have instituted policies to ameliorate the material situation of potentially criminal groups. Such a 'societal' policy would, however, have run counter to basic political principles of early (and, as we shall see, also late) capitalism. The disciplining of individuals remained the main way out.

This brings us to our own situation, and to our own 'Criminal Policy Paper'. After the Second World War, Norway and a good many other capitalist countries have seen a more or less unequalled economic growth, which also has entailed an increase in the standard of living for large groups of people. Such an increase in the standard of living is no 'kind gift' from capitalism, but basically the result of capitalism's own need to be able continually to sell more. But disregarding this, and regardless of the fact that the growth is now beginning to show its limits and limitations, the development has created a new situation in criminal policy: the large mass of traditional crime – the thefts – may no longer as easily be explained as understandable materially oriented acts, committed by individuals against the background of their total material situation. To be sure, the sociologist may still argue that theft, especially in the recidivist form, is associated with a lack of material resources and with material need.[10] But in the light of the general material growth, it is politically very difficult to uphold such a lack and such a need as a basic causal principle.

If the crimes of theft had largely remained on the same level (or, even more, if their number had gone down), it would still probably have been possible to continue rather undisturbedly the reliance on the old, individually oriented types of sanctions. The problem, however, is that coinciding with the most successful period of growth in the history of capitalism, *the registered theft-rate has increased by leaps and bounds*. The result is that the state stands without a reasonable explanation of – and without measures which may be expected to be effective towards – a pattern of behaviour which, through its dramatic increase, *in fact is beginning to threaten the legitimacy of the regime*. A shift in understanding and in measures seems near at hand.[11]

It is precisely such a *shift of understanding and of measures* which the 'Criminal Policy Paper' of 1978 foreshadows. Let me emphasise right away: far from a complete shift is announced. Imprisonment is to a very large extent maintained as a measure despite its lack of efficiency – and despite the fact that this lack of efficiency is pointed out in the paper.[12] But the new departure which is intimated is probably important in terms of principle and long-term policy.

First, a few words about the new understanding of crime in the

'Criminal Policy Paper'. The old individually oriented understanding is abandoned, a 'societal' understanding has taken its place. It is emphasised that crime may 'be traced back to structural and organisational features of society' (p. 77 in the paper).

In more detail, a societal understanding of crime is emphasised which maintains that crime manifests itself as a consequence of weakened 'social control'. The industrialisation and urbanisation which our society has witnessed, especially after the Second World War, has presumably brought with it such a weakened 'social control'. This point of view runs through the paper as a whole, and a separate chapter is devoted to it under the title 'Societal conditions and the causes of crime' (ch. 7).

What is the effect of the emphasis on weakened 'social control' as the cause of crime? There are two effects. In the first place, it brings crime back to the sphere of rationality. In the last century and far into the present century, crime – especially theft – could be explained as an understandable materially oriented act. By emphasising weakened 'social control', crime may again be given a rational explanation. Secondly, and simultaneously, this emphasis provides an opening for new measures which may be instituted. Because if society's 'social control' is so weakened that crime flourishes, it is *natural to try precisely to strengthen society's 'social control'*.

A weakening of society's 'social control' is not the only possible 'societal understanding' which would have brought crime back to the sphere of rationality. Another basic hypothesis, namely, that social problems – including crime – are external symptoms of being expelled (especially of being expelled from work life) in our society, would also have had this function. However, such a basic hypothesis would not – if it was taken seriously – have opened the way for new measures which might appropriately have been instituted: if mechanisms of expulsion of this kind were behind the problems, it would in fact be necessary to change fundamentally the very system of production in society. This is a type of measure which would be inconceivable as a state measure in a capitalist society. But *increased 'social control', on the background of a presumed preceding weakening of this 'control', is conceivable as a state measure in such a society*.[13]

Thereby the new societal understanding of the 'Criminal Policy Paper', and the measures foreshadowed in it, are *integrated into a social democratic understanding of society and politics*. This is actually not so strange – after all, a social democratic government has drafted the paper. The interesting fact is that with the 'Criminal Policy Paper', criminal policy is being integrated into the series of fields in which a social democratic policy has superseded an individualistic mode of thought. The similarity with the development of the

social democratic economic policy, which took place before and after
the Second World War, is striking: an economic policy based on an
individualistic, liberal understanding of society broke down. A new
interventionist state policy developed on the basis of a new, and less
individualistic, understanding. But all the time a policy was maintained which did not break basically with the framework conditions.

Criminal policy is – with the 'Criminal Policy Paper' – perhaps the
last field of society to be 'social democratised'.

Now, it must be added that the concrete instructions of the 'Criminal Policy Paper' as to measures, on the basis of the new understanding of crime, are actually sparse. The new viewpoint is expressed
many times, but largely in general terms. But on three points the paper
is concrete.

The first point concerns the proposal to appoint a 'Council of
Crime Prevention'. Following a pattern from Sweden and Denmark,
'the establishment of a Norwegian crime preventive council' (p. 91) is
advocated. 'The Council', it is emphasised:

> must itself be able to initiate the bringing forth, and the communication,
> of knowledge and viewpoints concerning the relationship between society
> and crime . . . The Council is in general supposed to function as a meeting
> place where representatives of important institutions [*områder*] in society
> come together and draw attention to how developments in their own field
> influence the development of crime. (p. 91)

In the light of the societal understanding which the paper relies on, it
is in other words fairly clear – if not directly stated – that a Norwegian
'Council of Crime Prevention' certainly is to have 'social control' as
its topic of concern. In this respect, the Swedish and Danish models
are clear. Furthermore, the Council is to have a corporative structure:

> If the Council is to function according to its goal, it is important that the
> members have a broad basis of experience. They should, among other
> things, have ties to industrial life, the labour market, and district develop-
> ment, schools and social policy institutions, in addition to the traditional
> criminal justice system. The Council should also comprise representatives
> of those research branches which are particularly important in relation to
> criminal policy issues. (p. 91)

The corporative structure of the Council is linked directly to its
mandate: 'If the Council is to operate according to its broad societal
goal, it is important that the traditional criminal justice system does
not dominate the composition of the Council' (p. 91).

The second point concerns the proposal for a development of
'crime care in the community'. A further integration of the aspects of
'control' and 'help' of probation is advocated: 'The Ministry of Justice assumes that a division of labour in probation and parole work,
for example, between social agencies and the police (the help and the

control functions respectively) should not be carried out despite the conflict situations which an integration apparently implies' (p. 145). An integration of the two aspects is underlined through the proposal 'that crime care in the community should *be integrated in the Ministry of Justice*, more precisely as a section which also comprises the present tasks of the Prison Department' (p. 147, the Ministry's italics). At the same time, there may 'according to the opinion of the Ministry . . . also be reason to consider whether one should introduce a *special* measure which consists of *sentencing directly to supervision*, but without an alternative imprisonment' (p. 146, the Ministry's italics).

The third point concerns the proposal to develop the structure and efficiency of the police. The development of the structure and efficiency of the police, which has included a centralisation and militarisation of the force, has been taking place – under the social democratic regime – all through the 1970s.[14] The White Paper devotes considerable space to increased police efficiency, though words like centralisation and militarisation are not used. According to the White Paper:

> The police play a central role in society's protection against crime. This role has several important aspects. First of all the police are to prevent crime. If this succeeds, the punitive system does not need to come into effect. Thereby, a great deal is gained. Through their preventive activities, the police are to attempt to make the criminal law more efficient as a means of influencing people's behaviour. (p. 56)

All of these statements – and several more of them – emphasise the significance of establishing a 'balance' between the weakened societal 'social control', which presumably is the cause of crime, and the state's own control measures. There is, in other words, an emphasis on establishing a balance between a *weakened informal social control* and *the state's formal control*. Let me give a few quotations which strongly underline the creation of such a balance. In the lengthy chapter on 'Societal conditions and the causes of crime' (in a section entitled 'Barriers to crime') it is stated, for example:

> The organised formal control which probably most directly influences people's behaviour, is the responsibility of the police. Society's need for this type of control increases as informal social control is being weakened. (p. 77)

The same point is also emphasised this way:

> Generally we have grounds for saying that people are becoming continually more alien to each other in modern industrial society, whereby social control in the smaller groups is also weakened. The result is a greater need for public control agencies, though they cannot fully compensate for informal social control. (p. 77)

And this way:

> If one wishes to reduce the extent of crime in society, it is therefore important both to improve the possibilities of control in the immediate environment [*naermiljoet*], and to invest in the development of various public control agencies. (p. 77)

And finally, this way, in connection with society's technological development – for example, automobilisation:

> The development of new technical measures and forms of production has, to repeat, contributed to a weakening of informal social control in society. There is reason to believe that a further development in the same direction will place still greater demands on the public, formal control system. The question, then, is how great a control task society after a while may manage to take on, and also how much public control is desirable. If society is going to manage to limit the development of crime, we must – in the time to come – be more disposed towards reducing *the possibilities* which people have of committing unwanted acts in a series of crime areas. This must be done through political decisions in areas which traditionally have not been viewed in relation to the development of crime. Also the general development in the direction of increased public participation and review within a continually larger number of areas of social life contributes indirectly to a new form of 'social control'. (pp. 78–9)

In short, in three concrete respects, and also in general terms, the 'Criminal Policy Paper' suggests new measures on the basis of the new political understanding of crime. They are all *geared towards increased formal control, out there in society, as a balancing of weakened informal control*.

Some threads may be tied together. The great reform in the first part of the nineteenth century built on an individualistic understanding of crime and foreshadowed an individualistic system of measures, with radical punitive isolation as a central method. The consideration of reform towards the end of the present century[15] builds on a societal understanding of crime, and foreshadows intensification of the general and official societal control system, out there in society. Another societal understanding – with an emphasis on the mechanisms of expulsion which in the last instance may be traced back to the dynamics of work life and mode of production – could have led to measures in the direction of fundamental change in this very mode of production. When confronted by this possibility, a social democratic state naturally halts – now as at earlier turning-points in history. With 'weakened social control' as a theoretical point of departure, measures which in no way imply such a fundamental change, but which in fact probably support prevailing relations of production, may be defended and introduced.

Some of the measures may certainly still show signs of being individualistic – like a conceivable future network of measures and types of compulsion in the mental health system, in the system for care of alcoholics and drug addicts, and in the proposed 'crime care in the community' which was mentioned above. Concerning these measures, Foucault's perspective on the prison-like features 'diffusing' into outside society will truly be an apt perspective.[16] But other conceivable measures may move fully away from individualism, and focus on *control of whole groups and categories* – through planned manipulation (with good intentions of establishing 'brakes on crime') of the everyday life conditions of these groups and categories. TV cameras on subway stations and in supermarkets, the development of advanced computer techniques in intelligence and surveillance, a general strengthening of the police, a general strengthening of the large privately-run security companies, as well as a whole range of other types of surveillance of whole categories of people – all of this is something we have begun to get, and have begun to get used to. These forms do not represent a further development of the individualising prison form, but rather a certain break with it – just as the prison in its time broke with physical punishment.[17] The new, genuinely societal forms of control – where whole groups and categories are controlled – may be woven together with the prison-like offshoots into a total control system.

The change of thinking, from the great reform during the first part of the nineteenth century to the principles of reform towards the end of the present century, at the same time mirrors a change *from open to hidden discipline*. It was one of the marks of individual liberalism that its disciplining not only was individualistic, but at the same time still relatively *open*. The disciplining was focused, as a direct measure, on the individual, and could thereby be clearly recognised by him or her, and by others in the environment. It is one of the marks of social democracy that its disciplining not only is societal, but – precisely on the basis of the specific type of societal understanding which underlies it – that it is also *hidden*. The new control out there in society is either completely outside the individual's range of vision, or at least quite a bit less visible than the control forms of pure individual liberalism.

To this I must add a couple of points, before I conclude. In the first place, it must be emphasised clearly, once again, that the 'Criminal Policy Paper' neither goes very far in actually suggesting a reduction of imprisonment nor very far in suggesting concrete non-individual and more hidden societal controls as alternatives to imprisonment. It is my personal political opinion that the former is bad and the latter is good. Secondly, it must also be emphasised that it will not be easy for the interventionist social democratic state (which has developed over time, and which functions in a social democratic way regardless of whether the concrete government comes from this or that bourgeois party) in the immediate future to find control forms out there in society which in fact will function effectively against crime. My view, at any rate, is that a 'combating of crime' must, as a necessary if not sufficient condition, involve deep alterations of the central mechanism of expulsion in our mode of production – bankruptcies, mergings, rationalisations and reductions of output – which, in turn, follow from the basic competitive and profit-oriented premise of the mode of production.[18] To repeat, the social democratic state halts in front of such alterations; the mechanisms are ameliorated, not abolished.

But the inefficiency of the control forms may, in fact, stimulate their growth: their inefficiency may long be utilised as a background for developing new and 'better' social controls. The inefficiency of imprisonment was for a long time used in this way: simply as a justification for building more and larger prisons.

In the late-capitalist, social democratic states, with state interventionism as a main characteristic, we may in other words – and this is, of course, a speculation – see the development of a new societal-control policy as the present century draws to its close – just as we saw some decades ago the development of a new (social democratic) economic policy. The great change in criminal policy during the nineteenth century was a rapid change – it was completed in 50–75 years. It is difficult to say whether the change which we are suggesting towards the year 2000 and thereafter will take place as rapidly. But with the technological level of our time, the possibility is present. If I were to venture a prediction, it would first be that the real prisons will live on for a rather long time. The prisons have important functions in society, and evidence from Sweden, Denmark, Norway, the UK and United States indicates that prison figures are again on the rise – after temporary downward trends.[19] But in terms of support and legitimacy, the prisons will be backed by less and less enthusiasm. At the same time – this is my second and main prediction – the external or societal-control system will gradually expand and become continually more extensive and important.[20] The expanding external control system (this is an additional prediction) will paradoxically provide the old prisons with some new legitimacy: in the shadow of the new control system, with its increased emphasis on the efficient control of whole categories of people, the prisons will regain a sense of rationality as a kind of last resort, used unwillingly against the utterly uncontrollable. In this way the control system as a totality may *expand rather than shrink* as a consequence of 'progressive' political initiatives such as the Norwegian 'Criminal Policy Paper'.

Interspersed with the new external or societal-control system, other elements may develop. It is something of a criterion of social democracy that it searches for, and finds, arrangements which to some degree ameliorate the most acute problems which people have, while the given basic structure – which creates the problems – is cemented. The ameliorating aspects at the same time have a legitimating function for the regime. Such a 'double character' developed in connection with the new economic policy of the 1930s and 1940s and it may be developed again in the social-control field. The conceivable future control arrangements may, for example, be combined with certain types of collective state intervention in the form of insurance or compensation to the victims of crime. We can already see the beginning of such arrangements today, and they may have a corresponding function of softening criticism against the regime in the field of crime.

The future control system, which we only see in outline in the 'Criminal Policy Paper', may – if it develops – have great political consequences. A developed state-interventionist criminal policy may fuse with the general hidden political control – and thereby disciplining – which is developing in society.[21]

All the more important, from a general political point of view, becomes the opposition to the development of the criminal-policy control system. By way of conclusion, a few words should be said about this opposition. Ten years ago[22] the state had no integrated policy in the penal field. The field was regarded as a technical, narrowly defined professional area. At that time it was possible for a conscious political opposition to 'break through', and to win the struggle for abolition of forced labour for alcoholics (abolished in Norway in 1970), abolition of the youth prison system (abolished in Norway in 1975), etc. – all of this *without* the state in advance having secured prison-like 'alternatives' to these systems. Today the state *has* begun to formulate an integrated policy – symbolised by the 'Criminal Policy Paper' – and if the analysis which is presented above is anywhere near correct, it will be significantly more difficult to 'break through' in this way in the decades to come. Put differently, the future opposition in penal and control policy must be highly alert to the development of 'alternative' arrangements of control. So we were earlier as well: we continually emphasised the importance of not giving control 'alternatives' of an even more dangerous kind a chance to appear elsewhere.[23] But now a double-tracked race must be run *in practice as well*: now we must, also in practice, not only conduct our struggle against the prison mode of control, but in direct opposition to the development of the 'alternative' arrangements as well.

Thereby the field of labour will be expanded. And – to repeat – be of much greater general political significance than just a few years ago.

Postscript

After the completion of this article (early 1979), a change took place on the criminal justice scene in Norway: during a general Cabinet 'overhaul' in the Social Democratic Party in autumn 1979, the Minister of Justice who stimulated and presented the 'Criminal Policy Paper' was given another ministerial post, and a new Minister of Justice was installed. In political circles and in the press, the change was widely viewed as a shift from a 'radical' to a 'conservative' Minister of Justice, caused by the mounting public criticism of the former minister, and her 'Criminal Policy Paper', for its radical stance in criminal policy matters.

Indeed, the press – primarily emphasising the aspects of the paper stressing depenalisation (see note 12) – had managed to define the paper as very radical. The new Minister of Justice quickly took a different view of the content of parts of it. In a parliamentary debate early in autumn 1979, and in various newspaper interviews, he came out forcefully *against* an adoption of any of the (mild) suggestions for depenalisation contained in the paper. In particular, he went against the suggestion of revising the use of imprisonment for theft (see details in note 12 above).

At the same time, the new minister *advocated*, in rather vague terms, 'reviewing the Criminal Policy Paper, focusing on what is best in it for future use in practical criminal policy' (*Aftenposten*, 3 November 1979). In this and similar statements the new minister in other words took a *selective* stand on the paper.

The *selective stand* was followed up and developed further in Parliament's treatment of the White Paper in spring 1980, as well as in the practical implementation of some aspects of the paper in 1980–1. In Parliament – in its committee on legal affairs and/or in the general debate – an emphasis was placed on establishing a council of crime prevention, on strengthening the probation system as a form of crime care in the community, and on strengthening the police. In addition, a committee to review the penal code was suggested – in line with the White Paper. On the other hand, very little emphasis was placed on depenalisation.

On this basis there is, indeed, *an even greater chance that the 'control aspects' of the 'Criminal Policy Paper' will be focused on and made into practical policy, whereas the 'depenalisation aspects' will be further reduced in importance.* If this occurs, the tendencies indicated in the present paper will be given further impetus.

The shift on the ministerial level, and the further treatment of the 'Criminal Policy Paper', show the danger of relying on the hope that a government policy paper is adopted *as a whole*. Rather, the process of political debate and legislation is selective, in the sense that proposals running counter to prevailing political tendencies are easily weeded out, whereas proposals supporting such tendencies are focused on and enhanced. For that reason, a well-intentioned policy paper may, in the end, be used for aims which were originally unintended. In this case, a highly amputated policy paper with a liberal intention will, if anything, end in supporting the conservative tendencies which are now in the making in criminal policy in Norway and other western countries.

Notes

1 Paper presented to the Conference of the European Group for the Study of Deviance and Social Control, Copenhagen 1979. The present paper is a translation of the final chapter – chapter 10 – of the author's book *Den skjulte disiplinerting* ('The Hidden Disciplining'), which appeared in Norwegian with Pax Publishers in 1978 with the addition of an updated postscript.

 The paper deals with a recent Norwegian White Paper on Criminal Policy, and the control policies which that White Paper may suggest for the future. It should be mentioned, as a context to readers from other European countries, that during the late 1970s comprehensive White Papers on criminal policy have appeared in all of the four Nordic countries – Finland, Sweden, Denmark and Norway. The Finnish and Swedish White Papers are to a considerable extent 'neo-classical' in orientation, emphasising a return to the classical principles of imprisonment. The Danish and Norwegian White Papers contain more of a 'control orientation' which is described and analysed for Norway in the present paper. The difference between the two sets of White Papers is not dealt with in the present paper, but constitutes an obvious further subject of analysis. The two main lines of development which the four White Papers suggest may, in fact, occur together and complement each other. This possibility is dealt with on a general level in the final section of this paper.

2 A content analysis of the press material has been undertaken (Hirsch, 1979).

3 Denmark and Sweden witnessed rather similar trends. The data on the rise and fall of the prison figures are presented by Nils Christie (1966). Christie explains the shifts in prison figures as reflecting changes over time in 'penal values'.

4 See George Rusche and Otto Kirchheimer (1939); Michel Foucault (1977a); Thomas Mathiesen (1972).

5 See Rusche and Kirchheimer (1939), and in contrast to them, L. P. Olaussen (1976); see also Mathiesen (1977).

6 See Foucault (1977a).

7 See Ludvig Kr. Daa (1843).

8 Some viewpoints on the question may be found in Mathiesen (1972).

9 There have been certain ameliorations of the individualistic principle – for example, the attempts of the 1960s at creating 'therapeutic communities'. But the attempts have been ameliorations, not breaks with the basic principle.

10 See, for example, Flemming Balvig (1977).

11 The fact that registered theft has increased during recent years appears with great clarity in one of the appendices to the 'Criminal Policy Paper' – see L. P. Olaussen: 'Vedlegg I' in the paper.

 Olaussen shows that between 1835 and 1955 the number of people punished for crimes (after 1923 including those with charges withdrawn) increased and decreased in cycles between 150 and 275 per 100,000 inhabitants in the country. Also in absolute figures, the number only showed a weak and uneven increase. From 1955 onwards, however, the curve per 100,000 inhabitants only shoots up, in 1968 the normal 'upper limit' of 275 registered criminals per 100,000 inhabitants is bypassed, 'and the increase has continued, even if somewhat more hesitantly during the last 3–4 years' (Olaussen, p. 183). The absolute figures also show an unmatched increase after 1955. Through the whole period it is theft which has dominated the picture. 'And the dominance of the thefts has become continually greater, the proportion of the thefts increasing from 65.9 per cent of all crimes in 1957 to 74.7 per cent in 1976. Accordingly theft must occupy a central position in an analysis of Norwegian crime' (Olaussen, p. 198).

Olaussen points to a relationship between the above-mentioned increase in thefts on the one hand and a marked increase, from the end of the 1960s, in paid theft insurance premiums on the other (p. 201). An increase in the number of those having an insurance may have contributed to the increase in the number of registered thefts, because more people may gain something by reporting thefts to the police. To the state, however, it is all the time the quantity of registered – known – crimes which is threatening to legitimacy. In addition, the insurance companies may very well be among the institutions which concretely press for a change in the direction of new measures in criminal policy.

12   Elsewhere I have given an account of how insignificant the 'Criminal Policy Paper's' suggestions concerning reduced imprisonment are (see Mathiesen, 1978a). I emphasise that I do not provide a full review of the content of the 'Criminal Policy Paper' in the present paper. For the benefit of non-Scandinavian readers, I here add a listing of the main suggestions and recommendations for reduced use of imprisonment contained in the White Paper.

It is suggested that *the age of criminal responsibility* should be raised from 14 to 15 years, after a 3–5 year transition period (to give the authorities 'a reasonable adjustment period') and on the condition that a strengthening of the social apparatus 'takes place before new legislation concerning the minimum age is put into effect'. *The use of remand* is recommended to be reduced to 'a smaller extent than presently', but the recommendation is not made concrete because a committee report on remand is awaited. It is recommended, that *the minimum period of punishment* – 21 days at present – should be reduced, for example to seven days, but it is admitted that such a reduction 'will only constitute a small contribution to the reduced use of imprisonment'. *Imprisonment for theft* is recommended to be revised, but the recommendation is not made concrete. *Imprisonment for life*, it is suggested, should be abolished, but this reform is suggested in order to create the possibility of renewed prison sentencing of life-termers who have committed new offences behind the walls. At present such offenders can only be sentenced to isolation, which, it is suggested should be abolished as a penal sanction (but retained as an administrative measure). *The use of security* for so-called 'abnormal' offenders – an indeterminate measure used against a relatively small group – should be virtually abolished. The proposal concerning 'security' is the most clear-cut 'anti-prison proposal' of the whole White Paper. In addition, some alternatives to imprisonment are suggested – especially 'community service'. British experience with 'community service', however, indicates that the sanction for a majority becomes an alternative to conditional sentences, whereby it constitutes an increase rather than a decrease of the total criminal justice control system – see Home Office Research Study No. 39, 1977. None of the suggestions or recommendations is binding on the government. They are presented as a basis for debate in Parliament. At the time of writing – early 1979 – that debate has not yet taken place, despite the fact that the White Paper appeared in May 1978. The debate is expected to take place in 1980.

13   The 'Criminal Policy Paper' could have found considerable theoretical and empirical support for an 'expulsion view' of crime in Knut Halvorsen (1977). The work is not even mentioned in the bibliography of the 'Criminal Policy Paper'.

I mention that also an 'expulsion view' may be 'incapsulated' or 'co-opted' and used as a basis for measures which hardly change the dynamics of production. We have seen this happen in various fields of social policy. It is this understanding taken in full seriousness, and followed up in full consequence (as in Halvorsen's book), which creates the opportunity for measures of a kind which transcend the existing order.

14   An account and analysis of the development of the Norwegian police may be found in Thomas Mathiesen (1979). See also Hakon Lorentzen (1977).

15 And almost to the year '1984'.
16 See Foucault, (1977a, final chapter); see also Mathiesen (1978b, ch. 9).
17 Foucault (1977a) emphasises that imprisonment also entails the surveillance of large numbers by the few, and that modern techniques of surveillance in outside society thereby are a 'continuation' of the prison form. I think this emphasis overlooks the even more basic − historical − difference between control of single individuals and generalised control of groups or categories.
18 Evidence favouring this view seems to be increasing. For Norway I refer to Mathiesen (1975), which shows in detail the great increase in bankruptcies, mergings and rationalisations during the 'growth years' of the 1960s and to L. P. Olaussen ('Vedlegg I' to the 'Criminal Policy Paper', pp. 194−5), which shows a clear relationship between the number of bankruptcies and registered crime between 1865 and 1940. See also Knut Halvorsen (1977). But, of course, the concrete links between the mechanisms of the production system and traditional criminal behaviour and/or criminal careers remain unravelled, and much research remains to be done.
19 One reference may be given by way of example: *Prison Statistics − England and Wales* (London, HMSO, 1978, p. 14). Excepting Norway, all of the countries mentioned saw a decline in their prison figures in the beginning of the 1970s, followed by new upward trends in the late 1970s. The upward trend is particularly conspicuous in England and the United States.
20 A similar prediction concerning the external or societal-control system has been presented in Stanley Cohen (1977); see also Cohen (1979b).
21 The latter measures of control − of which political surveillance and tendencies towards 'Berufsverbot' are only two − are discussed at length in the book from which the present paper is taken. (See Mathiesen, 1978b, and also Mathiesen, 1980a, final chapter.)
22 The Norwegian organisation KROM − organising prisoners and others in opposition to the official criminal policy − was founded exactly ten years before the 'Criminal Policy Paper' was published.
23 See Thomas Mathiesen (1974), pp. 83−100.

7 Community Corrections: Panacea, Progress or Pretence?[1]

Andrew Scull

In the last few decades, we have been witnessing what appear to be the beginnings of a major shift in the ideology and apparatus of social control – a change that may come to rival in importance the early-nineteenth-century shift toward institutionally based modes of segregative control. Like that earlier transformation, the current developments are widely hailed as a beneficent and progressive reform. Like their predecessor, they are accounted the product of humanitarian instincts and our increasing knowledge about the control and rehabilitation of errant human beings. And like that prior episode of 'reform', the reality is at once more complex, less benign and more morally ambiguous than its apologists would have us believe.

In this paper, I shall concentrate on providing an analysis and critique of one segment of this broader series of inter-related changes, the developments in the criminal justice sector that American criminologists generally encapsulate as the rise of community corrections. They refer here to a wide variety of policies and programmes, whose major shared characteristic is that they constitute versions of formal social control operating outside the walls of traditional penal institutions, both juvenile and adult. Apart from expanded reliance upon 'conventional' probation services, community correction thus embraces a wide spectrum of approaches: pre-trial diversion schemes, half-way houses and day centres, and programmes of behaviour modification, as well as several new British sanctions such as Community Service Orders and 'intermediate treatment'. Indeed, the community-correction label is attached to almost anything which so much as *sounds* as though it involves increasing community responsibility for the control of crime and delinquency. Through a careful examination of both the ideology and the practice of this movement, focusing largely on developments in the United States, I hope to contribute to our understanding of these transformations which appear to be taking place in modern control structures.

Nothwithstanding the manifestos of the labelling theorists and the programmatic statements of their conflict-theory critics, the macrosociology of social control has been a strangely neglected topic in modern sociology. Much of the most important work in this area has been done by historians (Rothman, 1971 and 1980; Hay *et al.* 1975; Thompson, 1975; Ignatieff, 1978; Katz, 1979), or by others whose researches, however avidly they may now be read and imitated, were once equally marginal to the mainstream sociological enterprise (Rusche and Kirchheimer, 1939; Foucault, 1965 and 1977a). Although in the last few years this defect has begun to be remedied (Scull, 1976, 1977a, 1977b and 1979a; Cohen, 1977 and 1979b; Fine, 1977; Rock, 1977; Spitzer, 1979b; Spitzer and Scull, 1977a and 1977b), the general field of control still lies uncharted. Isolated studies of particular prisons, asylums and reformatories; more or less sensitive discussions of the police and their lot; or even such synoptic works as Goffman's classic essay (1961) on the total institution – none of these have contributed in any marked degree to a portrait of the larger structure that orders these particularities. Still less can we look to the mass of low-level evaluative studies of individual programmes – those parodies of 'value-free' social science, with their configuration analyses, their Automatic Interaction Detector computer packages, their feedback and cybernetic systems – for any understanding of the broader network of social control. And, of course, the ideological proclamations of the proponents of current reforms are about as reliable a guide to the antecedents, characteristics and significance of what is happening in the real world as the collected works of the brothers Grimm (see Chapter 5).

The modern system of social-control institutions
The contemporary drive towards decarceration – the emptying of mental hospitals, the advent of community corrections and their analogues – involves a sustained assault on the intellectual (and to some degree institutional) foundations of a control system whose hegemony has lasted almost two centuries. As I have argued at greater length elsewhere (Spitzer and Scull, 1977a; Scull, 1979a), the central features of this earlier system were: (1) the substantial involvement of the state, and the emergence of a social-control apparatus that was highly rationalised and, in general, centrally administered and directed; (2) the treatment of many types of deviance in institutions providing a large measure of segregation – both physical and symbolic – from the surrounding community; and (3) the careful differentiation of various sorts of deviance and the consignment of each variety to the ministrations of 'experts'; with the inevitable corollary of (4) the development of professional and semi-professional 'helping

occupations'. Throughout Western Europe and North America, all these features of the modern social-control apparatus were substantially a product of the eighteenth and nineteenth centuries, a period that saw the coincidence of the need and the ability to organise the necessary administrative structures and to raise the substantial sums required to establish an institutionally based control system. Ultimately (although I do not have the space to analyse these developments here), one must view the move towards this type of social-control apparatus as a reflection of the underlying transformations of the social structure associated with the maturation of the capitalist market system (Spitzer and Scull, 1977b; Katz, 1979; Fine *et al.*, 1979; Scull, 1979a: esp. ch. 1, and 1979b.).

Although they were not immune to criticism, sometimes of a very fundamental sort (Scull 1977a, chs. 6 and 7), the basic elements of this nineteenth-century system have proved remarkably resilient. This is not to say, of course, that nineteenth-century control structures remained wholly immune to change. Particularly in the early years of the twentieth century, 'reforms' were mooted and certain changes subsequently implemented which did in fact modify the character of the social-control apparatus in important ways.

David Rothman and the 'Progressive revolution'
David Rothman has recently contended that these 'Progressive Era' reforms mark the second 'major divide' in American society 'in attitudes and practices toward the deviant, creating new ideas and procedures to combat crime, delinquency, and mental illness' (Rothman, 1980: 43). For Rothman these were of revolutionary importance, ranking, along with the earlier 'discovery of the asylum' (Rothman, 1971), as a major watershed in the history of social control in America. For reasons that in Rothman's account still remain somewhat obscure, the nightmarish institutions which existed at the turn of the century as prisons, reformatories and mental hospitals suddenly began to lose their legitimacy, and were swept up in a wave of reforming zeal that sought to break with the 'rigid, inflexible, and machine-like' qualities of inherited approaches, and to replace them with 'open-ended, informal, and highly flexible policies [and programmes]' (Rothman, 1980: 43). This programme of reform, above all, emphasised the need for a discretionary response to the individual case, and this was combined with a blithe self-confidence in the reformers' own capacity to design and implement effective forms of treatment and a dangerous faith in the benevolence of the state and its agents. The result was a whole series of changes that widened the scope of state action.

Within the criminal justice sector, for both adult and juvenile offenders, the Progressives attempted to widen the range of 'treatment' available to the authorities, while granting the behavioural 'experts' in charge of the system greater freedom to match diagnosis and therapy. Use of the medical metaphor grew apace, for it legitimised both heightened official discretion and the emphasis on individual variability. For adult criminals, the new approach was most visible in the rapid spread of probation as an alternative weapon in the state's armamentarium (Rothman, 1980: 44; Young, 1976). But changes were also introduced that were aimed at the more serious offender – most especially, parole and the indeterminate sentence, the means, according to those introducing them, by which 'the prisoner becomes the arbiter of his own fate. He carries the key to the prison in his own pocket' (Rothman, 1980: 69). By the early 1920s, almost half of the prisoners released were on parole. Meanwhile, within the prisons themselves, routines were allegedly modified to correspond with the reformers' emphasis on a more flexible response to the individual offender.

In the sphere of juvenile justice, parallel changes occurred with similar speed. The Juvenile Court emerged in Chicago at the turn of the century (cf. Platt, 1969); it quickly spread nationwide and 'revolutionized social policy toward the delinquent' (Rothman, 1980: 205) by replacing punishment with the rehabilitation of the individual child. Redirecting the wayward required not a response to a single delinquent act, but a global reformation of character, using techniques expertly tailored to the requirements of the individual case. And if this meant abandoning procedural safeguards and granting extraordinary latitude to intervene, then, as Rothman clearly demonstrates, Progressive reformers were willing – indeed eager – to do so.

On the surface, therefore, it is not unreasonable to claim that the Progressive changes in the criminal justice system marked a revolutionary break with past practices. But to rest content with such an assessment is to confuse intentions with consequences, to ignore the discrepancy between words and action that looms so large in all forms of 'social-control talk' (see Chapter 5 above). On more sober reflection, the largely rhetorical nature of the Progressive 'revolution' is all too apparent. Though he resolutely avoids confronting the implications of his own findings, Rothman himself presents a remarkable array of evidence demonstrating that as far as *prisons* were concerned most of the progressive reformers' sound and fury in reality signified nothing: 'therapeutic innovations had little effect on prison routines' and 'change never moved beyond the superficial' (Rothman, 1980: 133–4).

On occasion, reform did not even penetrate skin deep, as with the change-over from striped convict uniforms to more ordinary dress.

Even when some new amenities were allowed – more exercise, more frequent visitors – the fundamental realities of prison life remained unaltered. The Progressives' dream, 'that they could transform a nightmarish prison, dedicated to punishment, into a community that would at once prepare the inmate for release and serve as a testing ground for society' (Rothman, 1980: 127), echoed the reveries of their Jacksonian counterparts. Reality once again turned out to be brutally different. Nor did alternative, non-institutional programmes fare much better. Probation was scarcely more than a sham in all but densely populated areas. Even here, 'the actual results were pitiful'. Conditions in the system 'not only made the fulfillment of case work principles well nigh impossible, [they] also prevented probation from carrying out a meaningful police function' (Rothman, 1980: 83, 91).

The records of the juvenile justice system reveal a similar litany of failure. Again and again, Rothman returns to the token quality of the Progressive emphasis on individualisation, psychiatric guidance and intervention, and to the persistence within institutional walls of quasi-military routines not essentially different from those that character-ised the nineteenth-century system. All the reformers' brave words about breaking with the ugliness and failures of the past had little practical effect. At best, 'the rhetoric of treatment provided only the external trappings. Inside, incapacitation and deterrence ruled, as befit a holding operation' (Rothman, 1980: 268, 283).

Wherever one looks, then, one discovers that under the pressures of administrative convenience, Progressive innovations were trans-formed into harsh caricatures of themselves. They served merely to advance the self-interest of the care-taker professionals, or, as with social work, virtually to create the profession that perpetuated them. For example, the introduction of probation and the indeterminate sentence multiplied the inducements to 'cop a plea', and plea bar-gaining enabled judges and prosecutors to shorten trials, ease crowded court calendars, and raise the conviction rate, as well as to insulate both their own and police conduct from further judicial scru-tiny and review. Prison wardens, meanwhile, welcomed the combina-tion of parole and the indeterminate sentence with open arms, for with it the 'reformers had delivered into their hands a disciplinary mechanism far more potent than the lash, and not insignificantly, far more legitimate' (Rothman, 1980: 74).

This is not to suggest that this whole episode is devoid of signifi-cance (see Garland, 1981). The greater emphasis placed on medical and therapeutic rhetoric helped to legitimise a policy of ever greater intervention. Parole and probation were important innovations, however far they departed from the reformers' intentions and how-ever half-hearted their implementation. Probation, in particular, 'expanded the scope of state action and state surveillance', and subjected new segments of the population to the risks of arbitrary state action (Rothman, 1980: 112).

In the last analysis, however, as I have indicated, the Progressive reforms supplemented rather than revolutionised existing arrangements, and left most of the underlying structures inherited from the nineteenth-century largely untouched. Only in very recent years has this modified system of segregative control once more confronted a serious ideological and practical challenge, in the form of the burgeoning 'community-corrections' movement. Unlike the Progressives, who mistakenly decided that 'the appropriate task was to reform incarceration, not to launch a fundamental attack upon it' (Rothman, 1980: 29), contemporary reformers have apparently opted for a fundamental assault on the logic of the system as a whole.

Community corrections and the critique of segregation
The insurgent movement has, in consequence, attacked on a broad front. Part of the present stress on the 'community' clearly draws upon reservoirs of opposition to centralisation and state intervention; certainly, the fashionable emphasis on 'the limits of benevolence' (Gaylin *et al.*, 1978) borrows much of its emotional freight from the existence of widespread suspicion of and antagonism directed towards all forms of bureaucracy and certified expertise. But this, for the most part, is window dressing – glittering phrases designed to dazzle the eye and attract a crowd. It is scarcely surprising that programmes developed by the high-level bureaucrats and intellectual experts, who are the movement's principal spokesmen, continue to rely heavily upon state initiative and sponsorship, and upon the advice and counsel of men and women such as themselves.

The central thrust of their critique lies elsewhere, in the contention that the institution is necessarily, always and absolutely a failure – a colossal mistake whose commission can only be redeemed by its abolition. Drawing particularly upon the work of the labelling theorists, stabilised deviance is seen primarily as a product of the reactions of others, and of the control institutions that represent societal reaction in its most crystallised, unambiguous and pernicious form. Not only does processing by such institutions inflict more visible, organised and ineradicable stigma than is commonly bestowed in informal interaction, but it exposes the inmate to the powerful socialising impact of institutional existence. And contrary to a century and a half of rhetoric by institutional custodians, the effect of this socialisation is not to cure or to rehabilitate, but to perpetuate and intensify the underlying pathology. Life in the mental hospital tends 'inexorably to the attenuation of the spirit, a shrinking of capacity, and slowing of the rhythms of interaction, a kind of atrophy' (Miller, 1974: 54). The same is true of its sister institution, the prison: with its cruelty, brutality and lawlessness, the exposure of inmates to a society permeated with corruption and dominated by the very worst elements, it must necessarily 'teach crime, instill crime, inure men to it, trap men in it as a way of life' (Wills, 1975: 8). Efforts to reform such places are useless. Their defects are not simply the consequence of administrative lapses or the lack of adequate funds, but rather reflect fundamental and irremediable flaws deeply embedded in their basic structure (for a popularisation of these notions, see Mitford, 1973).

The obverse of this profound pessimism concerning the 'correctional effects of corrections' has been an equally far-reaching optimism about the merits of the proposed alternative – treatment in the community. Such an approach is said to permit the reintegration of the offender, while 'avoiding as much as possible the isolating and labelling effects of commitment to an institution' (Task Force Report, Corrections, 1967: 20). It is at once both more humane and cheaper. Moreover, the inexpensive redemption which the community offers extends not merely to the decarcerated deviant, but in significant measure to all of us:

> the destination is a degree of community participation and effectiveness which has all but departed our lives as people living together. Part of the powerlessness and frustration which so many sense at this juncture will be resolved in this trend, to the benefit not only of inmates or clients or patients or criminals now in institutions – but of the community as a whole. (Alper, 1973: viii)

Such idyllic visions are curiously familiar to those acquainted with the history of reform movements. For the *adoption* of the asylum, whose *abolition* is here pictured as having such universally beneficent results, aroused millennial expectations among its advocates which are almost precisely parallel. Furthermore, it is at least mildly curious to portray modern society as a collection of little organic villages where neighbour will help neighbour and families willingly minister to the needs of their own troublesome members – when surrounded by the reality of the increasingly privatised, rationalised and atomised existence which is characteristic of late capitalism.

It is significant, I think, that what effort the decarceration movement *has* made to provide some empirical underpinning for its claims has been concentrated on demolishing the pretensions of the institutions that have traditionally processed our deviant populations. In this connection the labelling literature, with its stress on deviance as an ascribed rather than achieved status, has provided an invaluable ideological account of the failings and ill effects of prisons, mental hospitals and juvenile reformatories. Coupled with this has been the adoption (from the same source) of the naive, unexamined and certainly fallacious notion that deviance responds primarily (or even exclusively) to efforts at control, and its corollary that simple changes in the control system can completely alter the nature and quantity of deviance in a society.[2] (Fortunately or unfortunately, deviance responds to much else besides.) The offspring of this alliance has been a ready acceptance of the superiority of 'radical non-intervention', the sweeping away of well-intended but mischievous controls, the removal of their erstwhile objects from the anti-therapeutic environment of the total institution and their consignment to the tender (if unexamined), mercies of the community. For, if deviance is the product of formal efforts at control, elimination of control must surely be an improvement – a point so obvious it scarcely requires demonstration. It is this that lends some credence to the claim that 'Diversion is the practitioner's operationalization of labeling theory' (Klein *et al.*, 1976: 106); for labelling theory has unquestionably smoothed the way toward abandonment, or at least major modification, of the system of segregative control, and it has allowed this development to be presented as motivated by humanitarian concern for the deviant as well as for the community as a whole.

The social basis of 'decarceration'

It is, of course, an 'illusion that a specific penal practice is bound up with a specific penal theory, and that it is sufficient to demolish the latter to set the former under way' (Rusche and Kirchheimer, 1968 edn: 141). One may grant the depths of current pessimism in intellectual circles concerning the value of institutional responses to deviance and recognise the degree to which decarceration has consequently been elevated to the status of a new 'humanitarian' myth, comparable only with that which attended the birth of the asylum. Yet social policy generally proves only mildly susceptible to shifting intellectual fads and fancies. What, then, accounts for the apparent success of the critics in this instance?

Certainly, it is not the originality or forcefulness of their arguments. Almost precisely parallel contentions about the anti-therapeutic consequences of confinement were made by several nineteenth-century critics, who drew conclusions remarkably similar to those of their twentieth-century counterparts. Yet such men, despite their unquestionable political skill and influence, had no success in changing existing social policies (Scull, 1977a, chs. 6 and 7). Analogous criticisms have been repeated insistently ever since, with little effect, at least until recently. Quite clearly, receptivity to and application of a given set of findings are dependent more upon the temper of the audience to which they are addressed than on the intrinsic merits of the propositions being advanced.

Further, there are serious lacunae in the arguments of contemporary advocates of the community approach. Extraordinary ignorance of the likely effects of such a policy persisted long after it had become official dogma. Among the mentally ill, the first group to 'benefit' from this shift in control strategies, and the population among whom it has had by far its greatest impact, 'the massive release of patients to facilities in residential neighbourhoods', *preceded* 'substantial data collection and analysis' concerning the likely effects of this change (Wolpert and Wolpert, 1974: 19). Deinstitutionalisation has accelerated rapidly, despite the absence of community after-care facilities, and even though we continue to lack substantiation that community care is advantageous for clients (Ahmed, 1974; Wolpert and Wolpert, 1976). The movement toward community corrections began much later and has not proceeded nearly as far (although the statistical data remain difficult to obtain and interpret) (Messinger, 1976; Scull, 1977a, ch. 3); this movement has recently encountered significant opposition (see below). But here, too, one of the most striking features has been our sheer lack of knowledge concerning the likely effects of decarceration on crime rates or the social order more broadly conceived (Vorenberg and Vorenberg, 1973; Greenberg, 1975). Even those who applaud these developments concede that 'there is not a wealth of sound evidence upon which to justify the current effort to deinstitutionalize correctional programs' (Empey, 1973: 37).

Perhaps more serious still, for those who contend that the change reflects our society's new-found humanitarianism, is the accumulating evidence that actual implementation of the policy (in contrast to its rhetorical claims) has had effects exactly the reverse of humane. Certainly, some of those decanted back into our midst have been reabsorbed quietly, if not without cost. This should scarcely be surprising. After all, many of those subjected to processing by the official agencies of social control have been virtually indistinguishable from their neighbours who were left alone. In this sense Goffman (1961: 135) rightly describes them as victims of 'contingencies'. They, at least, can be expelled from institutions without appreciable risk. And the burden of care for those released mental patients whose family ties are reasonably intact can be shifted on to the shoulders of their relatives, where it becomes largely invisible, if none the less real (Brown *et al.*, 1966).

But for many others, especially ex-mental patients, the outcome has been much less favourable. In discussions of deinstitutionalisation there is constant reliance upon 'boo' words and 'hurrah' words (Stevenson, 1944). But the concrete referents of 'hurrah' words like 'community care' remain unknown or undiscussed: their desirability is instead suggested by implicit comparison with the nastiness of the institutional alternatives. For ideological purposes, it is just as well that these concepts remain unexamined, since all too often the 'community' consists of the social wastelands that form the core of our cities, and 'care' is another word for malign neglect. Exploratory research in this area has revealed:

> the growing ghettoization of the returning ex-patients along with other dependent groups in the population: the growing use of inner city land for institutions providing services to the dependent and needy . . . and the forced immobility of the chronically disabled within deteriorated urban neighbourhoods . . . areas where land-use deterioration has proceeded to such a point that the land market is substantially unaffected by the introduction of community services and their clients. (Wolpert and Wolpert, 1976: 37, 39)

In the absence of any expansion of state-provided services for the burgeoning ex-inmate population, such 'social junk' (Spitzer, 1975b: 645) has become a commodity from which various professionals and entrepreneurs extract a profit, the basis for a whole emergent industry battening upon derelicts and discharged mental patients. As a result, 'deinstitutionalisation' for many has meant little more than a transfer from a state to a private institution or quasi-institution, where 'one form of confinement has been replaced by another and the former patients are just as insulated from community attention and care as they were in the state hospital' (Wolpert and Wolpert, 1974: 61). What has changed is the packaging of their misery, not its reality. My earlier research on this subject (Scull, 1976 and 1977b) suggests that both the sources and the outcome of the movement away from segregative institutions can best be understood as a response to broader social-structural changes. I shall argue later in this paper that the picture I drew there now requires some reconsideration and modification, particularly as it applies to the treatment of criminals. But first let me sketch the basic components of my original approach to these issues.

Briefly, the creation and expansion of the welfare state, providing minimum subsistence for elements of the surplus population, generates structural pressures to curtail sharply the costly system of segregative control by creating some viable alternative. Previously, the highly restrictive welfare policies, which were characteristic of the United States until well into the present century, meant that asylums, prisons and the like represented one of the few costs of reproduction that were socialised, that is, administered by the state rather than the private sector. As a result, fiscal pressures on the state from this source were relatively slight, and the expenses associated with a system of segregative control were readily absorbed. Moreover, there was little or no choice but to keep the chronically insane in the asylum, since, although the overwhelming majority were harmless, they could not provide their own subsistence, and no other sources of support were available to sustain them in the outside world.

The advent of a wide range of welfare programmes providing just such support sharply increased the opportunity cost of neglecting community care in favour of the institution, which was inevitably far more costly than the most generous scheme of welfare payments. The comparative advantage of the non-institutional approach was further strengthened by the widespread unionisation of state employees, since, in the mid-1950s, the 'advent of the eight hour day and forty hour week in state institutions . . . virtually doubled unit costs' (Dingman, 1974: 48). Moreover, greater state expenditures on welfare were only part of a much broader and more massive expansion of the state's role in civil society, engendered by the need of advanced capitalism to socialise more and more of the costs of production (O'Connor, 1973; Braverman, 1974). The fiscal pressures created by this expansion have been intensified by the failure of productivity in the state sector to keep pace with that in the private sector, with the necessary consequence that a rising expenditure is required merely to maintain existing levels of activity. Hence there was an emergence and persistence of efforts at retrenchment in at least some sectors of the social-control apparatus, even at a time when general expenditure on welfare items was expanding rapidly. (Subsequently, of course, with the intensification of the fiscal crisis and the growing political dominance of monetarist recipes, spending cutbacks have become the rule rather than the exception for the social services.)

State hospital populations stabilised and began to decline in the early 1950s and, as welfare programmes markedly expanded during the 1960s and 1970s, the movement to empty the asylums accelerated. More devices were developed to divert potential inmates away from institutions, and existing ones were applied with greater urgency and effect. With the intensified effort to control soaring costs came the extension of deinstitutionalisation to the criminal justice sector, at first in the form of tentative, small-scale, experimental programmes, but soon on a much wider scale. The growing fascination of criminal justice planners and policy-makers with diversionary programmes coincided with a declining concern for imprisonment as a means of retribution and deterrence.

The decarceration movement today
At the end of 1975, when I completed my book on *Decarceration*, the advocates of deinstitutionalisation clearly dominated public debate in

the United States about the proper approach to the mad and the bad. Even in Europe, where the idea of abolishing or creating alternatives to incarceration was much slower to take hold, such notions began to circulate much more freely. Opposition, if not silent, was muted and fragmented, and often could simply be dismissed as self-interested. Among the public at large, it took the form of protest by the residents of particular communities against the placement of ex-inmates of any kind in *their* neighbourhood. Sometimes this involved harassment, threats of vigilante action, even arson; but in the politically more sophisticated and better organised communities, the favourite tactic was exclusionary zoning (Coates and Miller, 1973: 67; Segal, 1974: 143 ff.; Greenberg, 1975: 28 ff.; Wolpert and Wolpert, 1976). Such particularistic activities were simply designed to protect the parochial concerns of residents, who clearly wished to minimise contact with the very deviants whom they should eagerly be embracing according to the decarceration ideology. Limited opposition of this sort, by its very nature, was not likely to coalesce into a more broadly based attack on the policy *tout court*. Provided the burden could be shifted elsewhere, to other less vociferous, less powerful populations, the discontent could readily be defused without serious modification of the underlying programme. These complaints just reinforced other pressures to deposit the decarcerated in the poorest, most deteriorated and least desirable of urban locations.

Attempts to stimulate a general repudiation of the movement were largely the work of state employee unions (for example, CSEA, 1972; AFSCME, 1975). They sought to create moral panics (Cohen, 1972) among the general population by skilled manipulation of 'exemplary tales' concerning the squalor of the conditions in which ex-inmates were living and the violence to which they were prone, and the deleterious effects of these on both property values and public order. But although such efforts were not without success – the most notable being the decision by the Reagan administration in California to modify sharply its plans to eliminate state hospitals for the mentally ill and mentally retarded[3] (Chase, 1973) – they were clearly vulnerable to the accusation that they expressed more than the vested interest of those with direct responsibility for the shortcomings of the institutional alternative.

Within the last few years, of course, the situation has changed rather markedly. Although the process of emptying mental hospitals continues substantially as before, our jail and prison population has once again increased (to record levels), overcrowding is rife, and old and discarded buildings are being reopened and crammed with prisoners (Flynn, 1978: 131–2). Moreover, a strong conservative backlash urges longer terms of imprisonment, mandatory fixed sentences, and so forth (Fogel, 1975; Van den Haag, 1975; Wilson, 1975; Von Hirsch, 1976), and finds its pale reflection in the rediscovery by liberals of the virtues of swiftness and certainty in punishment (Martinson, 1974; see generally, Greenberg and Humphries, 1980). What are we to make of these developments, and what implications do they have for the future of the decarceration movement?

Let me confess at the outset that they suggest serious limitations to studying prisons and asylums as a unitary phenomenon. It is not that such assimilation is never theoretically or empirically justified, or that I feel I was completely wrong in invoking similar imperatives to explain the drive to decarcerate prisoners and patients. But I now recognise how important it is to remain sensitive to crucial differences that modify policy outcomes (Christie, 1978).

Ironically, the casual dumping of the disoriented and the senile has been made easier by the fact that the measures designed to dispose of them are ostensibly undertaken from a benevolent and humanitarian concern for their welfare. However great the discrepancy between the ideology and the reality of asylum existence – indeed, precisely *because* of the magnitude of that discrepancy (Orlans, 1948) – enormous energy and substantial resources have been devoted for more than a century and a half to elaborating, disseminating and perpetuating the illusion of concern with the inmate's welfare.[4] As someone who is sick and therefore cannot be held responsible for his condition or situation, the mental patient is the recipient of treatment 'for his own good'. If it is concluded that traditional approaches are destructive and anti-therapeutic, then non-intervention, dressed up as community treatment and promoted in the name of the very virtues once attributed to the asylum, can be advocated on the grounds of its advantages for the client. But prisoners are not clients, and pain, privation and suffering are seen by many as their just desserts. Because they 'chose' to offend, retribution is in order. The 'humanity' of community corrections is thus its Achilles' heel, precisely the feature most likely to alienate (fiscal) conservatives and indeed the public at large, who might otherwise be attracted by the idea. Criminals recidivate because of an innate or acquired depravity, and if prisons are unpleasant places, that is exactly what they should be.

The social legitimation that punishment derives from the positivist approach, and public opposition to whatever smacks of leniency toward criminals clearly delayed and inhibited the expansion of deinstitutionalisation to the criminal justice system. (As we shall see, they may also have affected its character.) If the structural pressures which I have identified ultimately prompted some movement in this direction, it was inevitable that such efforts would remain more labile and susceptible to retrenchment than their mental health counterparts.

If a public obsessed by crime in the streets has recently demanded that more (lower-class) criminals be locked up (and for longer periods of time), that has not discouraged the more utilitarian students of the criminal justice system. Quite the contrary; the overcrowding, tension and violence incident to such a reversal of the downward drift of prison populations has led at least some to speculate that 'a trend diametrically opposed to non-institutional alternatives, may finally force the development and implementation of plans for prison population reduction and de-institutionalization' (Flynn, 1978: 133). The criminologist's task is, then, the purely technical one of devising the means for 'the classification for risk . . . and the concomitant development of criteria on the basis of which a process of deinstitutionalisation – or at least a substantial population reduction – can be implemented' (Flynn, 1978: 134). Such a 'classification system should seek to identify those offenders who commit serious predatory crimes and violence, in order to separate them from offenders who do not represent any serious risk to the safety of the public'. The latter should then be 'classified out' of the criminal justice system, so as to reduce 'the social and economic costs of wholesale incarceration' (Flynn, 1978: 135, 148). The ethical and constitutional objections to such an approach (Greenberg, 1975) and its intensification of the class-biased character of the punitive system are passed over in silence. More cynically (or, perhaps, just more honestly), Ken Pease, a British criminologist, has proposed that we simply employ a sliding scale of remission for good conduct in prison, varied according to the numbers entering the system and the target for the total prison population – a sort of 'hydraulic, cybernetic model of prison life, whereby, if a lot come in this end then a lot go out that end' (Taylor, 1978: 204). Nagin (1978) has presented data that suggest this has been the implicit policy in the United States for several decades now.

In all probability, some such techniques will be devised and implemented to keep the lid on the potentially explosive conditions in our jails and penitentiaries and to permit some modest reductions in institutional populations. Indeed, in Britain, at least, there have been increasingly frantic government pronouncements about the 'necessity' for reductions in prison populations, to be achieved even at the price of greater and more automatic remission of sentences, and the introduction of restrictions of judicial sentencing powers. (see Fowles, 1980; Home Office, 1980; Parliamentary All Party Penal Affairs Group, 1980; Abolitionist, 1981; Pease 1981; Walker, 1981). To cite a further example, Michigan has enacted a programme whereby, whenever its prisons exceed capacity for thirty consecutive days, the governor must reduce all minimum sentences by ninety days (see Rutherford *et al.*, 1977).[5] But the significance of the revolt against excessive 'leniency' towards criminals is much broader than this. It affects the very substance of community 'alternatives' to imprisonment, and impels decarceration here to assume a guise quite different from that found in the deinstitutionalisation of the mentally disturbed – and one that is much more heavily interventionist in character.

Decarceration and the extension of control

My earlier critique of decarceration's humanitarian claims (Scull, 1977b) rested in large parts on evidence that 'decarceration' meant the substitution of a policy of non-intervention which actually amounted to neglect and exploitation and not the glorious therapeutic alternative its advocates proclaimed so loudly. I remain convinced that for the sub-population of deviants with whom *Decarceration* was primarily concerned, the mentally ill, this is essentially an accurate representation. But further research (and criticism of that book) has made me realise that for other groups, particularly the criminal, the problem is not so simple: here the humanitarian dangers, though still present, often come from just the opposite direction.

To be sure, deinstitutionalisation has meant little more than token efforts at control and 'supervision' for a good many discharged delinquents and criminals. The massive expansion of the population dealt with through non-institutional dispositions has not been matched by the development of a comparable infrastructure capable of providing community supervision and control, with the result that community treatment is often present in name only. In this situation it would be difficult to contend that the alternative disposition is less humane than the prison (from the offender's viewpoint).[6] Appalling though our ghettos may be, conditions there still are not quite as nasty, brutish and degrading as those in our penitentiaries. But what is generally neglected in such cost-benefit equations is that, although community treatment may be more humanitarian to those who are spared incarceration, it clearly is not so to anyone whom the community subsequently victimises. After all, 'whatever else it does or does not do, institutionalization does tend to ensure that these persons, anyway, will not visit depradations on the community while they are institutionalized' (Messinger, 1976: 90). And although, given the present state of knowledge about deterrence, 'one can only speculate about this possibility . . . to the extent that the effectiveness of a deterrent threat depends on the certainty of punishment . . . diversion programs at the pre-trial level or non-institutional sentences like probation could well lead to higher crime rates' (Greenberg, 1975: 8).

The problem I now have in mind, however, becomes significant as and when the slogan 'community corrections' actually begins to take on some substance. It is hinted at by Norval Morris in *The Future of*

Imprisonment (1974), and treated more seriously and at greater length in recent papers by David Greenberg (1975) and Stanley Cohen (1979b). Community programmes, precisely because of their less overtly punitive content, may become the occasion for significantly widening the reach and scope of the social-control apparatus. As Morris (1974: 10) puts it, 'We risk substituting more pervasive but less punitive control mechanisms over a vastly greater number of citizens for our present discriminatory and irrational selection of fewer citizens for more punitive and draconian sentences.'

Evidence is now accumulating that the development of so-called 'diversionary programmes' leads to 'a more voracious processing of deviant populations, albeit in new settings and by professionals with different names' (Cohen, 1979b: 350; see also Cressey and McDermott, 1974; Lerman, 1975; Klein *et al*., 1976; Messinger, 1976; Rutherford and Bengur, 1976; Blomberg, 1977). This tendency is hardly surprising, for neglect, pure and simple, has clear disadvantages as a social-control strategy, at least when dealing with criminals and some delinquents. Although the advocates of diversion consistently ignore or downplay the importance of the deterrent and retributive functions of punishment, to the extent that crime represents a 'rational' form of activity, the erosion of sanctions threatens to elicit more of it. The crazy and the senile can, by and large, be contained and isolated, even while being neglected. Their very lack of resources, immobility and absence of initiative, reinforced by such practices as exclusionary zoning and the centralisation of welfare services, can be exploited to secure their ecological separation into twilight zones where decomposition can proceed without offence to either the sensibilities or the operations of the larger society, subject only to routine and straightforward policing of the boundaries of these human sewers to ensure that their contents do not spill out and become a public nuisance (Bittner, 1967; Aaronson, Dienes and Musheno, 1978). Even were we to grant the attractions of unpoliced ghettos, those cannot be secured by releasing criminals, the targets of whose victimisation are insufficiently selective and not adequately geographically concentrated or controllable. The pressures thus generated for visible (and perhaps even effective) supervision are further reinforced by public perception of the criminal as someone whose activities are blameworthy and warrant – indeed require – the infliction of pain (cf. Christie, 1978).

The demands this situation creates dovetail nicely, in turn, with the organisational instincts of the correctional bureaucracies for self-preservation and expansion. By playing upon the fears and mobilising the disquiet of the public, the correctional staff can readily justify a substantial expansion of the amount and intensity of professional involvement and activity. Thus, one may anticipate that Lerman's

(1975) findings on the way the California Community Treatment Project has been manipulated by and in the interests of the correctional establishment will turn out to be applicable much more generally.

The convergence created by the special problems involved in controlling crime – 'the occupational interests of correctional and prison employees and administrators, and public demands, partly instrumental and partly symbolic, for sterner measures to stop increasing crime' (Greenberg, 1975: 16) – merely reinforces the tendency toward greater intervention already signalled in the pervasive and uncritical stress on rehabilitation so deeply entrenched in the community-corrections literature and practice. Battered by assaults on its constitutionality, effectiveness and moral justification (Leifer, 1969; American Friends Service Committee, 1971; Kittrie, 1972; Gaylin, 1974), the therapeutic ethic now appears to be losing ground in institutional settings. From both right and left, there are renewed calls for fixed sentencing based upon deterrent and retributive considerations, rather than rehabilitation (Fogel, 1975; Van den Haag, 1975; Wilson, 1975; Von Hirsch, 1976; Clarke, 1978). What seems to be happening, however, is that the self-same therapeutic rationalisations and practices are being reinvoked, as the basis for the new community programmes.[7]

The discretionary decision-making that forms an integral part of any programme of coercive 'rehabilitation' is a crucial feature of community corrections at all levels of its operations. It is most obvious in decisions about who is eligible for community dispositions in lieu of the harsher sanction of imprisonment. The very sense that the former is less punitive (or even non-punitive) and can actually *prevent* more crime diminishes concern with whether the 'client' has actually committed the offence that nominally brought him to the attention of the authorities. Instead of an adjudication focused on prior conduct, there is an assessment of whether the accused can benefit from the services provided by the programme, a decision that frequently entails intentional avoidance of due process and systematic obfuscation of the whole issue of guilt and innocence. The selection of 'suitable cases for treatment' relies upon 'critical predictor variables': age, prior institutional commitments, institutional adjustment, marital status, type of (unadjudicated) current offence, prior record, employment record, family and community ties, and so forth – the intent being to avoid releasing those who are dangerous or who might recidivate (Flynn, 1978). As Cohen comments:

> while the traditional screening mechanisms of the criminal justice system have always been influenced to a lesser or greater degree by non-offense related criteria (race, class, demeanour), the offense was at least considered. Except in the case of wrongful conviction, some law must have been broken. This is no longer clear. (1979b: 346)

The basic thrust toward making treatment criteria and dispositions independent of legal scrutiny and review is equally evident at later stages in the process. Once placed in a programme such as the Manhattan Court Employment Project:

> the recommendation of the project staff is obviously of critical importance to the defendant. The consequences of an unfavorable decision may include not only a resumption of prosecution, but possibly, if convicted, a more serious sentence, since a judge may be reluctant to grant probation to someone whose performance in the community program has been judged inadequate. Yet this decision is left to administrative staff to be made according to extremely subjective criteria. There is no procedure for appealing a negative recommendation, and given the nature of the criteria employed e.g. 'changes in attitude and lifestyle', it is hard to see how there could be. (Greenberg, 1975: 21)

Or again, as Lerman's (1975) study of the California Community Treatment Project has shown, short-term custody, which is so large a part of its procedures, is not governed by legal rules or due-process safeguards (just as the other 'treatments' within the programme are the product of discretionary decisions by programme personnel). Therefore the lack of accountability, threats to 'client' rights, and feelings of injustice and arbitrariness on the part of those manipulated are simply built into the system (see also Boorkman *et al.*, 1976).

In the words of those running the system, even 'such relatively nondelinquent offenses as missing a group meeting, "sassing" a teacher, showing an uncooperative attitude, or the threat of an emotional explosion' could prompt short-term incarceration (project report, cited in Lerman, 1975: 37). Indeed, the mere *belief* on the part of the staff that a subject might fail to comply with the programme's norms could do so. The whole approach thus brings with it the danger 'of highly intrusive intervention concerning matters of personal choice that have no direct bearing on criminal activity' (Greenberg, 1975: 6). And to the extent that these features generate further perceptions of injustice or unfairness, the long-run tendency must be for them to undermine further the legitimacy of a criminal justice system already regarded as inequitable and arbitrary.

This outcome is in no sense an aberration. On the contrary, in 'corrections', as in other social-control systems, the more control comes to be legitimated in terms of diagnosis and treatment rather than rules, responsibility and punishment, the more likely it is to intrude into the emotions, thought and behaviour of the individual and to be concerned with generalised behavioural 'problems' rather than specific acts. The threat thus looms of a massive extension of official intervention into the lives of millions who had previously escaped notice or attention – all under the guise of 'helping' them. In fact, 'the more benign, attractive, and successful the programme is defined as being . . . the more it will be used and the wider it will cast its net' (Cohen, 1979b: 348; see also Mathiesen's discussion of 'hidden disciplining', in Chapter 6).

In conclusion: crime control and social justice
I am not sanguine, therefore, about recent trends toward community corrections or about the likely impact of this movement on efforts to 'rehabilitate' offenders. As I suggested earlier, many of the more extravagant claims and expectations advanced by advocates of deinstitutionalisation derive from a serious overestimation of the strength of the casual link between crime and the apparatus of repression. *Pace* the assertions of the more starry-eyed devotees of labelling theory, 'the amount and structure of criminality is determined by other social forces: the system of crime control plays only a modest role' (Antilla, 1978: 197). As David Greenberg has suggested (1975: 5–6, 25), a serious attack on the 'crime problem' would probably involve, at a very minimum, 'efforts directed at reducing unemployment, barriers to teen-age entry into the job market, and other structural features of the labor market that impede the pursuit of "a lawful style of living in the community" '. Even these changes, any one of which is exceedingly unlikely, would probably be insufficient; we may well need, in addition, a broader attack on inequalities in both income and the ownership of productive property. Yet contemporary changes in the political economy of the United States point in precisely the opposite direction (O'Connor, 1973 and 1974; Wilson, 1978).

Thus there seem to be few immediate prospects for social change in the direction of increased equity and equality (although I, like most sociologists, am a bad prophet and so retain some hope that I shall be proved wrong). Without such change, I see little likelihood of anything more than minor incremental gains and further cosmetic 'improvements' (that, more often than not, are actually regressive) dressed up as major advances towards a more just and humane criminal justice system. On the whole, though, I think a realistic pessimism is to be preferred to a synthetic comfort built upon baseless fantasies of the dawn of the therapeutic milennium; or even upon more modest illusions about the possibilities of humanising a fundamentally inhuman system.

Let me conclude by saying that I am well aware of the pressures to be more than 'negatively critical'. It is not enough, according to the conventional wisdom, to speak harsh words about contemporary institutions. One 'should have the decency to provide a detailed blueprint for change and improvement, and should offer his suggestions in the spirit of one who is thankful for our collective blessings and, at all costs, hopeful' (Boyers, 1979: 28). This I cannot do, for I lack the necessary faith in the managerial approach to the problem. Indeed, I question the very legitimacy of the idea, implicit in such terminology, that the problem of crime and imprisonment can be 'solved' by internal technical adjustments. The social roots of our difficulties are too deep. This leaves me in a distinctly uncomfortable position: only a confirmed Pangloss can view the realities of a traditional penal system with equanimity; but what I have learned about the community-corrections movement simply reinforces my conviction that tinkering around with the criminal justice system in a radically unjust society is unlikely to advance us very far toward justice, equity or, come to that, efficacy. Perhaps the best I can do is to persuade others to share my sense of discomfort.

Notes

1 I am grateful to Steven Spitzer, Richard Abel and David Greenberg for their comments on an earlier draft of this essay. The current version has also benefited from comments and suggestions from David Garland and Peter Young.
2 For an empirical critique of this claim, confronting what is generally taken to be its strongest evidence — drug addiction — see Scull (1972); for a more wide-ranging dissent from such romantic notions by one who might be seen as the putative father, see Lemert (1972).
3 See *Los Angeles Times*, 29 January 1974.
4 That many of those employed to run such places are not hypocrites but true believers does not detract from the falsity of those beliefs. The benefits of such mythologies accrue largely to those who perpetrate them, not to their alleged beneficiaries. Inmates are generally all too aware of the emperor's missing clothes (save where sharing the illusion makes their lives more bearable).
5 See *Wall Street Journal*, 18 August 1981.
6 This assumes, of course, that those 'diverted' to the community would otherwise have been institutionalised. Where this is not the case, even the token supervision entailed by probation may be substantially more intrusive than prior dispositions would have been, not to mention the fact that the probationer is now far more vulnerable to serious sanctions in the future. Even from this narrow perspective, therefore, the humanity of community corrections is dubious. I shall discuss this point at greater length below.
7 This transfer of the therapeutic rationalisation from the sphere of formal incarceration to that of community corrections obviously deserves more extended treatment than I can give it here. One of the most critical questions it raises, of course, is *why* this flip-flop is occurring. Richard Abel (personal communication) has suggested one plausible explanation — that community dispositions are both less visible and, because they are less imbued with state action, less subject to constitutional scrutiny. Elsewhere, he has made an analogous point about the relationship between the distribution of bias in the criminal justice system and the visibility of that bias in the behaviour of official agents (Abel, 1978).

8 Neglected Features of Contemporary Penal Systems
Anthony E. Bottoms

This essay has a threefold but essentially modest purpose. I wish, first, to draw attention to some features of contemporary western penal systems, which in my judgement have been unduly neglected by those interested in the sociology of punishment. I shall argue, secondly, that these neglected matters cast very serious doubt upon an influential recent thesis concerning 'the extension of discipline'. Thirdly, I shall contend that a main lesson of the analysis is that developments in contemporary punishment have to be viewed in much closer relationship with certain central features of post-liberal western societies than they typically have been hitherto. If my argument is correct, it opens up a large research agenda; but it is not my purpose here to map that agenda, let alone to provide a complete analysis of contemporary punishment.

Some features of contemporary punishment
Let us begin with some empirical observations about punishment for adult offenders in the jurisdiction I know best – that of England and Wales. In Table 8.1 I have summarised the data on the sentencing patterns for adults convicted of indictable offences in 1938 (the last full year before the commencement of the Second World War) and in 1980 (the latest data available at the time of writing), with a midpoint year (1959) included for the sake of completeness. It might be helpful to explain at the outset that an indictable offence in England is one which can in principle be tried before a jury at a higher criminal court, and that the list of indictable offences includes what most people commonly think of as 'crime', such as homicide, most violent and sexual offences, burglary, robbery, theft, fraud, forgery and so forth.

The first thing that strikes one from the data in Table 8.1 is the proportionate decline in the use of imprisonment over the period analysed: from 33 per cent to 15 per cent. The next feature is much more surprising. For, contrary to what many would expect, it is not

Table 8.1   Adult indictable offenders: types of sentence

Type of sentence	Percentage of offenders[a]		
	1938	1959	1980
Prison service			
Imprisonment[b]	33.3	29.1	14.8
Probation service			
Probation	15.1	11.9	7.1
Community service	—	—	3.8
Suspended sentence with supervision	—	—	0.6	11.5
Other			
Fine[c]	27.2	44.8	52.6
Discharge	23.4	13.1	9.4
	50.6	57.9	72.4
Suspended sentence without supervision	—	—	10.4
Other penalty	1.0	1.1	1.3
Total	100.0	100.0	100.0
N[d]	38,896	75,358	243,651

Notes: [a]Includes all persons finally sentenced in England and Wales in the year shown.

[b]In 1938, includes penal servitude, and also Borstal training (then available for offenders up to age 23); in 1959 includes corrective training and preventive detention.

[c]In 1938, figures for persons aged 21 and over fined at higher courts are not separately available. This calculation assumes that all 116 offenders of all ages fined by higher courts were in fact adults.

[d]In 1938 the total excludes persons convicted at the magistrates' court but sent to a higher court for sentence. No age-specific data are available for this group, but the total for all ages was very small (377). Age-specific data are also not available for the same group in 1959, but it has been assumed that all persons sent to the higher court under s. 29 of the Magistrates' Court Act 1952 were 21 and over, unless the sentence they received was Borstal training.

Source: Relevant annual volumes of the *Criminal Statistics* for England and Wales.

probation which has been filling the gap caused by the proportionate decline in the use of imprisonment – indeed, probation itself has declined in its proportionate use (from 15 per cent to 7 per cent). Rather, the penalty which has shown the greatest increase in the period under review has been the fine, which has roughly doubled in its proportionate use (from 27 per cent to 53 per cent) at the expense of imprisonment, probation and the discharge.

This *rise of the fine* is a most important matter, and one might expect that it would have attracted great attention among penal analysts in Britain, especially those concerned with the sociology of punishment. This expectation is reinforced when one recalls that in one of the pioneering works on the sociology of punishment, Otto Kirchheimer wrote a chapter on the fine as one of his additions to Georg Rusche's text prepared for the Frankfurt Institute (see Rusche and Kirchheimer, 1939: ch. X). In this chapter, Kirchheimer presented data from a number of different European countries, showing *inter alia* that from the latter part of the nineteenth century:

> imprisonment remained the central point of the whole system, but it received increasing competition from the fine . . . This phenomenon is not merely the result of new crimes, like violations of purely police measures regulating traffic, but is also the consequence of a general policy of substituting the fine for imprisonment. (Rusche and Kirchheimer, 1939: 166–7)

But despite Kirchheimer's pioneering efforts, the rise of the fine for indictable offences in England has been almost wholly neglected as a significant penological phenomenon, not only by sociologists of punishment and social control, but even by policy-oriented penologists (although for brief, recent policy-oriented discussions, see Softley, 1978; Morgan and Bowles, 1981).

We must be careful, however, not to misstate the evidence about the rise of the fine. In the first place, it has not been an even development as between different countries. In the United States, for example, although good national data are very hard to come by, the pattern does seem very different.[1]

> Successive presidential commissions and reform groups have pointed to the fact that for offenses other than traffic violations the fine is used only sparingly in the United States . . . At the same time, the English gave probation in only five per cent of all cases – compared to more than 50 per cent of all cases in the United States. (Carter and Cole, 1979)

In Canada, on the other hand, the position of the fine is midway between the English and the American usage. On the latest available national data (that for 1973), the fine was used in the Canadian provinces in 34 per cent of indictable offences (see Griffiths, Klein and Verdun-Jones, 1980: 173).[2]

Even in England, the rise of the fine for adult indictable offenders has not been one of steady progress. The first great growth came in the late nineteenth century, but thereafter the proportionate use of the fine remained fairly static until the Second World War, during and after which there was a further great increase in use (for relevant data from 1900 to 1968, see Walker, 1972: Table 15.1). There have also been considerable fluctuations in the post-1945 growth of the fine, with, for example, little increase since 1970 (Home Office, 1981:

Figure 7.4). These detailed variations clearly need to be accounted for in any full explanation of the phenomenon.

Returning to Table 8.1, a second obvious feature to be noted is that there are now more penalties available to the English courts when sentencing adult offenders than there were in 1938. The two new-comers are the *suspended sentence of imprisonment* (available both with and without the complementary supervision of a probation offi-cer) and the *community service order*. These two measures were intro-duced respectively in the Criminal Justice Acts of 1967 and of 1972, and were both intended specifically to provide the courts with addi-tional alternatives to imprisonment. They are thus part of the recent thrust, by successive governments of different political persuasions, towards a policy of decarceration, although in practice these partic-ular measures have by no means always had the expected decar-cerative effect (see Sparks, 1971b; Pease, Billingham and Earnshaw, 1977; Bottoms, 1981).

For the purposes of this essay, rather different implications may be drawn from the introduction of these two penalties. As regards the suspended sentence, this was a measure borrowed by England from continental jurisdictions where it had a long history and was the legal foundation of the *mise à l'épreuve*, or the equivalent of the probation system (see Ancel, 1971). In England, however, the suspended sentence is mostly available only without the concomitant supervision of the offender,[3] and therefore, if there is no reconviction within the operational period of the suspension, it is functionally equivalent to discharge. This explains why in Table 8.1 the suspended sentence without supervision is placed together with the fine and the discharge as an 'other' penalty, in contrast to those measures supervised by the prison service (imprisonment) or by the probation service (probation; community service; suspended sentence with supervision). When this division is made, it is seen that in percentage terms, since 1938 these *penalties not involving continuing supervision by a penal agent* have grown, whereas both imprisonment and (to a lesser extent) probation-supervised sentences have declined.[4] This development is, of course, closely connected with the rise of the fine, but the suspended sentence without supervision has also contributed to the trend since its creation in 1967.

Community service is important for a rather different reason. Originally introduced only upon an experimental basis in six local probation areas, it quickly won support, and from 1975 was made available to all areas in England and Wales which wished to adopt it. A rapid expansion in use followed, so that in 1980 it was used in 4 per cent of cases involving adult indictable offenders, and 8 per cent of cases involving young adults aged 17–21 (these figures might seem small until one realises that the corresponding figures for probation are respectively only 7 per cent and 9.5 per cent). In the Criminal Justice Bill of 1981–2, community service is being further extended to juvenile offenders aged 16. Meanwhile it has proved eminently exportable, at least to other common-law jurisdictions, and has indeed enjoyed a very rapid geographic spread.

> England was the first country to use community service work as a penal measure in itself. Since then, however, similar legislation has been introduced in British Columbia, Ontario and other provinces in Canada, several states in the United States and Australia, and New Zealand. Community service is also used in some parts of the United States as a form of non-statutory pre-trial or pre-sentence diversion. (Young, 1979: xi)

All this has occurred less than ten years from the original tentative introduction of community service in England. Although it is still too early to make more than a provisional judgement about this sentence, it would seem that it could be one of the more important penal developments of the late twentieth century.

Finally, in this brief empirical survey, we need to note one further penal development in England which does not appear at all from an inspection of Table 8.1. This development is the *rise of victim compensation*. The most obvious and well-known manifestation of the growth of victim compensation is the proliferation of state-financed compensation schemes for victims of crimes of violence. Since these schemes involve the payment of moneys by the state directly to the victim (without any necessary involvement of the offender),[5] they are not usually considered as part of the penal system in their respective countries. This is, in my judgement, a profound mistake, for the schemes undoubtedly are a part of the official societal response to crime in the given jurisdiction. One of the policy documents which led to the introduction of the Crminal Injuries Compensation Scheme in Britain was quite clear about this linkage. Any 'fundamental re-examination of penal methods', it argued:

> must consider the fundamental concepts underlying our treatment of offenders, and examine not only the obligations of society and the offenders to one another, but also the obligations of both to the victim . . . The assumption that the claims of the victim are sufficiently satisfied if the offender is punished by society becomes less persuasive as society in its dealing with offenders increasingly emphasises the reformative aspects of punishment. (Home Office, 1959: 7)

The first criminal injuries compensation scheme was set up in New Zealand in 1963; Britain followed suit in 1964, and in subsequent years all Australian and most American and Canadian jurisdictions have also developed schemes. According to one recent text, although continental European countries have not introduced this type of measure, 'even there the political impetus today is in this direction', and Japan is also contemplating a similar development (Burns, 1980: 3, 399). By 1978, the British scheme received over 20,000 applications in a full year, and the total cost was over £10 million (Atiyah, 1980: 358, 524). The schemes have, however, run into substantial criticism, especially on the ground that if the state is to make grants to the victims of misfortune, there is no reason to single out the crime victim; rather, it is argued, the movement should be (as in New Zealand it has been) towards a more general scheme of state insurance and compensation for personal injuries (see Miers, 1978; Atiyah, 1980).

A related development also worthy of brief notice lies in the growth of victim-support schemes, whereby local volunteer support groups offer counselling and related help to victims of many kinds of crime. Although based on the voluntary principle, these groups are nonetheless closely connected to various official agencies, and especially to the police, upon whom they depend for initial notification that a person has been the victim of a criminal incident. The first victim-support scheme in England was established in Bristol as recently as 1974, yet by 1979 there was already a registered National Association of Victim Support Schemes, with a full-time National Officer and 75 per cent funding from the national government; during the first year of existence of the national association, the number of local schemes rose from 34 to 67 (NAVSS, 1980). Clearly, this movement looks like developing further in the years to come. Once again, there are similar developments in other countries, varying of course by national context (see, for example, Norquay and Weiler, 1981).

Although both the criminal injuries and the victim-support schemes are clearly important innovations, they are nevertheless not integrally related to the criminal trial or to the offender. This cannot be said of the third kind of development to be considered, that of the direct payment of compensation by an offender to the victim by order of the criminal court which tries the offender. In England, even before the Second World War there were some legal provisions allowing criminal courts to require the payment of compensation as an ancillary order, but these provisions were patchy and very little used. As a result of some strengthening of the provisions in 1948, the decade 1950–9 saw some compensation being ordered in just under 3,500 criminal cases per year (Home Office, 1961: 2), although with substantial local variation (Elkin, 1957: 58). However, even on the unlikely assumption that all these cases involved indictable offences, this constituted less than 3 per cent of the average annual number of persons found guilty of indictable offences during the decade. Thus the author of the first British criminology textbook was fully justified in claiming during the 1950s that 'the possibility of restitution is rarely considered by British courts of criminal jurisdiction nowadays' (Jones, 1956: 117).

As a result of a complex series of initiatives, the law was further simplified and broadened in the Criminal Justice Act 1972, which contained a general provision allowing the courts to make a compensation order as an ancillary order in any case where 'injury, loss or damage' had resulted. A study of the Crown Court in London before and after this provision came into force showed clearly that the Act had resulted in a significant increase in the use of compensation (Tarling and Softley, 1976). Subsequently, there has been further growth, especially in the magistrates' courts, as is evident from the data in Table 8.2. By 1980 the annual total of offenders ordered to pay compensation was as high as 128,000, and in magistrates' courts substantial proportions of defendants in all kinds of indictable cases (save sexual offences) were given compensation orders.[6] The position of compensation is further boosted by a provision in the Criminal Justice Bill of 1981–2 that where a fine and a compensation order are both ordered by the court, 'the court shall give preference to compensation'.

All this represents a great change from the 1950s; but, once again, the development has not been confined to Britain. Several American states have enacted legislation to enable or require a criminal to make restitution (Chesney, Judson and McLagen, 1977). In a number of places in the United States matters have gone further with the development of so-called mediation schemes; these take the case outside the criminal courts altogether and into a forum where the two parties (victim and defendant) are encouraged to reach a settlement, usually involving compensation and/or promises as to future behaviour. Although these schemes seem to be used mainly for minor crimes where the parties already know each other, they are a most noteworthy development, especially as evaluative research has shown that victims view them in a relatively favourable light as compared with the traditional court procedures (see Garofalo and Connelly, 1980). Taken together with the earlier developments described (criminal injuries compensation, victim-support schemes and the growth of compensation orders), there is surely here strong evidence that concern with the victim has become a powerful motif in contemporary western societal responses to crime.

We have identified, then, three developments in contemporary western penal systems which are worthy of further attention: first, the growth of the fine (and the related growth of penalties not involving continuing supervision by any penal agent); secondly, the birth of

Table 8.2   Indictable offenders ordered to pay compensation (all ages)

	1976[a]	1978[a]	1980[a]
Magistrates' courts			
Violence against the person	9	16	18
Sexual offences	1	1	1
Burglary	27	32	36
Robbery	15	22	21
Theft and handling	12	14	17
Fraud and forgery	33	37	46
Criminal damage[b]	70	71	68
Crown Court			
Violence against the person	6	8	11
Sexual offences	*	*	*
Burglary	9	9	7
Robbery	4	4	4
Theft and handling	8	9	8
Fraud and forgery	14	16	17
Criminal damage[b]	13	26	28

Notes: *Denotes less than 0.5 per cent.
          [a]Figures relate to England and Wales, and indicate persons ordered to pay compensation as a percentage of all offenders sentenced in the relevant category.
          [b]The definition of indictable criminal damage altered between 1978 and 1980, and the 1980 figures include only cases involving damage of £200 or more.
Source: Home Office (1981), Table 7.25.

community service; and thirdly, the growth of compensation and related matters. Yet none of these developments can be said to have received the attention it deserves from penal analysts, especially sociologists of social control.

The dispersal of discipline thesis
At this point it is useful to change the focus of attention, and to look closely at what might be described as the 'dispersal of discipline thesis'. This is a theme derived from recent articles by two very influential sociologists of social control, Stanley Cohen (1979b) in England and Thomas Mathiesen (1980b and Chapter 6 of this volume) in Norway.

I shall begin with an analysis of Cohen's essay on 'The punitive city' (1979b). This starts from an acceptance of the existence of the so-called 'great transformation' of punishment from the corporal to the carceral at the end of the eighteenth century and into the nineteenth, as described by Rothman (1971), Foucault (1977a) and Rusche and Kirchheimer (1939). The thesis then argued by Cohen is essentially a more elaborated version of that which he put tersely in an earlier essay:

> Foucault described one historical take-off in terms of the move from 'simple' punishment to the concentrated surveillance of the asylum. We are living through another change: from the *concentration* to the *dispersal* of social control. (Cohen, 1977: 227, italics in original).

This 'dispersal of social control' of course refers to the community-corrections movement. Much of Cohen's concern, in his 1979 article, is to describe in detail (and, for the most part, very tellingly) some of the key features of this movement. These include:

(1) *'Blurring'*. This is the breakdown between the old and simple institutional/non-institutional distinction, as institutions develop leave programmes, hostels, etc., and community agencies develop residential and day-attendance facilities. These developments 'beckon to a future when it will be impossible to determine who exactly is enmeshed in the social control system' (Cohen, 1979b: 346).

(2) *'Widening the net'*. This concept brings within the ambit of an allegedly beneficial community programme not only those who would otherwise have been the subject of formal social control (for example, in institutions), but also others who would not (for example, who would have been given an informal warning). This development therefore acts 'to increase rather than decrease the total *number* who get into the system in the first place' (1979b: 347, italics in original).

(3) *'Thinning the mesh'*. Although this fishing metaphor is more obscure than the previous one, its import is that the new community programmes may increase the *amount* of intervention directed at many deviants in the system. 'There is little doubt that a substantial number – perhaps the majority – of those subjected to the new programs will be subjected to a degree of intervention higher than they would have received under previous non-custodial options like fines, conditional discharge or ordinary probation' (1979b: 347).

(4) *Penetration*. This concept essentially sums up Cohen's thesis: the *formal* social-control agencies of the state are seen as penetrating more deeply into the *informal* networks of society. In the end, it is 'the sheer proliferation and elaboration of these other systems of control – rather than the attack on the prison itself – which

impresses' (1979b: 358). Moreover, these developments are throwing up whole new groups of professionals, and 'each set of experts produces its own "scientific" knowledge: screening devices, diagnostic tests, treatment modalities, evaluation scales' (1979b: 358).

In the last two pages of his article, Cohen relates his thesis to that of Foucault in *Discipline and Punish* (1977a). Just as Foucault had seen 'discipline' as the key concept in the emergence of the prison as the dominant form of punishment at the beginning of the nineteenth century, so Cohen, after speaking of 'indefinite discipline', asserts boldly that 'the "new" move into the community is *merely* a continuation of the overall pattern established in the nineteenth century' (1979b: 359, my italics).

No one who has any familiarity with the penal scene in western countries – especially in relation to juveniles – would deny that much of what Cohen describes is indeed occurring. In the British context, for example, one could readily produce examples from the field of so-called 'intermediate treatment' for young offenders which clearly illustrate 'blurring', 'widening the net' and 'thinning the mesh'. Perhaps for this reason, there has been a widespread acceptance of Cohen's general thesis, not only in Britain but elsewhere (for example, Chan and Ericson, 1981; Hylton, 1981). The same kind of thesis has also been argued by others writing independently of Cohen, and probably more crudely than he would accept.[7] So if his is an incomplete or mistaken thesis, it is of more than trivial significance to dispute it.

We can concentrate initially on Cohen's use of Foucault. Cohen recognises, of course, that Foucault in *Discipline and Punish* spoke of discipline as a new form of power, applied not only in the prison, but also in other areas of society: 'is it surprising that prisons resemble factories, schools, barracks, hospitals, which all resemble prisons?' (Foucault, 1977a: 228). Thus Cohen sees the new alleged 'dispersal of social control' as merely a continuation of this pattern into new areas. But this presupposes that all the dispersed forms of social control are *disciplinary*, in Foucault's sense; and this may be questioned.

In approaching this issue, it is important to be very clear about the concepts used. In one of the most illuminating passages of *Discipline and Punish*, Foucault (1977a: 130–1) draws some clear contrasts between three ideal types of punishment mechanisms (what he calls 'technologies of power') available at the end of the eighteenth century. These may be described as the *corporal*, that exemplified in the old punishment system of the *ancien régime*; then the *juridical*, that proposed by the classical reformers such as Beccaria (1764), but never generally implemented; and finally the *carceral*, or that which found expression in the prison, the overwhelmingly dominant punishment of the nineteenth century. In a summary sentence (the second full sentence on p. 131), Foucault expresses succinctly the main differences between these three mechanisms; these I have systematised and slightly elaborated to produce Table 8.3.

There are crucial differences between the juridical and the carceral systems. In the juridical system, just enough punishment is applied to act as a deterrent to the offender and to others; punishment must, as Beccaria firmly insisted, be always *preventive* in ultimate intent. But the intended preventive message of punishment is provided simply by representations and signs ('behave or you will be punished', etc.); there is no specific penal administrative apparatus designed to mould offenders into obedient subjects. Moreover, when the punishment is completed (and, of course, for the classical jurists it must be of a fixed duration, proportionate to the seriousness of the offence), then the punished subject rejoins society as a full member; he is, in Foucault's words, a 'juridical subject in process of requalification' as a fully equal member of the social pact.

In the contemporary context, a seemingly trivial but nevertheless very instructive example of this kind of juridical punishment can be seen in the game of ice hockey. Here, a player who breaks the rules may be given a 'penalty'; this is a term of fixed duration (perhaps two minutes or five minutes) during which he must leave the ice. For this period, he is placed in a 'penalty box', a special spatial area at the side of the rink, in clear view of the public but symbolically placed on the opposite side of the ice from the other members of the offenders' team who are awaiting their turn to play. Thus by symbolic representation the infraction of the player is marked, both for himself and for others; and, since teams do not wish to lose players, the overall purpose of the system is clearly to prevent breaches of the rules of the game. Once the player has 'sat out' for the required period, however, he may return to the ice without disgrace: he is now a 'requalified subject'. As Foucault (1977a: 104 ff.) explains the project of the classical reformers, punishment was to be *school* rather than *ceremony* (for the offender, and especially others, to learn to obey); punishment should be public, the better to impress others; and punishment should be as unarbitrary as possible (to protect the liberties of the citizens in the social contract). To comply with all of these requirements, there must be a complex of punitive signs (or coded sets of representations) which both reduces the desire that makes crime attractive, and increases the interest that makes the penalty feared, to a just sufficient extent (but no more) to preserve the overall social order. This message must be widely disseminated throughout society:

Table 8.3   Central features of three mechanisms of punishment

	Corporal	*Juridical*	*Carceral*
(a) Locus of the power to punish	Sovereign and his force	Social body	Administrative apparatus
(b) Intended residual object of the power to punish	Ritual marks of vengeance	Signs (coded sets of representations)	Traces (behavioural habits of obedience)
(c) Mode of penalty	Ceremony of power	Representation	Exercise
(d) Status of offender	Vanquished enemy	Juridical subject in process of requalification	Individual subject to immediate coercion
(e) Body/soul	Tortured body	Soul with manipulated representations	Body subjected to training (to produce compliance of the soul)

Source: Adaptation of passage in Foucault (1977a: 130–1).

This, then, is how one must imagine the punitive city. At the crossroads, in the gardens, at the side of roads being repaired or bridges built, in workshops open to all, in the depths of mines that may be visited, will be hundreds of tiny theatres of punishment. (Foucault, 1977a: 113).

But none of this is *discipline*, in Foucault's sense. To return to the ice-hockey example, no one does anything to the offending player while he is in the penalty box; he just sits there. In the ideal project of the carceral system of punishment, on the other hand, there is an explicit apparatus of punishment established whereby the offender is intendedly *trained*. The forms of this prison training may vary, as Mathiesen notes (Chapter 6, p. 133 above), for example, from *religious exercises* to *work* to *schooling* to *quasi-medical treatment*; but in each case, specific exercises are performed with and upon the offender. Like the classicists' juridical punishment, all this is intendedly preventive; but 'what one is trying to restore in this technique of correction is not so much the juridical subject, who is caught up in the fundamental interests of the social pact, but the obedient subject, the individual subjected to habits, rules, orders, an authority that is exercised continually around him and upon him, and which he must allow to function automatically in him' (Foucault 1977a: 128–9). Thus, in the carceral project, 'work on the prisoner's soul must be carried out as often as possible' (1977a: 125), for disciplinary punishment's intended corrective effect is '*obtained directly through the mechanics of a training'* (1977a: 180, my italics). It is this *training* which requires knowledge of the offender as a whole person (and not just as someone who can be placed into a penalty box), with the correlative apparatus of expertise, judgements, professionalism and so forth.

Cohen (1979b: 360) is aware that Foucault draws some distinctions between the classical reformers and the prison project, but he does not by any means fully explicate the presence of discipline (or coercive soul-training) in the one scheme and its absence from the other. Thus, although the main argument of his paper leads up to a description of the new community-corrections movement as 'indefinite *discipline*' and as '*merely* a continuation of the overall pattern established in the nineteenth century' (1979b: 359, my italics), Cohen nevertheless actually derives the title of his paper from Foucault's passage about the 'punitive city' of the classical reformers, as cited above. Indeed, he even (and most incongruously) places the passage itself in a place of honour at the beginning of his argument.

I have drawn particular attention to this contrast between the juridical and the carceral projects because of its relevance to an understanding of contemporary punishment. For when we juxtapose this juridical/carceral contrast with the developments outlined in the first section of this paper, immediate doubt is cast at least upon the universal applicability of Cohen's 'dispersal of discipline' thesis. Cohen nowhere mentions the growth of the fine, and the modern fine is clearly more of a classical than a disciplinary punishment.[8] Neither the rise of the fine, nor the growth of compensation, nor the general increase in penalties not involving supervision by a penal agent look remotely congruent with a general thesis of a thrust towards 'indefinite discipline'.

Community service, however, appears to be an altogether different case, and both Cohen (1979b) and Mathiesen (Chapter 6 above) refer to it in their respective essays. It therefore merits some close attention. Cohen says that 'the stress on community absorption has found one of its most attractive possibilities' in the community service order; it is attractive because it 'appeals not just to the soft ideology of community absorption but the more punitive objectives of restitution and compensation' (1979b: 357). Mathiesen (in Chapter 6, n. 12) refers to the British experience with the community service order as tending, for a slight majority of recipients, to be imposed in place of another non-custodial sentence rather than in place of prison (citing here Pease *et al.*, 1977). Thus, argues Mathiesen, 'it constitutes an increase rather than a decrease of the total criminal justice control system' or in other words, in Cohen's terms, it is an example of 'thinning the mesh'.

Both authors undeniably have a point. Community service does sometimes have a 'thinning the mesh' effect (for example, in replacing the fine); and some of its specific work projects ('helping in geriatric wards . . . painting and decorating the houses of various handicapped groups, building children's playgrounds etc.' as Cohen puts it) do look like punishment penetrating deeply into the informal social fabric. Nevertheless, we do need to ask one crucial question: is this an extension of *discipline*, in Foucault's sense?

Here we must go back to *Discipline and Punish* once again. There we find Foucault noting that the juridical reformers 'almost always proposed public works as one of the best possible penalties' (1977a: 109). 'Public works' as a penalty meant two things; it signified the collective interest in the punishment, and also its visible, verifiable character. Later, Foucault draws a sharp contrast between the classical reformers and the carceral project so far as the link between work and punishment is concerned. For the reformers, work in prison or in public works projects could be 'an example for the public or a useful reparation for society' (1977a: 240), but in the carceral project:

> Penal labour must be seen as *the very machinery that transforms* the violent, agitated, unreflective convict into a part that plays its role with perfect regularity. The prison is not a workshop; it is, it must be of itself, a machine whose convict-workers are both the cogs and the products. (Foucault, 1977a: 242, my italics)

When we look at community service against this background, to which model does it more closely approximate – that of public works or penal labour? A clue may be gleaned from considering a passage by Warren Young (1979) in which he notes three distinctions between what he describes as the respective 'modes of rehabilitation' attempted under a probation order and a community service order:

> First, the traditional approach of the probation service, based essentially on social casework principles (however they are for the time being defined) has been preoccupied with the offender's shortcomings and failures . . . The community service order, on the other hand, is concerned with utilising the positive attributes of the offender. In essence, it is an ability-oriented rather than a problem-oriented approach . . . Secondly, while the requirements of the probation order are normally fulfilled within the sanctuary of the office or home interview, work under the community service order is usually performed in full view of the outside community . . . Thirdly, the community service order has a fixed and limited content directed towards the fulfilment of a clearly defined objective ordered by the court . . . in stark contrast to the vague, diffuse and often global objectives of the probation order. (Young, 1979: 40–1)

This statement is probably rather too precise, for we know from elsewhere that community service is a concept sufficiently flexible to develop in a number of different directions in different local areas

(Pease and McWilliams, 1980: esp. ch. 9). Nevertheless, in the context of the present discussion Young's statement is of great interest. Developments away from preoccupation with the offender's shortcomings, towards a more public penality and towards greater precision of punishment are *precisely* what one would expect, if a disciplinary project (in Foucault's terms) were being eroded and replaced by a more juridical one. This view is reinforced when one considers aspects of the choice of work placement in community service, as discussed by Pease and McWilliams (1980: 22–4). They note that in most local areas 'the work placement is largely chosen by the offender rather than by the organiser'; that in all areas the offender will be shown a list of tasks and asked which interests him most; and that there is everywhere an implication that his choice will be a reasoned one, consistent with a view of the offender as an autonomous moral actor. None of this looks much like 'discipline'.

This conclusion should not be overstated. In the first place, community service is still in its infancy and could yet be developed in a more disciplinary form. Secondly, there is known to be substantial local variation in the way this penalty is administered. Thirdly, it is possible that with rising unemployment levels magistrates will increasingly intend community service as disciplinary for unemployed offenders, even if the mechanism of the application of the penalty does not appear specifically disciplinary in its actual administration. Nevertheless, despite these caveats, it is safe to conclude that community service is rather less disciplinary than Cohen at least supposes.

If the foregoing is correct, the following conclusions may be drawn. First, none of the major penal developments noted in the first section (the growth of the fine, compensation and community service) are fully consistent with the 'dispersal of discipline' thesis, for none of them is primarily disciplinary. Secondly, although community service may not be primarily disciplinary, it does appear to involve some of the specific mechanisms which Cohen describes, namely, 'thinning the mesh' and 'community absorption' (although the latter might be better described in other terms, as we shall see in the next section). The juxtaposition of these two main conclusions suggests that we need a different kind of theoretical apparatus to the one Cohen employs, if we are successfully to explain some of the developments which he describes.

At this point we may usefully turn to look in more detail at Mathiesen's essay (Chapter 6 above and also 1980b), to which reference has already been made. At first sight, Mathiesen's thesis might seem to be almost identical to that of Cohen. Thus, for example, Mathiesen's 'main prediction' for the future of control systems is that 'the external or societal control system will gradually expand and become continually more extensive and important' (p. 140 above) – a prediction which Mathiesen himself recognises as being similar to Cohen's (see Chapter 6, n. 20). But, on closer analysis, matters are not quite so simple. Discussing a recent Norwegian White Paper on the control of crime, Mathiesen first notes that in the language of the document there appears to be some shift of emphasis from the typical conceptual underpinning of crime-control strategies in the nineteenth century. In that era, control was 'distinctively individualistic': that is, 'the disciplining, through the criminal justice system, of that part of the working class which was registered as criminal, took place *as a disciplining of individuals*; a disciplining of the law-breakers "one by one" ' (p. 132 above). In the new White Paper, however, 'the old individually oriented understanding is abandoned, a "societal" understanding has taken its place' (p. 135 above). At a subsequent point in the argument, when discussing future societal-control strategies, Mathiesen suggests that some future measures (such as those of alcoholics, the mentally ill, and in 'crime care in the community') might retain the old individualistic focus, so that 'concerning these measures, Foucault's perspective on the prison-like features "diffusing" into outside society will truly be an apt perspective' (p. 139 above). (Again note that this is very similar to Cohen). However, Mathiesen continues, other measures could 'move fully away from individualism, and focus on *control of whole groups and categories*' (p. 139 above). These measures will increasingly impinge on the everyday lives of these groups and categories; this, Mathiesen explicitly argues, will represent a certain *break* with individualism as the organising focus of social control (p. 139 above). As examples of this new kind of control Mathiesen gives the following (see p. 139 above):

> TV cameras on subway stations and in supermarkets, the development of advanced computer techniques in intelligence and surveillance, a general strengthening of the police, a general strengthening of the large privately-run security companies, as well as a whole range of other types of surveillance of whole categories of people – all of this is something we have begun to get, and have begun to get used to.

Mathiesen is surely right to draw attention to these developments as significant recent features in social control. However, it is noteworthy that he still wishes to call this 'discipline', and indeed refers to the changed style of social control as 'a change *from open to hidden discipline*' (see p. 139 above). It is in this sense that he can be characterised, together with Cohen, as espousing a 'dispersal of discipline' thesis. Yet in Mathiesen's case this terminology contains the seeds of confusion. At an early point in his essay Mathiesen clearly links the concept of discipline to Foucault's work (see Chapter 6, n. 6). For Foucault, discipline, epitomised in *Panopticon*, involves both *surveillance* and *the mechanics of a training* aimed at producing obedient subjects. But Mathiesen's 'control of whole groups and categories' depends almost exclusively simply upon the mechanisms of surveillance, using (especially) the devices of advanced technology and enhanced policing; there is little or no hint in any of the examples which he gives of 'the mechanics of a training', and, significantly, in the passage cited above it is actually the word 'surveillance' rather than 'discipline' which is used.[9] A similar point may be made concerning Shearing and Stenning's (1981) otherwise excellent analysis of the growth of the private security industry in modern western societies. These authors suggest that private security is helping to precipitate a reorganisation of policing towards a more preventive mode, and that this is a part of 'a more general phenomenon in the transformation of social control' (1981: 236). Principal contentions are that the scope of surveillance undertaken by private security has increased enormously, and that the nature of surveillance has been transformed in the process (1981: 213). The work of Foucault (1977a) is specifically invoked, and Shearing and Stenning talk explicitly about the emergence of a more complete 'disciplinary society'. Yet, although aspects of surveillance in modern societies are brilliantly analysed, there is little suggestion in Shearing and Stenning's paper of any development of 'the mechanics of a training' upon the bodies and souls of individuals, in the manner suggested by Foucault.

Thus despite the apparent similarity of Mathiesen's and Cohen's work in presenting a 'dispersal of discipline' thesis, at a deeper level Mathiesen's proposition concerning the apparent shift from individualistic to collective social control actually produces a clear divergence of emphasis as against Cohen. In the remainder of this essay I shall assume (following on from the arguments presented above): first, that Mathiesen is right in perceiving a shift towards collective social control in modern western societies; but, secondly, that at least in the sphere of punishment the dispersal of discipline thesis is not a particularly helpful characterisation of some current developments. In order to make sense of these differing conclusions, it will be necessary to consider the nature of law and social control in post-liberal capitalist societies.

Before proceeding with the substance of that analysis, one important point of a methodological nature must be made. Some writers (for example, Chan and Ericson 1981; Hylton 1981) have recently sought to extend Cohen's thesis by arguing that many modern western penal systems are experiencing an extension and expansion of social control; *both in and out* of institutions; that is, that imprisonment rates are going up, just as community supervision is also rapidly increasing. However, when we look at the data used, it is found that these all relate *either* to the absolute number of people imprisoned or put on probation, *or* alternatively to the rate of prison or probation sentences per 100,000 of the general population; data on the *proportion* of convicted defendants given imprisonment or probation are given little or no attention.[10] Some simple calculations from the figures in Table 8.1 will show that English data calculated on the same basis as that of these analysts would give the same kind of result as, for example, Hylton's data for Saskatchewan. Thus, for example, we can calculate from Table 8.1 that the number of adults given prison sentences in England and Wales rose from less than 13,000 in 1938 to 36,000 in 1980, despite the fact that the proportion of convicted defendants given imprisonment fell sharply over the same period.

Two comments may be made upon this approach to the issues. First, ignoring the proportionate data could result in missing some key trends. In the English case, since the numbers sent to prison have increased, despite a declining proportion of indictable offenders sent to prison, and since the fine has increased in its *proportionate* use, it necessarily follows that the fine has increased numerically very much faster than has the level of prison committals. But analyses of Hylton's type, concentrating solely upon prison and probation numbers and rates per 100,000, would simply ignore this vital data on the fine, and would thus fail to realise that in England the penalties involving active control by a penal agent (prison, probation, etc.) are not those which have been increasing the most rapidly.

Secondly, we have to ask what underlies the two different approaches. The numerical approach is obviously particularly concerned to measure the absolute level of the state's punitive power exercised over its subjects. The proportionate approach is more inclined to be interested in the balance of different punitive methods used by the state at different periods upon those who have been convicted of crime. What produces the dramatic differences in results between the two approaches is, of course, the huge rise, in most western countries in the post-war period, in the number of persons convicted – in England, the number of adults convicted of indictable crimes rose from under 40,000 in 1938 to over 240,000 in 1980 (see Table 8.1). But could this rise itself indicate an extension of state power, thus lending support to the numerical approach?

The rise in convictions is, on closer examination, found to be largely the product of the sharp increase in the number of registered crimes over the period in question (that is, it is not due to an increase in the detection rate, or other variables of a like kind). The increase in registered crimes could be the result of (1) a real increase in crime; (2) an increased willingness on the part of the public to report crimes to the authorities; (3) an increased readiness on the part of the police to record crimes reported to them; (4) an increased tendency on the part of the police to discover crimes on their own initiative, and not through public reporting ('direct discovery'); or, of course, a combination of any two or more of these possibilities. For present purposes, the fourth possibility can be effectively discounted, since several studies (for example, Mawby, 1979; Bottomley and Coleman, 1981) have shown that over 80 per cent of recorded indictable offences in England are reported by the public, and that 'direct discoveries' of offences by the police are very few and far between (about 5 per cent of recorded indictable offences). The third of the four possibilities (recording) is likely to affect *detected* crime (the sole focus of attention when considering convictions) only in so far as the police now prosecute those whom they may have previously informally warned without recording the matter at all; the little evidence that there is indicates that, at least for adults, this is not likely to have occurred in anything other than small numbers. Accordingly, it is probable that the main reason for the increase in registered convictions in the post-war period is *either* a real increase in crime, *or* an increased willingness by the public to report crimes, some of which are detected. For present purposes, it does not much matter which of these possibilities has had the greater influence; either way the public is reporting more crime to which the social-control system has to respond in some way or other. Of course, it is very important that many more people are being sent to prison per annum now than before the Second World War; but it is also of great importance that, proportionately, very many fewer of those being identified as criminal (after a member of the public has reported the matter) are being sent to prison. Neither piece of information on its own conveys the full picture of what is occurring; and to think of these data as simply about the expansion and extension of state control is highly misleading.[11]

Punishment and post-liberal society

In the third part of this essay, I shall try to take further some of the preceding strands. The ultimate question which one ideally needs to confront is, of course: 'if the empirical developments outlined in the first section cannot be brought within a "dispersal of discipline" thesis, how can they be characterised'? However, a definitive answer to that question would require much further research. Hence, it is necessary to take a more modest approach. I shall content myself with the following issues: first, is it at least possible to provide tentative hypotheses as to how a particularly rapid growth of non-disciplinary elements of the penal system might have taken place; and secondly, how does this relate to Mathiesen's apparently correct perception of social control being increasingly about 'the control of whole groups and categories'?

We may begin in a sphere almost wholly ignored by sociologists of punishment – the non-indictable offence (or its equivalent in other jurisdictions). The point of starting here is that this is an area where in almost every country the fine is the routine penalty applied: taking English non-indictable (or 'summary') offences in 1980, for example, the courts 'imposed a fine . . . on 99 per cent of those sentenced for summary motoring offences, and on 89 per cent of those sentenced for other summary offences' (Home Office, 1981: para. 7.2). Perhaps something can be learned about the growth of the fine for indictable offences from this area of routine application elsewhere.

When we look at what constitutes the 'summary offence' in England, two classes stand out. The first is the summary motoring offence, which accounted for nearly 75 per cent of all persons sentenced for summary offences in England and Wales in 1980, and where, as we have seen, almost all convicted defendants were fined (although one should note that some were additionally disqualified from driving – another penalty of the juridical type). The second major class is that of prosecutions by public agencies other than the civil police (for example, government departments, local authorities, or special statutory agencies such as that concerned with the enforcement of television licensing in Britain). A recent study of prosecutions by such agencies in England and Wales showed that, in a survey of twelve courts, well over 95 per cent of such cases resulted in a fine (Lidstone, Hogg and Sutcliffe, 1980: app. A); moreover, the cases themselves were much more numerous than many have assumed, and according to estimates produced by the study, agency prosecutions probably account for as many as a quarter of all non-motoring cases (summary and indictable combined) involving persons aged 17 or over (Lidstone *et al.* 1980: 30–3). If this is right, then a further calculation suggests that agency prosecutions are responsible for over 40 per cent of the non-motoring summary cases for the same age-group;[12] in which case, motoring offences and agency prosecutions between them account for almost seven-eights of all persons over 17 prosecuted for summary offences in England and Wales.

In considering these types of offence, the typology of Kamenka and Tay (1975) is helpful. They suggest that law can be considered in terms of three broad types: '*gemeinschaft*-type law', '*gesellschaft*-type law', and 'bureaucratic-administrative law'. They explain the difference as follows:

> *Gemeinschaft*-type law takes for its fundamental presupposition and concern the organic community. *Gesellschaft*-type law takes for its fundamental presupposition and concern the atomic individual, theoretically free and self-determined, limited only by the rights of other individuals

. . . . In the bureaucratic-administrative type of regulation, the presupposition and concern is neither an organic human community nor an atomic individual; the presupposition and concern is a non-human abstracted ruling interest, public policy or on-going activity, of which human beings are subordinates, functionaries, or carriers. The *Gesellschaft*-type law concerning railways is oriented toward the rights of people whose interests may be harmed by the operation of railways or people whose activities may harm the rights of the owners or operators of railways seen as individuals exercising individual rights. Bureaucratic-administrative regulations concerning railways take for their object the efficient running of railways or the efficient execution of tasks and attainment of goals and norms which are set by the authorities, or the community, or the bureaucracy as its representative. (Kamenka and Tay, 1975: 138, italics in original)

In the terms of this typology, law enforcement in the spheres of both road traffic and the public agencies may be regarded clearly as bureaucratic-administrative law. In the case of the public agencies, this emerged very clearly from the research by Lidstone *et al.*; almost all the agencies saw their law-enforcement role as primarily *preventive* rather than as prosecutorial, and in each case the law-enforcement style was closely related to the agency's perception of its own primary function. Thus, for example, the Factory Inspectorate was much more interested in obtaining safe factories by persuasion of employers, enforcement notices, and the like, rather than prosecuting; the television-licensing agency was much more interested in collecting licence revenue than in prosecuting; both agencies prosecuted only as a last resort, in some considerable contrast to the civil police. Similarly in motoring law: although prosecutions are proportionately more frequent here, it is clear that the civil police and traffic wardens are essentially interested in the safe and efficient flow of traffic, rather than with stamping out morally undesirable behaviour or with the protection of traditional individual rights and liberties – indeed it is in motoring offences that the criminal law most readily lays aside its traditional apparatus of *mens rea* in favour of strict liability.

The fine itself, of course, is not bureaucratic-administrative; rather, as previously noted (see n. 8) it accords with some of the central features of classical jurisprudence, being calculable, unarbitrary and public. It is, therefore, in these two specific contexts a *gesellschaft*-type penalty used to back up an essentially bureaucratic-administrative law-enforcement system.

One lesson of particular importance to be derived from the study of these two types of offence is that in both instances the primary locus of social control lies elsewhere than in the punishment system. The Factory Inspectorate and the television-licensing authority each have elaborately developed bureaucratic systems of control in their respective spheres; both regard the court, and the possibility of punishment, very much as a last resort, on the fringe of their respective control systems. In the road-traffic sphere, the primary mode of social control is environmental, through what Karl Llewellyn (1940) in his law-jobs theory called the 'preventive channelling' of traffic lights, stop signs, parking restrictions, adequate road design and street lighting, and so forth. In both these areas of 'modern crime', therefore, we have preventive social-control systems backed up by the fine (and other juridical penalties such as disqualification). *Disciplinary punishment is not necessary to achieve control.*[13] The overall style of social control developed in these contexts is rather similar to that which Shearing and Stenning (1981) see emerging in the field of private security. Might it be more generally applicable, even to the area of the traditional crimes in the indictable sphere?

We will return to this issue. For the moment, we may make the obvious point that neither the motoring offence, nor the agency prosecution, nor any other kind of bureaucratic-administrative law existed at all in the late eighteenth century/early nineteenth century, that is, the time when we see the beginning of the dominance of the carceral system of punishment. To understand the rise of the fine in these specific areas, therefore, we clearly need to set the discussion in the context of the change from the early industrial capitalism of 1800 to the much more technologically advanced welfare-capitalist society now operative in Britain; for without this social change neither the motor car nor the present range of specialised public agencies would have developed. Once having made this point, it obviously also seems likely that this social change from early to advanced capitalism might additionally be related to some of the other penal developments outlined in the first part of this essay. Of course, it is not the case that all late-twentieth-century law is bureaucratic-administrative law; but it surely is possible that the change in the nature of society from 1800 to 1980, just as it has produced certain kinds of bureaucratic-administrative law like the agency prosecution, may also be affecting other penal developments. On the face of it, therefore, simple extrapolations from Foucault's description of the penal system from the early nineteenth century to the present are very unlikely to be adequate.

Without attempting a full analysis, three features of the change from 1800 to the present day are worth attention. These are: the rise of advanced technology; changes in the nature of work; and the growth of welfarism and corporatism. These may be considered seriatim.

Technology
The technological distance between 1800 and 1980 is vast. We take for granted colour television, computers, pocket calculators, communi-

cations satellites, air travel and international direct-dial telephones. In 1800 there was not even a railway system or a postal service, let alone an electricity supply.

Recent technological developments have direct implications for social control. Mathiesen's quotation, given earlier, clearly recognises this: 'TV cameras on subway stations and in supermarkets, the development of advanced computer techniques in intelligence and surveillance . . . ' Police practice has been revolutionised by the two-way radio, and by intelligence storage on police national computers. At roadside check-points in Northern Ireland, for example, car numbers are routinely fed through to a computer which then returns a security grading, indicating whether the car should be stopped and searched, and/or its occupants questioned. Additionally, private security has developed elaborate technologies of screening when entering public buildings, and television surveillance when inside (Shearing and Stenning, 1981). These developments greatly facilitate a new form of social control (Mathiesen's 'control of whole groups and categories'), and perhaps this new form of social control makes disciplinary punishment less necessary, just as it is not necessary in the preventive social control of the non-police agencies.

More indirect consequences of the spread of technology are also possible. Berger, Berger and Kellner have endeavoured to analyse the characteristic mind-set produced by what they call 'modernity'. These authors explicitly accept the view that '*all* societies with a certain degree of technological/economic sophistication have significant common characteristics, *regardless of the ideological and political differences between them*' (1974: 17, my italics). In excavating the concept of modernity, they consider that *technology* and *bureaucracy* are the 'primary carriers of modernization', and they further see these as related in that 'while technological production may be viewed as a basic structuring force of modernity, modern man commonly copes with its impact on his own everyday life via various bureaucracies' (1974: 16, 61). Analysing the 'essential concomitants' of technological production and of bureaucracy on the 'everyday consciousness of ordinary people' (1974: 29), Berger *et al.* identify a number of key notions. As concomitants of technology are listed componentiality; interdependence of components and sequences; separability of means and ends; segregation of work from life; anonymous social relations; self-anonymisation and a componential self; multirelationality; and possible alienation (1974: ch 1). As concomitants of bureaucracy are suggested orderliness; taxonomic propensity; general and autonomous organisability; predictability; a general expectation of justice based on impersonal weighing; a non-separability of means and ends (cf. technology); moralised anonymity; and explicit abstraction (1974: ch. 2).

One could of course dispute almost any of these items, and the concept of 'modernity' itself, as applied by Berger *et al.*, is a very difficult one (cf. the related concept of secularisation, also prominent in Peter Berger's work, but which, if it is to be meaningful, has to be broken down into discrete elements: see Gill, 1975). Nevertheless, the basic idea that habitual exposure to technology and to bureaucracies does have important effects upon everyday consciousness is by no means implausible.

If at this point we return to motoring offences and agency prosecutions, it is noteworthy that they seem to mirror exactly the two 'primary carriers' identified by Berger and his colleagues, since clearly the mass-produced motor vehicle is one of the crucial technological innovations of the twentieth century, and the public agencies which control factory safety, television licensing and the like are a main exemplar of modern bureaucracy.[14] And certainly one aspect of Berger *et al.*'s analysis is very important here. A main feature of technological production is *componentiality*, that is, 'the components of reality are self-contained units which can be brought into relation with other such units . . . reality is *not* conceived as an ongoing flux of juncture and disjuncture of unique entities' (1974: 32). A main feature of *bureaucracies* is that of *limited competence*: 'each jurisdiction and each agency within it is competent *only* for its assigned sphere of life and is supposed to have expert knowlege appropriate to this sphere' (1974: 46). In the context of the present discussion, these features produce *specificity of social control*. Thus the Factory Inspectorate is interested in the factory manager only qua factory manager, not as a whole human being; similarly, the television-licensing authority treats the individual only as a television user, and the social control of motoring tends to concentrate upon the individual only as a motorist. (Interestingly, those individuals who have both motoring and non-motoring convictions – on which see Willett (1964) – tend to find the police citing only previous motoring convictions in motoring cases, and only previous non-motoring convictions in other cases). This specificity of social control is very different from the holistic approach of disciplinary punishment, investigating all aspects of the offender's life and often showing much more interest in the offender as a person than in his specific offence (see any standard textbook on therapeutic approaches with offenders). The specific social-control approach of the agencies and of motoring law is so pronounced that no one thinks it at all surprising that the diagnostically oriented social-inquiry report (or 'pre-sentence report' as it is called in some countries) is almost wholly absent when the courts consider those types of case. The fine as an impersonal and calculable penalty, then, fits well into the mind-set produced by this specificity of social control. If the offender has not been and is not to be investigated as a whole person, it scarcely makes sense to subject him to specific disciplinary and corrective techniques designed to bring the soul in the body into the status of obedient subject – the essence of Foucault's disciplinary apparatus.

Does any of this have any relevance for the recent growth of the fine, and other non-disciplinary penalties, in *indictable* as opposed to summary offences? Possibly for certain offences a directly analagous set of processes might have occurred. For example, in shop-lifting the change from the small corner shop to the large supermarket not only increases the opportunity and the temptation to steal, it also brings with it a much more impersonal and componential relationship between the shopper and the store, and the creation of a new kind of social-control agent – the store detective (aided, of course, by television) – whose role tends towards specificity. However, for most indictable crimes, the relationship between developing technology and the punishment system is probably more complex and indirect – as we shall see.

Changes in the nature of work

In the context of the present discussion, a point of particular interest which arises from the preceding analysis is the relationship of developing technology, and the consciousness it may produce, to that of 'discipline'. This substantive point has been taken up by John Lea (1979) in a perceptive essay in which (like other Marxist theorists such as Melossi and Pavarini, 1981: app.) he tries to relate Foucault's *Discipline and Punish* more directly to the world of the factory and to the forces and relations of production. According to Lea, in the factory of early capitalism the worker had to be 'disciplined', in Foucault's sense, for the capitalist to ensure production; with the development of automated technology, however, there is also an automation of the worker himself, a 'conversion of the worker from a machine operator into part of the machinery'. This has crucial consequences for discipline:

> Only when the worker stood in contrast to and, in terms of method of operation, confrontation with the automatism of the machine was the disciplining of his body fused with, and contingent upon, his subordination to the authority of capital. With the fusion of worker and machine, discipline is built into the design and pacing of the machinery . . . Indeed, as Gramsci remarked, *the new automation of the labour process frees the worker mentally from subordination to the authority of capital.* (Lea, 1979: 85, my italics)

Moreover, argues Lea, taking the analysis further, this is only part of a whole shift in the nature of social control produced by the movement from early industrial capitalism to modern western states in which monopoly capitalism and advanced technology are decisive features:

> Under the new system of control the terrain upon which compliance is generated shifts outside the factory — the door is finally closed upon Panopticon — *and* outside the market . . . into a new relationship between the two, into a trade-off of gains in the market, in the price of labour, in return for compliance in the labour process. (Lea, 1979: 87 italics in original)

This conclusion is closely echoed, yet taken further, in a couple of essays by Melossi (1979 and 1980). Lea's analysis is explicitly limited to structures of control in and around the process of economic production; Melossi is more directly interested in penal and policing developments. Just as Lea sees the discipline of the body declining in the factory, and the locus of industrial control shifting into corporate bargaining, so for Melossi:

> The entrustment of discipline to the machine in the taylorized factory shifts the emphasis of social control to the learning of discipline as a highly automatized process, to be carried on for everybody at an early age. For adults, consensus and legitimization are needed. At the same time, social control follows the movement of capital from within the factory to the outside: the city itself, the urban areas must be controlled . . . Social control goes back to outdoor relief, which the strict liberalism of the previous century had scornfully abandoned. The new epoch of welfare is announced. And with it the era of policing . . . Both the welfare system and policing are much older creations but they knew their first generalization and massification in the twenties. (1980: 392)

More generally, Melossi argues, the predominating tendency in modern social control is, first, away from reliance upon secondary social control (through the penal arena, for example), and towards control of primary relations; and secondly, within the sphere of secondary social control, 'to displace control away from detention (incarceration) towards police measures of various forms of social surveillance' (Melossi, 1979: 96).

These analyses by Lea and Melossi are of great interest. They clearly link with Mathiesen's perception of a shift from carceral individualism towards 'control of whole groups and categories', yet make this shift more intelligible in terms of other economic and social developments (see Chapter 6 above). They also link with our earlier discussion of technology, and of the possibility (perceived first through the non-indictable offence) that modern social control may increasingly use the penal system only as a last resort, relying primarily upon other forms of social control. They therefore help to explain why 'discipline', in the strictly Foucauldian sense, may be of relatively declining significance within the *penal* system (as opposed to the social-control system as a whole).

Welfarism and corporatism

If all this is correct, we need to know *how it is* that social control is achieved (outside the factory, outside the secondary institutions) in modern society. As we have seen, part of the answer to this lies in modern technology, and another part in the mechanics of corporate bargaining. A further aspect of relevance is the growth of monopoly capitalism, which allows *inter alia* the development of 'mass private property' in public areas (shopping malls, airports, and the like), facilitating the expansion of private security with its preventive control techniques (Shearing and Stenning, 1981). But, as Melossi's analysis suggests, yet another dimension is undoubtedly to be found in the social-control possibilities of state welfare systems. This necessitates a fuller discussion of the implications of welfare developments.

Unger (1976: 192 ff.) clearsightedly identifies as two key features of western 'post-liberal societies' what he calls welfarism and corporatism. 'Welfare tendencies', or 'the overt intervention of government in areas previously regarded as beyond the proper reach of state action', of course refers to the growth of such things as social security, public housing, socialised medicine, and so forth. 'Corporatist tendencies' are described as 'a set of attributes of post-liberal society [which] is but the reverse side of the events just enumerated: the gradual approximation of state and society, of the public and the private sphere' (Unger, 1976: 193). It is not difficult to see that both sets of 'tendencies' have implications for the possibilities of social control.

Without entering into the enormous complexity of the debates about the welfare state and about corporatism (and, in particular, whether corporatism is a necessary accompaniment of a welfare-state society), four points of general importance to the present discussion may be made. First, the general development of corporatism in welfare-state societies reminds us that the public and the private spheres do interpenetrate in many areas of social life outside the criminal justice system – industrial development, health policies, and so on – and hence we should not be particularly surprised to find similar features developing in some aspects of community corrections, as Cohen (1979b) shows in detail that they do.[15] Moreover, these developments in various non-criminal spheres are not necessarily sinister, which should perhaps make us at least pause before painting too blackly the 'penetration' and 'community absorption' which Cohen identifies as a key aspect of community corrections.[16] Indeed, this public–private admixture can even be seen in some other aspects of the criminal justice system itself, in contexts where there is no implication of the state acting in any overbearing or improper fashion – the victim support schemes are a clear illustration.

Secondly, it is quite important, when considering developments of this kind, not to paint too simple a picture of 'penetration' or of 'the state'. This can be specifically illustrated as regards the growth of the fine in England between 1945 and 1965. This period is, with justification, generally regarded as the time of maximum growth in the influence of the ideal of the scientific rehabilitation of offenders. Yet it was precisely during this period that a major growth in the fine occurred in England – to the active dismay of some liberal and reformist commentators (for example, Elkin 1957: 39), and despite the disapproval of the senior permanent official in the Home Office at the time (see Fry, 1951; 115). To understand this paradox, it is necessary to realise that different groups of people were involved. The concept of scientific rehabilitation gained its dominant hold mainly upon probation officers, senior prison personnel, governmental officials and academics. The judges and magistrates in the courts, however, were relatively isolated from this development; and they apparently saw the fine as an increasingly appropriate penalty during the same period (perhaps connected with the growth to a full employment economy at the time). So who (if anybody) is 'the state' – the courts or the government officials? Similarly, if we argue a 'penetration' thesis as Cohen suggests (the formal social-control agencies of the state penetrating more deeply into the informal networks of society), then who exactly is penetrating whom? More radically, is the whole division between 'the state' and 'civil society' (going back, of course, to Marx and beyond him to Hegel) an over-simplified or even a false one?

The third point to be made moves us away from corporatism towards welfarism. Here a highly relevant analysis is to be found in a paper by Philip Abrams (1978) about lay community care (defined as 'the provision of help, support and protection to others by lay members of societies acting in everyday domestic and occupational settings'). According to Abrams, there are specific social forces in advanced welfare-capitalist societies such that 'extensive and effective community care is uncommon and improbable in our type of society' (1978: 79). There is, moreover, an identifiable economic logic that underpins this negative relationship:

> From a public point of view the provision of expert services is of course very costly and the provision of neighbourliness very cheap. But from the point of view of the individual the position is reversed: the costs of community care are exorbitant, those of the welfare state are low – or at least unavoidable . . . [There is] a decline of effective community care, local attachment, neighbouring and so forth in these societies. (Abrams, 1978: 80).

This economic logic might not be directly applicable to the provision of official services in relation to offenders, but the indirect effects are likely to be of great importance. In the first place, the decline in lay care in welfare-capitalist societies almost certainly contributes to the growth of registered crime, either because a decline in lay care actually produces a real growth in crime (a very plausible hypothesis), or because it encourages people to turn to an official agency (the police) and to report an incident as 'a crime', rather than to deal with it themselves within informal community networks (also highly plausible). And this, of course, would certainly help to explain the paradox noted by Mathiesen (see p. 134 above) that 'coinciding with the most successful period of growth in the history of capitalism, the registered theft-rate has increased by leaps and bounds'. Or again, the development of a mind-set which becomes accustomed to calling upon and mobilising official services rather than informal care networks could certainly help to explain phenomena such as: the perceived need for victim-support schemes; the provision of an unpaid offender workforce to perform needed community tasks for which no one is volunteering (a typical scenario with community service orders); or the suggestion that various activities for children organised by professional social workers are highly desirable and that children 'at risk' should attend them as well as offenders (the origin of many 'widening the net' developments in relation to 'intermediate treatment' for juveniles in Britain). Viewed in this light, Cohen's 'penetration' and 'community absorption', and Mathiesen's 'external control system gradually expanding' take on a somewhat different aspect.

Fourthly, an analysis of this type might help to explain the British–American contrast in the use of the fine and of probation. At first sight, it might seem paradoxical that the more developed welfare-state society (Britain) should make *less* use of probation (a welfare-oriented sanction). But perhaps the very fact that Britain has developed more extensive state welfare provision allows a degree of social control in the informal structures of society such that the formal supervision of offenders – by, in effect, disciplinary means – becomes less necessary. This is inevitably a highly tentative suggestion, but perhaps one worthy of further research.

At this point we may return to Foucault, and note that, surprisingly enough, he might not disagree too much with the tenor of this discussion. Although there is a passage at the end of *Discipline and Punish* which appears to support Cohen's argument about the extension of discipline more widely into the community,[17] this is not the end of the matter. As Barry Smart notes in his essay (Chapter 3), Foucault in later work has drawn an important distinction between the '*anatomo-politics of the human body*' and the '*bio-politics of the population*' (see especially Foucault 1979a: 135–45). Post-eighteenth-century societies have replaced the ancient right of the powerful to take life or let live, with a more general power 'to foster life, to disallow it to the point of death'. As well as developing disciplinary controls over individual human bodies (in factories, schools, prisons, etc.), societies have:

> focused on the species body, the body imbued with the mechanics of life and serving as a basis of the biological processes: propagation, births, and mortality, the level of health, life expectancy and longevity, with all the conditions that can cause these to vary. Their supervision was effected through an entire series of interventions and regulatory controls. (Foucault, 1979a: 13a)

This, in turn, produces a change in the nature of law:

> I do not mean to say that the law fades into the background or that the institutions of justice tend to disappear, but rather that the law operates *more and more as a norm*, and that the juridical institution is increasingly incorporated into a continuum of apparatuses (medical, administrative, and so on) whose functions are for the most part regulatory. (Foucault, 1979a: 144, my italics)

As Smart indicates, Foucault's later work suggests 'a relative decrease in the significance of techniques of discipline, and a concomitant increase in the importance of mechanisms of insurance and security; it represents the insertion of a "principle of cohesion" in the very fabric of society, the constitution of a particular kind of solidarity' (see above, p. 80). This conclusion is obviously congruent with some of the main lines of argument sketched above, particularly those derived from Mathiesen, Lea and Melossi. It also, very interestingly, dovetails with Kamenka and Tay's (1975) analysis, since Foucault sees law developing 'more and more as a norm', and bureaucratic-administrative law as identified by Kamenka and Tay takes for one of its central objects 'the attainment of goals and norms'.

If the above analysis has any merit, what may therefore have been happening in contemporary western penal systems is that, as societal power in the form of 'the bio-politics of the population' has developed (through welfarism, corporatism, technological developments, and so forth), so individual discipline ('the anatomo-politics of the human body') has become less necessary to the penal apparatus.[18] Adequate social control can in many instances be developed externally to the penal system in the strict sense. The implication would be that the penal project of the classical reformers failed at the end of the eighteenth century because it did not in itself produce order (cf. Foucault's comment on the disorders surrounding the early public-works programmes – Foucault, 1977a: 125 and n. 11), and there was insufficient social control exercised elsewhere in society to make the classical/juridical project possible. In modern states, however, such power does exist, and so the schemes of classical penality render themselves as more realistic possibilities, at least for some crimes and some offenders.[19]

I should repeat (out of abundant caution) that I do not claim that the preceding analysis adequately explains contemporary punishment. I have been concerned merely to show that there are plausible ways of theorising about a possible relative decline in the significance of disciplinary punishments within the total apparatus of social control, and hence also to raise hypotheses about the specially rapid growth of non-disciplinary penalties for crime. When penal developments are looked at in this way, many of the specific mechanisms which Cohen identified ('widening the net', 'thinning the mesh', 'penetration', etc.) can also be considered without adopting Cohen's own 'dispersal of discipline' thesis. The key to the whole debate, as I have by implication suggested, is to obtain a clearer grasp of the transformation from early to late capitalism than Cohen attempts.

Some concluding qualifications
Lengthy as it already is, this essay nevertheless cannot be concluded without some qualifying remarks upon three topics: differentiation; the moral evaluation of crimes; and political initiatives in crime control.

Differentiation
The foregoing analysis should emphatically not be read as an argument that disciplinary punishment is dead or dying; it is an analysis only of the specially rapid growth of non-disciplinary penalties.[20] It follows that some attention needs to be given, in any full discussion of contemporary punishment, to which cases are deemed to require disciplinary punishments and which not: to the *differentiation* of discipline.

One point of general importance is that disciplinary punishments appear to be proportionately much more common amongst juvenile offenders (the foregoing analysis is deliberately restricted largely to adults). This difference is not too surprising: disciplinary control is far more often applied to the child in our society generally (in school, the family, youth organisations, etc.), so it is to be expected that this will be reflected in the penal system.

A few years ago, I coined the term 'bifurcation' to describe some recent penal developments for adult offenders: 'put crudely, this bifurcation is between, on the one hand, the so-called "really serious offender" for whom very tough measures are typically advocated; and on the other hand, the "ordinary" offender for whom, it is felt, we can afford to take a much more lenient line' (Bottoms, 1977: 88). Subsequently, the self-same concept of bifurcation was used independently by Matthews (1979: 107) in a sociological analysis of contemporary punishment; from where it was picked up and applied to Canadian trends by Chan and Ericson (1981: 67). Back in Britain, the concept has been defended in policy terms by Floud and Young (1981: xv), in their prestigious report on the dangerous offender, as 'the rational response to indications of welcome changes in penal policy'. Mathiesen has also made a prediction which sounds very like a future bifurcation strategy (see p. 140 above:) 'in the shadow of the new control system with its increased emphasis on the efficient control of whole categories of people, the prisons will regain a sense of rationality as a kind of last resort, used unwillingly against the utterly uncontrollable'. Of course, it does not follow, just because many writers are using the same idea, that they are correct in discerning a trend. Assuming, however, that they are, then the differentiation between the 'serious' and the 'ordinary' offender could be an important contemporary trend which may be linked to the disciplinary/non-disciplinary divide. As yet, however, we have no really adequate understanding as to why bifurcation is emerging.[21]

One aid to the differentiation of discipline may be the social-inquiry report. In England and Wales, the proportionate use of these diagnostic tools *more than doubled*, in the adult courts, between 1956 and 1971 (Davies, 1974: Table 3). It might seem odd that this should be so, at a time when non-disciplinary forms of punishment were increasing especially fast, since the diagnostic inquiry seems so closely linked to the disciplinary form. But perhaps, on the contrary, it is only when the courts have available to them the enhanced possibility of calling upon a diagnostic tool of this kind that they feel able to discriminate adequately between indictable offenders – to decide that, although some need the expert attentions of social workers, or a taste of the prison's disciplinary apparatus, for an increasing number of others more juridical penalties will suffice. This is a little speculative; to demonstrate the thesis more clearly we would need to know in detail in what kinds of cases reports are called for, especially in the lower courts, and we would also need to know about the comparative sentencing patterns in cases disposed of with and without a report. As far as I am aware there is only a small amount of research evidence on the second question and none at all on the first, so the matter must remain open. Nevertheless, one might suggest that the argument sketched above has at least prima-facie plausibility.

Taking it a little further, one might also argue that here lies a crucial difference in the use of the fine for motoring offences and agency prosecutions as opposed to the indictable offence. In the former cases, the social-inquiry report is literally unknown, and the fine completely routine. For the indictable offence, even in England, where a majority of such cases receive a fine, the position of this penalty perhaps remains more precarious, so that arguably its widespread use remains dependent still upon the *possibility* of a disciplinary penalty being applied in appropriate cases – and hence also upon the social-inquiry report being used to help identify those cases.

Moral evaluation of crimes

Durkheim (1973) taught us that the explanation of changes in punishment may lie in a changed social evaluation of the moral seriousness of crimes. This insight may be of particular importance as regards the recent moves towards a more victim-oriented approach to criminal justice, to which relatively little specific attention was paid in the previous section of this essay. In an earlier paper, I attempted to apply Durkheim's theorisation directly to the moves towards compensation for victims:

> [According to Durkheim] we can distinguish two kinds of crime – crimes against collective things, such as religion and public customs and authorities, and crimes against individuals, such as theft and violence. Less developed societies tend to include within their penal laws only the first type; such crimes are seen as deeply odious, and elicit very strong sanctions. As societies developed, the contents of their criminal codes became more individualistic and less collective or religious; and punishment became less severe because the harm to the victim, and the subsequently meted out harm to the criminal, were seen to be of the same type – so respect for the human dignity of the offender could therefore attenuate the penalty in a way not possible for the collective or religious crimes. In such a movement one can well expect that the logical end result would be a tendency to redress the imbalance between the offender and the victim, rather than simply to mete out sanctions against the offender. (Bottoms, 1980: 16–17)

I went on to remark (in a footnote) that of course in his earlier *Division of Labour in Society* Durkheim had suggested a general historical move from repressive to restitutive sanctions, but that there was no doubt that he was ignorant of the great extent of restitution in primitive societies. 'There has been no adequate exploration', I concluded, 'of the way in which the State took over these restitutive sanctions and turned them into repressive ones – which it now seems to be about to reconvert' (Bottoms, 1980: 23). Others have made much the same point, and have dubbed the apparent restitution–repression–restitution movement a 'curvilinear' trend (see Spitzer, 1975a: 633; Bottomley, 1979: 156–7).[22]

Two points may be made arising from this. First, I remain of the view that an explanation of a broadly Durkheimian kind, taking very seriously changes in the moral evaluation of crimes as a likely key to the change in punishment style, represents the best hope of making sense of the recent moves towards victim compensation – and perhaps of some other penal developments. At the same time, it now seems clear that we cannot simply 'read off' Durkheim for an adequate explanation of the contemporary situation as regards victim compensation. Rather, we shall need to research very carefully into changing moral evaluations of law and crime, and other forms of social regulation, and attempt to relate them in a sensitive manner to some of the changing forms of social organisation from early to late capitalism, as discussed in the previous section. This will be a matter of very considerable complexity (see, for example, Corrigan, 1981).

Secondly, some caution is also needed in embracing the 'curvilinear' hypothesis. An apparently similar punishment-type applied in different societies at different times may, in fact, be a very different kind of punishment in sociological terms.[23] For example, we learn from a recent essay by the distinguished Islamic law scholar, Sir Norman Anderson (1980: 66–7), that 'under the classical Islamic law . . . murder, manslaughter and wounding . . . were treated, for the most part, as civil wrongs rather than crimes, and it was left to the "heirs of blood" to demand either talion or "blood-money", or even to pardon the aggressor, in suitable cases'. Further investigation shows, however, that in most Islamic societies this conceptualisation of murder as a civil wrong – and hence as a matter which may be settled by the payment of compensation – is only possible because it occurs in a societal context where the concept of honour is a central feature (this is clear from current Saudi experience: see Saudi Arabia, 1980). This may also be true of modes of compensation in the penal codes of other (non-Islamic) non-western penal systems, and of compensation in pre-medieval European law. Yet, as Berger *et al.* (1974: 78–89) point out, the concept of honour is dead or dying in modern western societies; it has 'an unambiguously outdated status in the *Weltanschauung* of modernity'. Hence, if western states do now recover an enhanced practice of compensation in their penal systems, it will certainly be based upon a very different conceptual foundation from some of these earlier practices.[24]

Political initiatives in crime control

Finally, it should be noted that political initiatives could be taken which could decisively affect some of the matters we have debated. Thus, even if it is true there is a relative decline in disciplinary punishments within the penal system, it does not follow that this is an irreversible trend. In Britain at the time of writing, the elected government is attempting (with some success) to reverse many of the central elements of the welfare-state society which was created earlier in the twentieth century; for example, by denationalisation, reduction of public spending in health and education services, and so on. *Inter alia*, this government was elected on a 'law and order' ticket, and as part of that programme has introduced a special regime of brisk discipline (a 'short sharp shock') into the detention-centre system for juvenile and young adult offenders. If this sentencing option is taken up by the courts (always problematic in view of the relative independence of the courts from government, but in this case a distinct possibility), then clearly it would lead to the reassertion of a more overt form of discipline at one point in the penal system; and this could spread. At the same time, in analysing developments of this kind, one does need to ensure that the declared policies of the government are being translated into actual practice; and/or that the practice is an even one as between different pieces of legislation or different parts of the state apparatus. It is easy to be seduced by a government's own rhetoric into believing that all relevant policies and practices at a given time are of one kind, and so fail to realise that a dominant political policy might not be being implemented by the courts, or might not be applied consistently by the government itself in different pieces of legislation. As an example of this unevenness we may take the previous Conservative government in Britain (1970–4), whose activities in the sphere of legal control were analysed at length by Stuart Hall and his colleagues. These authors took the view that as a result of various initiatives (legislative, judicial and social) around 1970, 'the times are exceptional; the crisis is real; we are inside the "law-and-order" state' (1978: 323). Yet the same authors had previously referred to the Conservative government's 1972 Criminal Justice Act (prominent in the first part of this essay because it introduced community service orders and gave a great boost to compensation orders) as a piece of 'permissive legislation' which 'aims to introduce more imaginative non-custodial alternatives', and which was seen as linked to some earlier 1960s Labour Party legislation by its 'softness' (Hall *et al.*, 1978: 35–6).

These necessary qualifications relating to differentiation, the moral evaluation of crimes and political initiatives in crime control bring home again the complexity of the task of understanding punishment in modern western societies. This essay has sought to tackle one part of that complexity by focusing attention upon certain neglected matters in contemporary punishment, and in doing so has attempted to consider some fresh theoretical issues. But there are, inevitably, more questions raised than resolved. As was indicated at the outset, if the argument of this paper is correct, it opens up a large research agenda for future work.

Notes

1 Oddly, Kirchheimer omitted American data from his pioneering chapter on the fine, despite the fact that this work was written and published in the USA.
2 Sentencing data on a national basis have not been available in Canada since 1973. Even the 1973 figures exclude the provinces of Quebec and Alberta, which did not submit returns.

3 This is because suspended sentences of imprisonment of six months or less cannot have a supervision requirement attached to them, and the great majority of suspended sentences are below this length. Interestingly, supervision requirements are also imposed only in a minority of cases where the length of the sentence makes supervision technically possible.

4 A very small number of fines do involve supervision by a penal agent, either because a 'money payments supervision order' is imposed concurrently with the fine, or because at the end of the day imprisonment in default of payment is ordered. However, neither practice is sufficiently widespread to affect in any way the general message of Table 8.1. About a quarter of suspended sentences of imprisonment are ultimately served as imprisonment, but again this does not affect the interpretation of Table 8.1, because all such activations of the suspended sentence are accompanied by fresh offences for which imprisonment is ordered (usually consecutively with the activated suspended sentence), so they would then appear in the table under 'imprisonment'.

5 Deliberately so, in order that the victim of an undetected offence of violence is not disadvantaged.

6 The lower rate of compensation orders in the Crown Court (as shown in Table 8.2) reflects the fact that courts are officially advised not to add a compensation order to a custodial sentence (save in exceptional circumstances), and custodial sentences are proportionately much more frequently applied to defendants in the Crown Court.

7 For example, Matthews (1979: 115): 'the introduction of parole, probation, indeterminate sentences, diversion programmes and the whole array of recent control strategies have served, *invariably*, to either increase lengths of incarceration, loss of liberty, or surveillance on one hand, and to introduce many, particularly the young, into the control net for "offences" that prior to the setting up of such programmes would have gone unnoticed or seem to be inconsequential' (*sic*) (my italics).

8 Because the fine is calculable, public and potentially free from arbitrariness, it accords well with the tenets of the classical school; hence it was attractive to the eighteenth-century reformers, although they saw a number of practical difficulties in its administration (see Heath, 1963: 79, 200, 254). I have, however, deliberately limited my comment to the 'modern fine', because in an earlier era the fine was often so closely connected with imprisonment through the default mechanism: in England and Wales, in 1910 almost 20 per cent of all persons fined were eventually imprisoned for default, but by 1940 this figure had dropped to 1 per cent.

9 Mathiesen's talk of 'a change from open to hidden discipline' is also somewhat confusing, since Foucault makes it clear that some of the power of the carceral mode of penality lay in its being performed away from the public gaze.

10 Hylton (1981) gives them no attention; Chan and Ericson (1981: 42) note the possibility of such data and briefly cite some from the USA, but note that no national data of this kind are available for Canada (the subject of their principal attention, and of all tables and figures in their monograph).

11 By implication, this analysis rejects Ditton's (1979) 'controlology' thesis as it applies to indictable crime; by contrast, Chan and Ericson (1981) are more sympathetic to Ditton. There is no space here for a full critique: suffice it to say that acceptance of Ditton's full thesis involves *inter alia* taking the view (1) that murders are not committed unless a conviction for murder is obtained; (2) that whether somebody becomes a murderer depends *exclusively* upon the actions of social controllers; and (3) that variations in the official murder rates are allowable as evidence of control-waves, but *never* of a real rise or fall in the number of murders. I imagine I am not alone in finding this implausible.

12 For technical reasons, all these estimates must be treated with some caution: for a discussion of the technicalities see Lidstone *et al.* (1980: 30–3 and app. C).

13 Foucault (1977a: pt 4, 277) additionally suggests that one of the hidden functions of prison is to constitute a criminal class; it 'fails to eliminate crime . . . [but] has succeeded . . . in producing the delinquent as a pathologized subject'. No such project is considered necessary in relation to the areas of 'modern crime' at present under discussion.

14 Cf. the admiring comment of Sidney and Beatrice Webb (1929: 243): 'not only in the manufacturing and other civilian departments of the Army, but at least equally in the gigantic Post and Telegraph service, together with the Customs and Excise and the Inland Revenue, the whole organisation, both central and local, exhibits no failure in the uniform execution of whatever is prescribed from the top, with results that are anything but inefficient'.

15 I have deliberately used the language of public/private here, *not* state/civil society (cf. Unger) in view of the difficulty in identifying 'the state' referred to subsequently in my text.

16 Both Cohen (1979b: 339) and Mathiesen (see Chapter 6, n. 15) refer in their respective essays to the spectre of Orwell's *Nineteen Eighty-Four*.

17 See Foucault (1977a: 306). This passage is relied upon by Cohen (1979b: 360) and implicitly by Mathiesen (in Chapter 6, p. 139).

18 Here and elsewhere in this essay, the use of certain of Foucault's terms for substantive concepts does not imply a general acceptance of Foucault's epistemology and method.

19 It is noteworthy that elements of classical theorising have enjoyed a more widespread renaissance in contemporary criminal justice systems that can be covered in the scope of this essay: for example, in the constitutionalist reforms of the US Supreme Court in the 1960s, and in Finnish and Swedish White Papers of the 1970s (see Chapter 6, n. 1). It is perhaps particularly interesting that this renaissance in *gesellschaft*-type law should be occurring in criminal justice and punishment at a time when in civil law (contract, public law, etc.) *gesellschaft*-type law is in some retreat.

20 In an earlier essay (Bottoms 1980: 20–1), I did tentatively suggest a more general retreat from discipline; I would not now wish to press this point.

21 In an earlier essay (Bottoms, 1977: 89–91), I made some suggestions on this point based on Durkheim (1973); these suggestions, however, would need amplification and refinement in any full explanation.

22 Bottomley (1979) relates this to the more general work of Black (1976); I would have reservations about this in view of the somewhat mechanical concept of law employed by Black.

23 This is probably also important in relation to the fine, which in its first great growth for indictable offences in England in the late nineteenth century was closely linked to the possibility of imprisonment in default (see above, n. 8); a link which had largely disappeared by the time of the second growth (1940 +). In an earlier era in England, the fine was even more closely linked to imprisonment, and defendants were routinely held in prison until the fine was paid.

24 A related point may be drawn from the works of the two most prominent contemporary theorists advocating restitution in penal systems, namely, Christie (1977) and Hulsman (1981–2). Christie's approach appears strongly geared to the recovery of the 'neighbourhood' as a meaningful social unit; this gives his work a *gemeinschaft*-type appearance which can make it seem very remote from modern industrialised societies. Hulsman, although sharing essentially the same vision, suggests that crime control should become more 'problem-solving', and that decision-makers should ask questions such as 'how do I minimise the social problems which are caused by the criminal justice system as it presently operates?' (1981–2: 154) This latter approach does not necessarily imply a *gemeinschaft*-type solution.

9 On Rights and Powers: Some Notes on Penal Politics
Pat Carlen

Theories of punishment have, traditionally, been concerned not with the *power* to punish, but with the *right* to punish. The retributive infliction of pain has perennially been seen as an inevitable component of the good social life, and its justification, first by faith and then by right, has been seen as the necessary prerequisite. All of the philosophical theories of punishment have depended for their logic on the juxtaposition of an individual either to God or to Society. Penology, on the other hand, has been more pragmatic, concerned with the *efficacy* of punishment, primarily as a means of social protection or criminal deterrence, secondarily as a reformative, retributive or expiatory social force (see Chapter 1). Yet, despite the strident appeal of its pragmatism, penology has had few successes, its history being the failure of punishment in general, and imprisonment in particular, either to diminish law-breaking or to reform those who engage in it.

Philosophies of punishment, by contrast, have enjoyed a continuing success. They have repeatedly supplied the punitive obsession with its justifications, they have repeatedly enmeshed new critique within their well-worn and ever-elastic juridical parameters. Subsequently, and contemporaneously, they have produced the new dichotomies of tautologous argument and already atrophied debate concerning treatment versus punishment, welfare versus legalism, individual versus society and 'capitalist' versus other types of justice. Central to all these debates is the language of rights. The aim of this paper is, first, to demonstrate why the language of rights needs to be displaced and, second, to specify and argue for some interventions into penal politics based not upon the language of rights, but upon calculated strategies for the socialisation/transformation of existing penal powers.

Rights and punishment
Whereas previous epochs were concerned with either the divine nature of royal punishment or the contractual nature of state punishment,

present debates emphasise the rights (divine, human, legal or other-wise) of individuals. There are several permutations. Twentieth-century justifications for invoking individual right in penal politics can still be located in God, although nowadays they are more likely to be presented as residing either in humanity (for example, Szasz, 1974), in law (Thompson, 1979) or, more frequently, in an often unexplicated existential philosophy of the individual's right to free-dom from interference by others (Tomasic and Dobinson, 1979). Thus, whereas both classical and neo-classical penal philosophers tended towards *social* (statist) discourses on rights, this century's penal campaigners have inclined towards *anti-social* discourses on rights. Furthermore, although legal theorists of rights have always claimed to marry the individual and the social interest, with the increase of administrative decision-making and the proliferation of welfare agancies charged with the redistribution of goods, income and different types of medical and social care, modern penal cam-paigners have tended to root their claims either in inalienable *human* rights to natural justice (see Taylor, 1980 on prisoners' rights) or in socialist doctrines concerning the dangers of increased statism (see Thompson, 1979). What has rendered the whole discourse of rights even more mystifying is that, with changed conceptions of gender, marriage, family, etc., rights have been invoked on behalf of practi-cally everyone whose interest conflicts with anyone else's.

That the concept of rights is problematic in any legal system has recently been argued by Paul Hirst (1980). Within penal politics, however, the discourse of rights is still all things to all persons, and although the substantive elements usually include, at the least, notions of state, society, the individual, humanity, God, freedom and oppression, their meanings emerge contradictorily and with diverse effects as they combine in discourses which are often either politically opposed or just discursively asymmetrical to each other. An examina-tion of three opposing ways in which the concept of rights is being used within contemporary penal discourse will demonstrate both the practical catholicity and the ideological tenacity of the concept. The first two examples indicate just how diffuse are the justifications for, and effects of, invoking individual rights. The third, the well-known example of the place of rights in contract theory, leads on to a consi-deration of to what extent it is necessary or useful for a radical penal politics to continue to invoke the language of 'rights' against the spectre of 'statism'.

The rights of the individual to (a) punishment and (b) freedom from treatment

C. S. Lewis and Thomas Szasz (amongst others) have both invoked the right to punishment as necessary to the recognition and guaranteeing of human freedom – a freedom to choose to act for good or bad and to know in advance the consequences of those acts. The ability to know in advance and for all time the consequences of one's acts is an instance of the Divine, whereas to err is, of course, human (Szasz, 1974). Thus, whereas C. S. Lewis manages to invoke God against humanism in the service of an evolutionary humanity whose knowledge remains for ever anti-social, rooted in natural states, Szasz manages to invoke humanity in the service of anti-psychiatry. With both Lewis and Szasz the right to punishment as opposed to treatment is predicated upon the assumptions: (1) that treatment (that is, the non-punitive intervention into an individual life with the aim of altering an antecedent condition) is always the opposite of punishment (the retributive imposition of pain); (2) that such treatment must, by definition, alter and thereby diminish the essential humanity of the individual; (3) that although there must be a concern to ask the question 'Who decides to treat what?' there is not the same urgency to ask 'Who decides to punish what?' because (4) the right to punish is rooted in God-made-Man. This deist theory of punishment, with the God of the Old Testament appearing with even greater authority as the New Testament God in naturally-sinful Man, has, despite its quaint antiquity, a partial and implicit currency today in some humanitarian and libertarian theories of punishment which rather uncritically invoke 'judicial process' against 'treatment'. The 'welfarism versus legalism' debate is, in fact, a debate about opposite sides of the same coin, a coin which, as we shall now see, represents the overdrawn (and almost bankrupt) concept of rights.

The right to full judicial process as opposed to quasi-judicial welfare intervention
Since the passing of the Children and Young Persons Act in 1969 juvenile justice has been officially presented as being the benign face of the English penal system. From the beginning, however, there has been concern about the working of the Act. Magistrates, policemen and some politicians have argued that the punitive element of criminal justice has been subverted by the 'treatment' philosophies of welfare agencies; lawyers and academics have argued that the judicial element in criminal justice has been subverted by social workers, whose decisions are not challenged in a court of law. Three recent books by criminologists, moreover, have claimed that as the 'treatment' meted out to juvenile offenders is often punitive in the extreme, there is all the more need for legal safeguards (see Morris and McIsaac, 1978; Morris *et al.*, 1980; Taylor, Lacey and Bracken, 1979). However,

whereas the magistrates and politicians are merely concerned that offending children are getting off too lightly, both Morris and Taylor are concerned with questions of rights. Unfortunately, their joint concerns serve mainly to demonstrate that the liberal concept of rights is still as impossible as ever. Thus, whereas Morris *et al.* (1980) claim that 'punishment is society's and the child's right', Taylor *et al.* (1979), more specifically, want rights for children against adults. Reynolds (1981), however, in criticising them both, wants even more and differently located rights – this time for parents and teachers against both children and other adults! And this is how it will go on – until, first the notion of right is restricted to one of its two possible legal meanings: either a capacity to act in a specified way, which capacity is bestowed upon an agent by other specifiable agencies of social decision-making; or a capacity to make a specific claim which has a guarantee of being upheld in a court of law; and second, the discourse of individual right is replaced by a programme for the socialisation of judicial powers.

The right to punish
Dominant contemporary assumptions about the right of the state to punish law-breakers stem from the contract theories of, for example, Hobbes and Locke. In contract theory, the state's right to punish law-breakers is based upon an assumption that the state is founded upon the citizens' consensual agreement to surrender their individual powers of punishment to the state's agencies in return for protection of their lives and property. In democratic states, the powers of the state agencies are themselves expected to be subject to due legal process.

There are many criticisms of contract theory. The major criticism relating to criminal justice has been that, in a state founded upon unequal property relations, criminal justice is, in the main, yet another means of oppression of the propertied by the non-propertied classes. Yet, despite their concern with questions of inequality, recent influential theories of justice (for example, see Rawls, 1972; Dworkin, 1977) have barely touched on questions of punishment, whereas radical interventions into criminal justice have been mainly under the banners of civil-rights campaigns. In criminology, Stanley Cohen is the only British criminologist who has more recently faced up to the extremely difficult substantive questions of punishment, and his answers are rooted in an essentialist humanism similar to that of Szasz and Lewis (see Cohen, 1979a; Carlen, 1980). Some Marxist writers, on the other hand, have also avoided contemporary issues of crime and punishment by analysing the historical forms and functions of penal politics. The radical authors of *Policing The Crisis* (Hall *et al.*, 1978), could not address questions concerning punishment at all! Yet some sections of the Left are, in fact, no less reluctant to make demands for intervention against law-breakers than is the Right. Their candidates for social censure may be different, but the substantive demand for regulation by penal sanction is the same. There are as frequent demands from left-wing pressure groups for the exposure and restraint of corrupt state agents and businessmen, rapists, wife-beaters and tax-dodgers as there are more general and popular demands for the punishment of 'thugs', 'vandals', 'muggers' and burglars. So why is there the radical reticence about theoretical and practical questions concerning the desirability, recognition, denial and concomitant control of the power to punish? Because, both in radical critique (for example, Althusser, 1971; Hall *et al.*, 1978) and in the radical press, the criminal justice system's power to punish is repeatedly represented as *ultimately* being *nothing more* than the repressive power of the state.

In the remainder of this paper I shall be arguing that the power to punish should be seen not only as being the crudest manifestation of the state's repressive power, but that it should also be constantly recognised and denied as being an element of political force which can, through a constant process of recognition and denial, be worked upon for socialist purposes. In this transformative process the language of legal rights could become secondary to the language of political powers.

Power and punishment

Recent interventions into penal policy by interested pressure groups have focused on four major areas: juvenile justice (for example, the Justice for Juveniles group); criminal process (for example, concern that the democratic basis of the traditional lay jury is being eroded); prisoners' rights; and on individual miscarriages of justice due to police corruption, radical prejudice, judicial/bureaucratic malpractice or someone's sheer incompetence. The only major theoretical intervention has been by Hall and his associates in their book about mugging (Hall *et al.*, 1978).

The logic underpinning most of the criminal justice campaigns has been well described by Clarke (1978) as a 'Justice Model of Corrections', supported by 'both the constitutionalists who urge a return to constitutionally guaranteed rights, due process and general formal legal rationality; and the transcendentalists who wish the criminal justice system to reflect and uphold universal human rights'. More specifically, all of these campaigns have been concerned with the protection of either accused persons at the pre-sentencing stage or convicted persons at the post-sentencing stage. Both rights campaigners and radicals in general have been silent about what to do with those who (after all possible judicial criteria have been met) have been found guilty of law-breaking. This is not only because many of them have reason to suspect that the power to punish is the unspeakable Other of all political power, nor because some libertarians have an unreasoned squeamishness about confronting any questions of authoritative regulation at all. It is because so many awkward theoretical, political and practical problems confront anyone who gets off the fence of 'pure' theory to intervene in the rather 'impure' politics which constitute the social response to law-breaking.

The remainder of this chapter will be addressed to a series of questions which are all related to a penal politics aimed at *socialising*, rather than reforming, criminal justice. As I agree with David Fernbach's (1981) point that to argue 'that Marxist political practice is ultimately governed by an ethical ideal is not an attempt to reinstate any form of idealism', let us take Phil Leeson's recent description of a socialist mode of production as the ethical ideal informing the rest of this paper. Leeson (1981) writes:

> An interpretation of what most socialists would hope for from the socialist mode of production would say that on the basis of public property there would be the maximum development of the forces of production by technical advance and by education. The relations of production would be such as to require the thoroughgoing democratisation of all aspects of public life via the development of popular participation at all levels and in all aspects of economic and political affairs.

What is to be done about criminal justice in the meantime?

A major fear underlying the popular punitive obsession is that any diminution in the numbers imprisoned will result in increased danger to life, limb and property. A close look at the prison population, however, suggests that, in the main, the criminal justice and penal systems are grinding away at huge cost to *process* (not necessarily even to punish or contain) those who have committed the least serious crimes. This is already well known to judges, policemen, social workers and prison officers. Witness, for instance, the recent words of the national Chairman of the Prison Officers' Association: 'There are a number of people in prison who should not be there. There are fine defaulters, debtors, prostitutes, drug addicts, drunks and certainly the particular bug that I carry around with me is the people who are mentally handicapped in one way or another.'[1] In a similar vein, the Governor of Winson Green Prison, Birmingham, claimed in 1980 that half of the people passing through his prison between the beginning of July 1979 and the end of June 1980 should never have been in prison at all.[2] So, then, what's new? We already know from the works of Foucault (1977a), Scull (1979a), Ignatieff (1978), Mathiesen

(1980a) and Williams (1981) that, at least since the seventeenth century, prisons, asylums and workhouses have been *consistently* used to confine and discipline the poor, the unemployed, the unemployable, the socially disadvantaged and the socially inept. In fact, of course, nothing's new. That is what needs explanation. I shall argue that at present the major impediments to socialising the criminal justice and penal systems inhere both in the secrecy surrounding them and in the jealously preserved independence of the judiciary. The secrecy needs to be undermined, the judicial independence redefined.

How can the secrecy of the judicial and penal processes be diminished?
The secrecy and mystification surrounding the judicial and penal processes has already been well documented (for example, Carlen, 1976; Cohen and Taylor, 1978). Recently, too, there has been political pressure for a Freedom of Information Act. What is more often overlooked, however, is just how little informed popular knowledge there is about the actual functioning of the criminal justice and penal systems. When public opinion is referred to by either judges or their radical campaigning adversaries, it is difficult to know what authority any of them are referring to (although one can surmise that, as often as not, they are invoking an imaginary body of popular belief which is at one with their own views!), for the criminal justice system, the penal system, the 'welfare' system, the penal reform movements and academic criminology operate both together and in opposition as a series of closed systems manned by both competing and non-competing elites. To open up the whole arena of penal politics, to reduce the secrecy and to engender responsibile public debate and policy, there must be an increase of informed popular knowledge of what the penal system is being used for, together with greater lay participation at the sentencing stage.

Calvert Dodge constantly emphasises the role to be played by the mass media in the creation of an ideological climate favourable to the reduction of prison populations. Of Holland, for instance, where (according to figures provided by the Home Office and published by the Howard League for Penal Reform) only 13.4 per 100,000 of the population are imprisoned as against 80 per 100,000 in the UK, he writes:

> the Dutch media devote considerable time to public service programs especially where rehabilitation is the message. The Netherlands' League for Penal Reform helps supply the media with the subject material and data for its programs . . . Emphasis is not placed on the deterrent effect of prison or penal sanction . . . and the Dutch have come to believe that punishment does not alter those situations or factors that lead to criminal behaviour. (Dodge, 1979: 153)

Sweden has also reduced its prison population; between 1971 and 1973 the number of prisoners fell from 4,600 to 3,600, which was 'the lowest number for ten years' (Short, 1979: 32). Again, Dodge emphasises the power of knowledge in facilitating change: 'Swedish citizens . . . are credited with knowing more about their prison system and its operations than most other populations. The Swedes take pride in the fact that this knowledge has aided them in reducing the number of prisons in Sweden and in maintaining the prisoners' civil rights during the process of resocialisation' (1979: 239). Lay access to 'expert' knowledge without an institutionalised lay agency, however, can only engender either innovative or reactive demands which may be accommodated by the existent system. So it has been with 'rights' campaigns. Penal campaigners, for instance, have usually concentrated on making either *innovative* substantive demands (for example, relating to the treatment of prisoners) or *reactive* demands (for example, against the erosion of the writ of habeas corpus, or the undermining of the democratic character of the jury). They have not tried to socialise criminal justice itself. A fundamental condition for the socialising of criminal justice would be for parliamentary legislation to redefine and redistribute the sentencing powers of the judiciary away from the criminal courts to lay tribunals governed by criteria, and endowed with powers, which are not primarily penal.

Why should the powers of the judiciary be redefined and redistributed?

The 'independence of the judiciary' has always been seen in the UK as being an indispensable constitutional guarantee against totalitarian rule. Yet how 'independent' of the executive have the judiciary really been? The history of the Habeas Corpus Suspension Acts, for instance, amply indicates the force of the political desire which limits (and defines) all legality. As Dicey comments, 'the unavowed object of a Habeas Corpus Suspension Act is to enable the government to do acts which, though politically expedient, may not be strictly legal' (Dicey, 1958: 234). Nor, at another level, have the judiciary been independent of the politico-moral prejudices of their class (see Griffith, 1977). In the area of criminal justice, moreover, their sentencing logic has, since the beginning of this century, been inseminated by the quasi-judicial welfare and medical judgements of professionals who, too often, are answerable only to the hidden demands of their own bureaucracies. The judiciary are only independent in one sense: they are independent of democratic control and review. As a result, in the area of sentencing they are often inefficient (that is, their sentencing policies exacerbate existing social problems and lead to a further waste of materials and labour). This wastage, however, does not result solely from the sentencing activities of the judiciary. It is also the inevitable result of an adversary system of criminal justice where the logic of prosecution demands that the strongest case be made against the accused in order to secure the highest penalty. In order to engender a more efficient (that is, less wasteful) response to law-breaking, therefore, I would suggest that both the decision to prosecute and the sentencing decision should be governed by criteria which are never primarily penal, and by agencies whose personnel are not predominantly professional.

Calvert Dodge (1979), describing the Dutch system of criminal justice, makes the point that 'more than 50% of Dutch criminal cases are handled through the expediency principle. This means that a public prosecutor may waive prosecution if the suspect agrees to attend a drug clinic, alcoholic rehabilitation program or similar treatment programme.' Furthermore, Dodge claims that 'for the last twenty to thirty years the rule has been to ask "Why prosecute?" rather than "Why not prosecute?" ' Admittedly, there is no lay element in Dutch criminal proceedings, and the adoption of the expediency principle on its own would most likely worry civil libertarians here. Yet, it seems to me that, if the expediency principle were to be adopted, together with both a greater lay element at the pre-prosecution and sentencing stages *and* procedural safeguards at all stages, the 'public', who are supposedly clamouring for increasingly severe penalties (and we do not actually know what proportion *is*!), would have to confront some of the extremely complex problems which, though they have provided some of us with our bread and butter for years, have not been spectacularly alleviated by either judicial or professional intervention. I am not, of course, suggesting that the more punitive sectors of the 'public' would immediately become less punitive once engaged in judging their fellows (in fact some of the sentencing antics of the secretly chosen and vetted lay magistracy suggest quite the opposite). Many actual crimes would in themselves continue to provoke feelings of fear, anger and revulsion. But the actual crimes can already be read about in the newspapers. What might surprise a lay person participating only infrequently in the criminal justice system might be: the parody of due process in which the courts and prisons too often engage; the intractable and extreme nature of many offenders' social circumstances; and the inappropriateness, both to the offender and to the community, of the court's final decision. To give but one example: for how long would the good people on the Clapham omnibus continue to send people to prison for not paying fines of, say, £50, once they knew that it costs well over £100 per person per week to keep them there? Might they not begin to question, at a fundamental level, the whole logic of present sentencing tariffs? And once they had so begun, might they not then go on to question the whole rationale behind the criminal justice and penal systems? I *think* that they might, and I think that they would then become increasingly perturbed about these systems' inefficiency, waste and sheer irrelevance even to the social problems they purport to address and alleviate.

How could the powers of the judiciary be redefined and redistributed?

One effect of the doctrine of the separation of powers (an effect which can be discerned in some judicial pronouncements) is that questions of judicial right are discursively segregated from questions of political will and power. Judges can quite openly deplore the social conditions which result in certain criminal proceedings, and yet, at the same time, locate all the guilt and responsibility in the individual law-breaker. The judge punishes: the social worker intervenes. However, whereas the judge has the full power to punish, the social worker has little power over the allocation of resources, and therefore lacks real power to intervene. I am suggesting that a more effective response to law-breaking would come about as a result of a policy of intervention, activated by lay tribunals which were empowered by Parliament to develop more non-penal community facilities at a local level. This is not so idealistic as it at first might seem.

For many years the ubiquitous notion of 'community' has been invoked as the imaginary backup to all kinds of social policies (see Chapter 5). The 'open door' policies of mental hospitals have been justified on the grounds that the 'mentally ill' should be coped with in the 'community'; the community service order has been hailed as the most imaginative penal innovation for years; there is always talk of getting the 'community' involved when there are difficult decisions to be made relating to housing, traffic, education, etc. All very worthy. The trouble is that 'communities', as spontaneously organising collectives, do not exist. Newly released mental-hospital patients and ex-prisoners are either exploited or have doors slammed in their faces; community service orders are organised by professionals on behalf of the courts, on one side, and specific organisations, on the other; and the long-suffering populations of derelict urban areas or isolated suburban housing estates remain just as alienated from, frightened of and powerless about the nature of law-breaking and the social response to it as they have ever been. Yet the lay jury is seen as a success. In Scotland, too, the response to advertisements for lay members of children's panels has been good. Why not, therefore, harness the public concern about law-breaking to a social intervention programme on which, for a specified period, all persons over a certain age would be eligible for either voluntary or compulsory service?

(Preparation for such service could be incorporated into social studies lessons in schools.) *I am suggesting that local lay tribunals, operating under the auspices of the expediency principle 'Why prosecute?', should initially process all juvenile and most other 'crime' where an accused person admits to breaking the law.* It would be essential that, at the least, such lay tribunals be chosen by non-secret methods; that ex-offenders not be barred; that tribunal members have voting powers on council finance and other committees. The judiciary would still fulfil a judicial function, but judicial intervention would follow upon the *lay* decision to prosecute. Thus, in practice, lay tribunals would provide a continuous review of police activities, while continuously defining and redefining the scope of the criminal justice system. Enough, however, of prescription! This proposal is not put forward as a blueprint for a socialised justice (which, whatever else it might be, should at least be forever changing!); it is just an example of one way in which the present system could be made more democractic and efficient. Yet even a more democratic system would have to confront the old questions concerning rights and powers of punishment.

Can the 'right to punish' be displaced by the power to intervene?
'The Dutch are efficient in handling criminal cases' (Dodge, 1979: 133). I would suggest that their efficiency inheres in their ability to separate the notions of social censure and regulatory intervention from the notion of punishment. A conceptual distinction between punishment and regulatory intervention can be made – even though sometimes individuals might experience the effects of regulatory intervention as being more painful than disabilities inflicted purely for penal purposes.

Punishment, if successful, intentionally causes pain and usually has disabling (physical, psychological or financial) consequences for the offender. Regulatory intervention, on the other hand, need have no penal intent; it could be defined as being merely the authoritative rectification of the particular social problems which both occasion, and are occasioned by, law-breaking. Thus, for example, in a more democratic (rather than elitist) system, a lay panel might, like the Dutch prosecutor, waive prosecution, if offenders agreed either to attend a drug clinic, an alcoholic rehabilitation centre, a day centre or some other programme, or to accept some other type of help, for example, services of a day nursery in cases of child neglect or abuse, or supervision by a lay supervisor (lay supervisors have been successfully used in Norway and Denmark). However, it would have to be mandatory that, when the lay agency empowered to define a problem and recommend a solution had so done, lack of the recommended facility (for example, work or housing for an offender) should not result (as it does at present) in incarceration or other punishment. But it might result in public debates in which much law-breaking would come to be seen as part and parcel of other social problems. For example, excessive numbers of alcohol-related crimes in one area might result not only in increased treatment facilities for those with a drink problem, but also in intensive programmes designed to educate the public about the dangers of alcohol and, in addition, the levies on those benefiting from its manufacture and sale might be increased. Or, in a different example, excessive youth crime might result in public debate about, and investigation and remedy of, the work and leisure opportunities for the youth in that area as well as a review of police practices in relation to youthful offenders; on the other hand, of course, it might not!

The points I am making are not those of utopian prophecy – although dozens of other possibilities could be cited. I am merely trying to indicate ways in which parliamentary legislation could make moves away from the present elitist and secretive judicial and penal systems which, although steeped in legal *right*, are completely lacking in the *power* to define effectively, and remedy, the social problems that, too often, occasion criminal proceedings. Which is why we have a repressive 'law and order society' increasingly incapable of delivering its own goods.

Are the foregoing arguments recipes for a mixture of libertarianism and statism?

No. First, I will answer the possible charge of libertarianism. I have not tried to argue that I can foresee a time when *no* individuals will be interpellated as guilty citizens worthy of social censure and even custodial restraint (although, of course, that is not to say that the time will not come!). Nor have I argued that punishment or the threat of punishment will have *no* part to play in a socialised justice. I would, however, expect such punishments as are imposed to be publicly justified and debated. (For example, although few British officials can think of any justification for our present policies of imprisoning the homeless, the mentally ill, the alcoholic and those who cannot afford to pay a fine, the Dutch and the Swedes can argue that their policies of imprisonment for dangerous driving and white-collar business crimes do, in fact, deter.) Furthermore, the argument has not been that social deprivation (however defined) licenses crime; poverty no more endows people with a 'right' to break the law than does political power endow the state with a 'right' to punish law-breakers. What I have argued for is, first, more informed public debate about the relationships between law-breaking, inequality and penal policy; second, and relatedly, more lay involvement in the prosecution and disposal of law-breakers; and finally, parliamentary legislation for the limitation of the powers of the judiciary and for the setting up of agencies empowered to respond to law-breaking in ways which would not be primarily punitive, where emphasis would be shifted, away from the *right* to punish, on to the *power* to remedy fractured social relations. It is at this point that one can hear protesting murmurs against the proliferation of bureaucracy, the increase of statism and the diminution of the civil rights which are *supposed* to protect against totalitarianism.

Undoubtedly any socialisation of the criminal justice system would require parliamentary legislation to create new types of agencies – agencies with a greater lay element – to respond to law-breaking. However, that does not mean that the road away from elitist specialism is necessarily via bureaucratic statism. Much of the power of the existent judicial and penal bureaucracies and professions inheres in the secrecy of their self-validating procedures and internal powers of review. The complexity of organisation necessary to any programme of socialisation would still entail the employment of people with specialist skills as well as the occupancy of offices endowed with specific powers. In a socialised system of justice, however, specialist bodies and public-office holders would have their spheres of competence defined externally (and not totally by central government), and their decisions would be open to lay review. (What, for example, I would hope *not* to have in a socialised system of justice, would be a situation as at present where doctors, social workers, psychiatrists and judges can all make penal decisions on the basis of reports never available for public scrutiny!)

Summary
These are not arguments for a popular justice. Justice will no more emanate from the 'people' than it has ever done from 'God', the 'State' or the 'Bench'. The requirements of due process must be constructed and reconstructed – that is, official action must still be governed by rules – although the rules' definition, interpretation and operation must, in turn, be governed by non-official agencies.

In a socialised system of justice individuals might still experience injustice, rules might still be broken and there would most certainly be continuous problems of organisation. But the system would be open to continuous and more democratic and informed review; its agencies would be empowered to define and resolve problems of law-breaking in terms of social regulation and justice in general; and finally, and most importantly, it would be empowered to experiment with modes of social intervention relevant to the changing nature of local problems of regulation and social justice.

In sum, it is the main theme of this chapter that a socialised system of criminal justice should move away from a system organised for the *administration* of justice by judicial right from above, towards one designed for the *construction* of justice within the more democractic organisation of competing interests and powers.

Notes

1   *Nacro News Digest*, March 1981.
2   *New Statesman*, 19 September 1980.

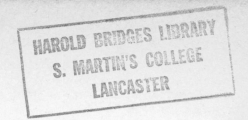

References

Aaronson, D. E., Dienes, C. T. and Musheno, M. C. (1978), 'Changing the public drunkenness laws: the impact of decriminalization', *Law and Society Review*, vol. 12, pp. 405–36.

Abel, R. L. (1978), 'From the Editor', *Law and Society Review*, vol. 12, pp. 333–40.

Abel, R. L. (1979), 'Delegalization: a critical review of its ideology, manifestations and social consequences', in E. Blankenburg *et al.* (eds.), *Alternative Rechtsformen und Alternative zum Reche* (Jahrbuch für Rechtssociologie Bund G), Opladen.

Abel, R. L. (1981), 'Conservative conflict and the reproduction of capitalism: the role of informal justice', *International Journal of the Sociology of Law*, vol. 9, pp. 245–67.

Abolitionist, The (1981), 'Parole reviews', *The Abolitionist*, vol. 9.

Abrams, P. (1978), 'Community care: some research problems and priorities', in J. Barnes and N. Connelly (eds.), *Social Care Research*, London, Bedford Square Press.

Acton, H. B. (1969), *The Philosophy of Punishment*, London, Macmillan.

AFSCME (1975), *Out of Their Beds and Into the Streets* Washington, DC, AFSCME.

Ahmed, P. (1974), 'New thrusts in unified mental health care systems, and the status of state mental hospitals', in *Where is my Home?* Washington, DC, National Technical Information Service.

Alper, B. (1973), 'Foreword', in Y. Bakal (ed.), *Closing Correctional Institutions*, Lexington, Mass., Lexington Books.

Althusser, L. (1969), *For Marx*, London, New Left Books.

Althusser, L. (1971), *Lenin and Philosophy and Other Essays*, London, New Left Books.

American Friends Service Committee (1971), *Struggle for Justice*, Philadelphia, Hill & Wang.

Ancel, M. (1971), *Suspended Sentence*, London, Heinemann Educational Books.

Anderson, J. N. D. (1980), 'Criminal sanctions', in J. Stott and N. Miller (eds.), *Crime and the Responsible Community*, London, Hodder & Stoughton, pp. 44–70.

Antilla, I. (1978), 'Control without repression', in J. Freeman (ed.), *Prisons Past and Future*, London, Heinemann Educational Books.

Atiyah, P. (1980), *Accidents, Compensation and the Law* (3rd edn), London, Weidenfeld & Nicolson.

Bailey, V. (ed.) (1981), *Policing and Punishment in Nineteenth Century Britain*, London, Croom Helm.

Ball, R. A. (1979), 'A theory of punishment', in P. J. Brantingham and J. M. Kress (eds.), *Structure, Law and Power*, Beverly Hills, Ca., Sage.

Balvig, F. (1977), 'Alternativer til frihedsstraf', *Information*, vol. 10, October.

Basaglia, F. (1981), 'Breaking the circuit of control', in D. Ingleby (ed.), *Critical Psychiatry*, Harmondsworth, Penguin Books.

Baxi, U. (1974), 'Durkheim and legal evolution: some problems of disproof', *Law and Society Review*, vol. 8, pp. 645–51.

Bayer, R. (1981), 'Crime, punishment and the decline of liberal optimism', *Crime and Delinquency*, vol. 27, no. 2, pp. 169–90.

Bean, P. (1976), *Rehabilitation and Deviance*, London, Routledge & Kegan Paul.

Bean, P. (1981), *Punishment*, Oxford, Martin Robertson.

Beccaria, C. (1764), *On Crimes and Punishments* (English translation by H. Paolucci, Indianapolis, Ind., Bobbs-Merrill, 1963).

Beck, B. (1979), 'The limits of deinstitutionalization', in M. Lewis (ed.), *Research in Social Problems and Public Policy*, vol. 1, Greenwich, JAI Press.

Becker, H. S. (1967), 'Whose side are we on?', *Social Problems*, vol. 14, no. 3, pp. 239–47.

Beit-Hallahmi, B. (1976), 'Psychological theories and correctional practise: a historical note', *Corrective and Social Psychiatry*, vol. 22, no. 4, pp. 38–9.

Bentham, J. (1962), *Principles of Penal Law*, New York, Russell & Russell.

Berger, P., Berger, B. and Kellner, H. (1974), *The Homeless Mind*, Harmondsworth, Penguin Books.

Berlin, I. (1978), *Russian Thinkers*, London, Hogarth Press.

Bittner, E. (1967), 'Police on skid row: a study of peace keeping', *American Sociological Review*, vol. 32, pp. 699–715.

Black, D. (1976), *The Behavior of Law*, New York, Academic Press.

Blomberg, T. (1977), 'Diversion and accelerated social control', *Journal of Criminology and Criminal Law*, vol. 68, pp. 274–82.

Blumberg, A. (1974), *Criminal Justice*, New York, New Viewpoints.

Bochel, D. (1976), *Probation and After Care*, Edinburgh, Scottish Academic Press.

Bolger, S., Corrigan, P., Docking, I. and Frost, N. (1981), *Towards Socialist Welfare Work*, London, Macmillan.

Boorkman, D. *et al.* (1976), *An Exemplary Project: Community Based Corrections in Des Moines*, Washington, DC, LEAA.

Bottomley, A. K. (1973), *Decisions in the Penal Process*, London, Martin Robertson.

Bottomley, A. K. (1979), *Criminology in Focus*, Oxford, Martin Robertson.

Bottomley, A. K. and Coleman, C. (1981), *Understanding Crime Rates*, Farnborough, Gower Publishing Co.

Bottoms, A. E. (1977), 'Reflections on the renaissance of dangerousness',

Howard Journal of Penology and Crime Prevention, vol. 16, no. 2, pp. 70–96.

Bottoms, A. E. (1980), 'An introduction to "the coming crisis" ', in A. E. Bottoms and R. H. Preston (eds.), *The Coming Penal Crisis*, Edinburgh, Scottish Academic Press.

Bottoms, A. E. (1981), 'The suspended sentence in England 1967–1978', *British Journal of Criminology*, vol. 21, pp. 1–26.

Bottoms, A. E. and McClean, J. (1976), *Defendants in the Criminal Process*, London, Routledge & Kegan Paul.

Bottoms, A. E. and McClintock, F. H. (1973), *Criminals Coming of Age*, London, Heinemann Educational Books.

Boyers, R. (1979), 'Review of Christopher Lasch, *Haven in a Heartless World*', *New Republic*, 19 February.

Bradley, F. H. (1927), *Ethical Studies*, Oxford, Clarendon Press.

Braverman, H. (1974), *Labor and Monopoly Capital*, New York, Monthly Review.

Brown, G. W. *et al.* (1966), *Schizophrenia and Social Care*, London, OUP.

Burchard, J. D. and Harig, R. T. (1976), 'Behaviour modification and juvenile delinquency', in H. Leitenberg (ed.), *Handbook of Behavior Modification and Behavior Therapy*, Englewood Cliffs, NJ, Prentice-Hall.

Burns, P. (1980), *Criminal Injuries Compensation*, Vancouver, Butterworths.

Burton, F. and Carlen, P. (1979), *Official Discourse*, London, Routledge & Kegan Paul.

Carlen, P. (1976), *Magistrates' Justice*, Oxford, Martin Robertson.

Carlen, P. (1980), 'Radical criminology, penal politics and the rule of law', in P. Carlen and M. Collison (eds.), *Radical Issues in Criminology*, Oxford, Martin Robertson.

Carson, W. G. and Wiles, P. (1971), *Crime and Delinquency in Britain*, London, Martin Robertson.

Carter, J. A. and Cole, G. F. (1979), 'The use of fines in England: could the idea work here?', *Judicature*, vol. 63, pp. 154–61.

Chambliss, W. (1976), 'Functional and conflict theories of crime', in W. Chambliss and M. Mankoff (eds.), *Whose Law? What Order?*, New York, John Wiley.

Chan, J. B. L. and Ericson, R. V. (1981), *Decarceration and the Economy of Penal Reform*, Toronto, University of Toronto Centre of Criminology, Research Report, no. 14.

Chase, J. (1973), 'Where have all the patients gone?', *Human Behavior*, 14–21 October.

Chesney, S., Judson, J. and McLagen, J. (1977), 'A new look at restitution: recent legislation, programs and research', *Judicature*, vol. 61, pp. 348–57.

Christie, N. (1966), 'De fratagbare goder', *Tidsskrift for Samfunnsforskning*, pp. 119–30.

Christie, N. (1977), 'Conflicts as property', *British Journal of Criminology*, vol. 17, pp. 1–15.

Christie, N. (1978), 'Prisons in society, or society as a prison: a conceptual analysis', in J. Freeman (ed.), *Prisons Past and Future*, London, Heinemann Educational Books.

Clarke, D. H. (1978), 'Marxism, justice and the justice model', *Contemporary Crises*, no. 2, pp. 27–62.

Clarke, M. (1976), 'Durkheim's sociology of law', *British Journal of Law and Society*, vol. 3, pp. 246–55.

Clarke, R. V. G. and Mayhew, P. (eds.) (1980), *Designing Out Crime*, London, HMSO.

Coates, R. B. and Miller, A. (1973), 'Neutralization of community resistance to group homes', in Y. Bakal (ed.), *Closing Correctional Insititutions*, Lexington, Mass., Lexington Books.

Cohen, S. (1972), *Folk Devils and Moral Panics*, London, Paladin.

Cohen, S. (1977), 'Prisons and the future of control systems: from concentration to dispersal', in M. Fitzgerald *et al.* (eds.), *Welfare in Action*, London, Routledge & Kegan Paul.

Cohen, S. (1979a), 'Guilt, justice and tolerance: some old concepts for a new criminology', in D. Downes and P. Rock (eds.), *Deviant Interpretations*, Oxford, Martin Robertson.

Cohen, S. (1979b), 'The punitive city: notes on the dispersal of social control', *Contemporary Crises*, vol. 3, pp. 339–63.

Cohen, S. (1981), 'Western crime control models on the third world: benign or malignant?', in R. Simon and S. Spitzer (eds.), *Research in Law, Deviance and Social Control*, vol. 4, Greenwich, JAI Press.

Cohen, S. and Taylor, L. (1977), *Escape Attempts: The Theory and Practice of Resistance to Everyday Life*, London, Allen Lane.

Cohen, S. and Taylor, L. (1978), *Prison Secrets*, London, National Council for Civil Liberties, and Radical Alternatives to Prison.

Corrigan, P. (1981), 'On moral regulation: some preliminary remarks', *Sociological Review*, vol. 29, pp. 313–37.

Corrigan, P. and Leonard, P. (1978), *Social Work Practice Under Capitalism*, London, Macmillan.

Cotterrell, R. B. M. (1977), 'Durkheim on legal development and social solidarity', *British Journal of Law and Society*, vol. 3, pp. 241–52.

Cressey, D. and McDermott, P. (1974), *Diversion from the Criminal Justice System*, Washington, DC, LEAA.

CSEA (1972), *Where Have All the Patients Gone?*, Sacramento, CSEA.

Daa, L. K. (1843), *Har Amerikas Erfaring bevist de Pensylvanske Faengslers Fortrinlighed?*, Kristiania, Krohn & Schibsted.

Davies, M. (1974), 'Social inquiry for the courts', *British Journal of Criminology*, vol. 14, pp. 18–33.

Davis, D. B. (1980), 'The crime of reform', *New York Review of Books* (26 June), pp. 14–17.

Davis, F. (1979), *Yearning for Yesterday: A Sociology of Nostalgia*, London, Collier Macmillan.

Dicey, A. V. (1958), *The Law of the Constitution*, London, Macmillan.

Dingman, P. R. (1974), 'The case for the state hospital', in *Where Is My Home?*, Washington, DC, National Technical Information Service.

Ditton, J. (1979), *Controlology*, London, Macmillan.

Dodge, C. (1979), *A World Without Prisons*, Lexington, Mass., Heath/Lexington Books.

Donzelot, J. (1979), 'The poverty of political culture', *Ideology and Consciousness*, no. 5, pp. 73–87.

Donzelot, J. (1980), *The Policing of Families*, London, Hutchinson.

Durkheim, E. (1957), *Professional Ethics and Civic Morals*, London, Routledge & Kegan Paul.

Durkheim, E. (1964), *The Division of Labour in Society*, New York, Free Press.

Durkheim, E. (1966), *The Rules of Sociological Method*, New York, Free Press.

Durkheim, E. (1973), 'Two laws of penal evolution', English translation by T. A. Jones and A. T. Scull, *Economy and Society*, vol. 2.

Dworkin, R. (1977), *Taking Rights Seriously*, London, Duckworth.

Edelman, B. (1979), *Ownership of the Image*, London, Routledge & Kegan Paul.

Edelman, M. (1964), *The Symbolic Uses of Politics*, Urbana, University of Illinois Press.

Elkin, W. A. (1957), *The English Penal System*, Harmondsworth, Penguin Books.

Empey, L. T. (1973), 'Juvenile justice reform: diversion, due process, and deinstitutionalization', in L. Ohlin (ed.), *Prisoners in America*, Englewood Cliffs, NJ, Prentice-Hall.

Erikson, K. (1966), *Wayward Puritans*, New York, John Wiley.

Etzioni, A. (1972a), 'Human beings are not very easy to change after all', in *Saturday Review* (3 June) (reprinted in *Annual Editions: Readings in Social Problems*, Dushkin, 1973).

Etzioni, A. (1972b), 'The grant shaman', *Psychology Today* (November).

Fernbach, D. (1981), 'Euro-communism and the ethical ideal', in M. Prior (ed.), *The Popular and the Political*, London, Routledge & Kegan Paul.

Ferri, E. (1917), *Criminal Sociology*, Boston, Mass., Little Brown.

Fine, B. (1977), 'Objectification and the contradictions of bourgeois power', *Economy and Society*, vol. 7, pp. 408–35.

Fine, B., Kinsey, R., Lea, J., Piccietto, S. and Young, J. (1979), *Capitalism and the Rule of Law*, London, Hutchinson.

Fitzgerald, M. (1977), *Prisoners in Revolt*, Harmondsworth, Penguin Books.

Floud, J. and Young, W. (1981), *Dangerousness and Criminal Justice*, London, Heinemann Educational Books.

Flynn, E. E. (1978), 'Classification for risk and supervision: a preliminary conceptualization', in J. Freeman (ed.), *Prisons Past and Future*, London, Heinemann Educational Books.

Fogel, D. (1975), *We Are the Living Proof: The Justice Model for Corrections*, Cincinnati, Ohio, Anderson.

Foucault, M. (1965), *Madness and Civilization*, New York, Mentor.

Foucault, M. (1977a), *Discipline and Punish: the Birth of the Prison*, London, Allen Lane.

Foucault, M. (1977b), 'Nietzsche, genealogy, history', in D. Bouchard (ed.), *Language, Counter-Memory, Practice: Selected Essays and Interviews by Michel Foucault*, Oxford, Basil Blackwell.

Foucault, M. (1979a), *The History of Sexuality Volume 1: An Introduction*, London, Allen Lane.

Foucault, M. (1979b), 'On governmentality', in *Ideology and Consciousness*, no. 6, pp. 5–23.

Foucault, M. (1980a), 'Body/power', in C. Gordon (ed.), *Michel Foucault: Power/Knowledge, Selected Interviews and Other Writings 1972–1977*, Brighton, Harvester Press.

Foucault, M. (1980b), 'Two lectures', in C. Gordon (ed.), *Michel Foucault: Power/Knowledge, Selected Interviews and Other Writings 1972–1977*, Brighton, Harvester Press.

Foucault, M. (1980c), 'Prison talk', in C. Gordon (ed.), *Michel Foucault: Power/Knowledge, Selected Interviews and Other Writings 1972–1977*, Brighton, Harvester Press.

Foucault, M. (1980d), in C. Gordon (ed.), *Michel Foucault: Power/Knowledge, Selected Interviews and Other Writings 1972–1977*, Brighton, Harvester Press.

Foucault, M. (1981), 'Questions of method: an interview with Michel Foucault', *Ideology and Consciousness*, no. 8, pp. 3–15.

Fowles, A. (1980), 'To reduce the prison population', in M. Brown and S. Baldwin (eds.), *The Yearbook of Social Policy in Britain 1978*, London, Routledge & Kegan Paul.

Fox, L. (1952), *The Modern English Prison*, London, Routledge.

Fry, M. (1951), *Arms of the Law*, London, Victor Gollancz.

Garland, D. (1981), 'The birth of the welfare sanction', *British Journal of Law and Society*, vol. 8 (Summer 1981), pp. 29–45.

Garland, D. (1982), 'Philosophical argument and ideological effect', in *Contemporary Crises* (1982) forthcoming).

Garofalo, J. and Connelly, K. J. (1980), 'Dispute resolution centers: Part II: Outcomes, issues, and future directions', in National Council for Crime and Delinquency, *Criminal Justice Abstracts*, vol. 12, pp. 576–611.

Garofalo, R. (1914), *Criminology*, Boston, Mass., Little Brown.

Gaylin, W. (1974), *Partial Justice*, New York, Knopf.

Gaylin, W. *et al.* (1978), *Doing Good: The Limits of Benevolence*, New York, Pantheon.

Gill, R. (1975), *The Social Context of Theology: A Methodological Enquiry*, London, Mowbrays.

Goffman, E. (1961), *Asylums*, Garden City, NY, Doubleday.

Gordon, C. (1980), 'Afterword', in C. Gordon (ed.), *Michel Foucault: Power/Knowledge, Selected Interviews and Other Writings 1972–1977*, Brighton, Harvester Press.

Gouldner, A. (1971), *The Coming Crisis of Western Sociology*, London, Heinemann Educational Books.

Grabosky, P. N. (1978), 'Theory and research on variations in penal severity', *British Journal of Law and Society*, vol. 5, pp. 103–14.

Greenberg, D. (1975), 'Problems in community corrections', *Issues in Criminology*, vol. 19, pp. 1–34.

Greenberg, D. and Humphries, D. (1980), 'The co-optation of fixed sentencing reform', *Crime and Delinquency*, vol. 26, pp. 206–25.

Griffith, J. (1977), *The Politics of the Judiciary*, London, Fontana.

Griffiths, C. T., Klein, J. F. and Verdun-Jones, S. N. (1980), *Criminal Justice in Canada*, Vancouver, Butterworths.

Hall, S. (1977), 'Rethinking the "base-and-superstructure" metaphor', in J. Bloomfield (ed.), *Class, Hegemony and Party*, London, Lawrence & Wishart.

Hall, S., Critcher, C., Jefferson, T., Clarke, J. and Roberts, B. (1978), *Policing the Crisis*, London, Macmillan.

Halvorsen, K. (1977), *Arbeid eller trygd?*, Oslo, Pax.

Harrison, B. (1974), 'State intervention and moral reform in nineteenth century England', in P. Hollis (ed.), *Pressure from Without in Early Victorian Britain*, London, St Martin's.

Hart, H. L. A. (1968), *Punishment and Responsibility*, Oxford, OUP.

Hay, D. *et al.* (1975), *Albion's Fatal Tree*, New York, Pantheon.

Healy, W. (1922), *The Individual Delinquent*, Boston, Mass., Little, Brown.

Heath, J. (1963), *Eighteenth Century Penal Theory*, London, OUP.

Hegel, G. F. (1967), *Philosophy of Right*, Oxford, Clarendon Press.

Hibbert, C. (1963), *The Roots of Evil*, Harmondsworth, Penguin Books.

Higgins, J. (1980), 'Social control theories of social policy', *Journal of Social Policy*, vol. 9, no. 1.

Hirsch, R. (1979), *Kriminaljournalistikk – salg, politikk eller saklig informasjon?*, Oslo, Institute for Sociology of Law, mimeo.

Hirst, P. Q. (1973), 'Morphology and pathology: biological analogies and metaphors in Durkheim's *The Rules of Sociological Method*', *Economy and Society*, pp. 1–34.

Hirst, P. Q. (1975a), *Durkheim, Bernard and Epistemology*, London, Routledge & Kegan Paul.

Hirst, P. Q. (1975b), 'Marx and Engels on law and morality', in I. Taylor, P. Walton and J. Young (eds.), *Critical Criminology*, London, Routledge & Kegan Paul.

Hirst, P. Q. (1979), *On Law and Ideology*, London, Macmillan.

Hirst, P. Q. (1980), 'Law, socialism and rights', in P. Carlen and M. Collison (eds.), *Radical Issues in Criminology*, Oxford, Martin Robertson.

Home Office (1959), *Penal Practice in a Changing Society*, London, HMSO (Cmnd 645).

Home Office (1961), *Compensation for Victims of Crimes of Violence*, London, HMSO (Cmnd 1406).

Home Office (1980), *The Reduction of Pressure on the Prison System*, London, HMSO (Cmnd 7948).

Home Office (1981), *Criminal Statistics (England and Wales) 1980*, London, HMSO (Cmnd 8376).

Honderich, T. (1976), *Punishment, the Supposed Justifications*, Harmondsworth, Penguin Books.

Hood, R. and Sparks, R. (1970), *Key Issues in Criminology*, London, Weidenfeld & Nicolson.

Hulsman, L. (1981–2), 'Penal reform in the Netherlands', *Howard Journal of Penology and Crime Prevention*, vol. 20, pp. 150–9, and vol. 21, pp. 35–47.

Hunt, A. (1978), *The Sociological Movement in Law*, London, Macmillan.

Hunt, A. (1981), 'The politics of law and justice', in *Politics and Power*, vol. 4, London, Routledge & Kegan Paul, pp. 3–27.

Hylton, J. H. (1981), 'Community corrections and social control: the case of Saskatchewan, Canada', *Contemporary Crises*, vol. 5, pp. 193–215.

Ignatieff, M. (1978), *A Just Measure of Pain: The Penitentiary in the Industrial Revolution*, London, Macmillan.

Jeffrey, C. R. (ed.), (1976), 'Criminal behaviour and the physical environment', *American Behavioral Scientist*, vol. 20, no. 2 (November–December).

Jessop, B. (1978), 'Marx and Engels on the state', in S. Hibbin (ed.), *Politics, Ideology and the State*, London, Lawrence & Wishart.

Jones, H. (1956), *Crime and the Penal System* (1st edn), London, University Tutorial Press.

Kamenka, E. and Tay, A. E.-S. (1975), 'Beyond bourgeois individualism: the contemporary crisis in law and legal ideology', in E. Kamenka and R. S. Neale (eds.), *Feudalism, Capitalism and Beyond*, London, Edward Arnold.

Kant, I. (1965), *The Metaphysics of Morals*, Indianapolis, Ind., Bobbs-Merill.

Katz, M. (1979), 'The origins of the institutional state', *Marxist Perspectives*, vol. 1, pp. 6–23.

Kittrie, N. (1972), *The Right to be Different*, Baltimore, Md, Penguin Books.

Klein, M. W. *et al.* (1976), 'The explosion in police diversion programs', in M. Klein (ed.), *The Juvenile System*, Beverly Hills, Ca, Sage.

Lasch, C. (1977), *Haven in a Heartless World: The Family Besieged*, New York, Basic Books.

Lasch, C. (1980a), 'Life in the therapeutic state', *New York Review of Books*, vol. xxvii, no. 10, pp. 24–32 (12 June).

Lasch, C. (1980b), 'Review of Rothman', Conscience and Convenience, *The Nation*, pp. 29–30 (14 June).

Lea, J. (1979), 'Discipline and capitalist development', in B. Fine *et al.* (eds.), *Capitalism and the Rule of Law*, London, Hutchinson.

Leach, E. R. (1970), *Political Systems of Highland Burma: A Study of Kachin Social Structure*, London, Athlone Press (1st edn, 1954).

Leeson, P. (1981), 'Capitalism, statism and socialism', in M. Prior (ed.), *The Popular and the Political*, London, Routledge & Kegan Paul.

Leifer, R. (1969), *In the Name of Mental Health*, New York, Aronson.

Lemert, E. (1967), *Human Deviance, Social Problems and Social Control*, New York, Prentice-Hall.

Lemert, E. (1972), 'Social problems and the sociology of deviance', in E. Lemert (ed.), *Human Deviance, Social Problems, and Social Control* (2nd edn), Englewood Cliffs, NJ, Prentice-Hall.

Lerman, P. (1975), *Community Treatment and Social Control*, Chicago, University of Chicago Press.

Lidstone, K. W., Hogg, R. and Sutcliffe, F. (1980), *Prosecutions by Private Individuals and Non-Police Agencies*, Royal Commission on Criminal Procedure Research Study no. 10, London, HMSO.

Llewellyn, K. (1940), 'The normative, the legal and the law-jobs: the problem of juristic method', *Yale Law Journal*, vol. 49, pp. 1355–400.

Lorentzen, H. (1977), 'Politiopprusting – aktører, interesser og strategier', *Retfaerd*, pp. 7–26; reprinted as 'Reinforcing the police – actors, interests and strategies', in *Scandinavian Studies in Criminology*, vol. 7, (1980), Oslo, Universitetsforlaget.

McKelvey, B. (1977), *American Prisons: A History of Good Intentions*, Montclair, NJ, Patterson Smith.

Mannheim, H. and Wilkins, L. (1955), *Prediction Methods in Relation to Borstal Training*, London, HMSO.

Martinson, R. (1974), 'What Works? Questions and Answers about Prison Reform', *The Public Interest* (Spring).

Marx, K. and Engels, F. (1970), *The German Ideology*, Lawrence and Wishart.

Mathiesen, T. (1972), 'Fengselsvesenets ideologi 1600–1970', in A. B. Syse (ed.), *Kan fengsel forsvares?* Oslo, Pax.

Mathiesen, T. (1974), *The Politics of Abolition*, London, Martin Robertson.

Mathiesen, T. (1975), *Løsgjengerkrigen*, Oslo, Sosionomen.

Mathiesen, T. (1977), *Rett og samfunn*, Oslo, Pax.

Mathiesen, T. (1978a), 'Berget som fødte en mus', *Dagbladet* (31 May).

Mathiesen, T. (1978b), *Den skjulte disiplinering*, Oslo, Pax.

Mathiesen, T. (1979), *Politikrigen*, Oslo, Pax.

Mathiesen, T. (1980a), *Law, Society and Political Action*, London, Academic Press.

Mathiesen, T. (1980b), 'The future of control systems – the case of Norway', *International Journal of the Sociology of Law*, vol. 8, pp. 149–64.

Matthews, R. (1979), 'Decarceration and the fiscal crisis', in B. Fine *et al.* (eds.), *Capitalism and the Rule of Law*, London, Hutchinson.

Mawby, R. (1979), *Policing the City*, Farnborough, Saxon House.

Mead, G. H. (1918), 'The psychology of punitive justice', in *American Journal of Sociology*, vol. 23, pp. 577–602.

Melossi, D. (1977), 'The penal question in capital', *Crime and Social Justice*, vol. 6 (Spring–Summer), pp. 26–33.

Melossi, D. (1979), 'Institutions of social control and the capitalist organisation of work', in B. Fine *et al.* (eds.), *Capitalism and the Rule of Law*, London, Hutchinson.

Melossi, D. (1980), 'Strategies of social control in capitalism: a comment on recent work', *Contemporary Crises*, vol. 4, pp. 381–402.

Melossi, D. and Pavarini, M. (1981), *The Prison and the Factory: Origins of the Penitentiary System*, London, Macmillan.

Messinger, S. (1976), 'Confinement in the community', *Journal of Research in Crime and Delinquency*, vol. 13, pp. 82–92.

Miers, D. (1978), *Responses to Victimisation*, Abingdon, Professional Books.

Miller, M. B. (1974), 'At hard labor: rediscovering the nineteenth century prison', *Issues in Criminology*, vol. 9, pp. 91–114.

Mills, C. W. (1943), 'The professional ideology of social pathologists', *American Journal of Sociology*, vol. 46, no. 2 (September), pp. 165–80.

Minson, J. (1980a), 'Review of Ignatieff and Scull', *Sociological Review*, vol. XVII (February).

Minson, J. (1980b), 'Strategies for socialists? Foucault's conception of power', *Economy and Society*, vol. 9, no. 1, pp. 1–44.

Mitford, J. (1973), *Kind and Usual Punishment*, New York, Knopf.

Morgan, R. and Bowles, R. (1981), 'Fines: the case for review', *Criminal law Review*, pp. 203–14.

Morris, A. and McIsaac, M. (1978), *Juvenile Justice?*, London, Heinemann Educational Books.

Morris, A., Giller, H., Szwed, E. and Geach, H. (1980), *Justice for Children*, London, Macmillan.

Morris, E. K. (1980), 'Applied behavior analysis for criminal justice practise: some current dimensions', *Criminal Justice and Behavior*, vol. 7, no. 2 (June), pp. 131–47.

Morris, N. (1974), *The Future of Imprisonment*, Chicago, University of Chicago Press.

Nagin, D. (1978), 'Crime rates, sanction levels, and constraints on prison population', *Law and Society Review*, vol. 12, pp. 341–66.

NAVSS (1980), *National Association of Victims Support Schemes: First Annual Report 1980*, London, NAVSS.

Neuman, F. (1964), *The Democratic and Authoritarian State*, London, Collier Macmillan.

Newman, O. (1980), *Community of Interest*, New York, Anchor Press.

Nisbet, R. A. (1962), *The Quest for Community*, New York, OUP.

Nisbet, R. A. (1966), *The Sociological Tradition*, New York, Basic Books.

Norquay, G. and Weiler, R. (1981), *Services to Victims and Witnesses of Crime in Canada*, Ottawa, Ministry of the Solicitor-General of Canada.

O'Connor, J. (1973), *The Fiscal Crisis of the State*, New York, St Martin's Press.

O'Connor, J. (1974), *The Corporation and the State*, New York, Harper & Row.

Olaussen, L. P. (1976), 'Avspeiler straffen arbeidsmarkedet?', *Sosiologi Idag*, pp. 33–40.

Orlans, H. (1948), 'An American death camp', *Politics*.

Orwell, G. (1949), *Nineteen Eighty-Four*, London, Secker & Warburg.

Parliamentary All Party Penal Affairs Group (1980), *Too Many Prisoners*, London, Barry Rose.

Pashukanis, E. (1978), *Law and Marxism*, London, Ink Links.

Pasquino, P. (1978), 'Theatrum politicum: the genealogy of capital – police and the state of prosperity', *Ideology and Consciousness*, no. 4, pp. 41–55.

Pasquino, P. (1980), 'Criminology: the birth of a special saviour', *Ideology and Consciousness*, no. 7, pp. 17–33.

Patton, P. (1979), 'Of power and prisons: working paper on *Discipline and Punish*', in M. Morris and P. Patton (eds.), *Michel Foucault: Power, Truth, Strategy*, Sydney, Feral Publications.

Pease, K. (1981), 'The size of the prison population', *British Journal of Criminology*, vol. 21, pp. 70–4.

Pease, K. and McWilliams, W. (eds.) (1980), *Community Service by Order*, Edinburgh, Scottish Academic Press.

Pease, K. Billingham, S. and Earnshaw, I. (1977), *Community Service Assessed in 1976*, Home Office Research Study no. 39, London, HMSO.

Plant, R. (1974), *Community and Ideology: An Essay in Applied Social Philosophy*, London, Routledge & Kegan Paul.

Plato (1981); see M. M. McKenzie, *Plato on Punishment*, Berkeley, Ca., University of California Press.

Platt, A. (1969), *The Child Savers*, Chicago, University of Chicago Press.

Platt, A. and Takagi, P. (1977), 'Intellectuals for law and order: a critique of the new "Realists" ', *Crime and Social Justice*, vol. 8, pp. 1–6.

Poulantzas, N. (1973), *Political Power and Social Classes*, London, New Left Books.

Poulantzas, N. (1978), *State, Power, Socialism*, London, New Left Books.

Probe (1980), *Journal of the NMAG*, (the NAPO members' action group).

Radzinowicz, L. (1966), *Ideology and Crime*, London, Heinemann Educational Books.

Ranulf, S. (1964), *Moral Indignation and Middle Class Psychology*, New York, Schocken Books.

Rawls, J. (1972), *A Theory of Justice*, Oxford, Clarendon Press.

Reynolds, F. (1981), 'In defence of the 1969 Act', *Howard Journal of Penology and Crime Prevention*, no. 1, pp. 6–14.

Richard, H. C. (ed.) (1977), *Behavioural Intervention in Human Problems*, New York, Pergamon.

Richter, M. (1964), 'Durkheim's politics and political theory', in K. H. Wolff (ed.), *Essays on Sociology and Philosophy by Emile Durkheim*, New York, Harper & Row.

Rock, P. (1977), 'Law, order, and power in late seventeenth and early eighteenth century England', *International Annals of Criminology*, vol. 16, pp. 233–65.

Rodman, B. S. (1968), 'Bentham and the paradox of penal reform', in *Journal of the History of Ideas*, vol. 29, pp. 197–210.

Rose, G. (1961), *The Struggle for Penal Reform*, London, Stevens & Sons.

Rothman, D. J. (1971), *The Discovery of the Asylum*, Boston, Mass., Little Brown.

Rothman, D. J. (1974), 'Prisons: the failure model', *Nation* (21 December).

Rothman, D. J. (1978), 'Introduction' and 'The State as Parent', in W. Gaylin *et al.*, *Doing Good: The Limits of Benevolence*, New York, Pantheon.

Rothman, D. J. (1980), *Conscience and Convenience: The Asylum and its Alternatives in Progressive America*, Boston, Mass., Little Brown.

Rusche, G., and Kirchheimer, O. (1939), *Punishment and Social Structure*, New York, Columbia University Press (reissued by Russell & Russell, New York, 1968).

Rutherford, A. and Bengur, O. (1976), *Community Based Alternatives to Juvenile Incarceration*, Washington, DC, LEAA.

Rutherford, A. *et al.* (1977), *Prison Population and Policy Choices*, Washington, DC, National Institute of Law Enforcement and Criminal Justice.

Saudi Arabia, Kingdom of (1980), *The Effect of Islamic Legislation on Crime Prevention in Saudi Arabia*, Riyadh, Ministry of the Interior, Kingdom of Saudi Arabia (translated, edited and printed in collaboration with the United Nations Social Defence Research Institute, Rome).

Schwartz, R. D. and Miller, J. C. (1964), 'Legal evolution and societal complexity', *American Journal of Sociology*, vol. 70, p. 159.

Scull, A. (1972), 'Social control and the amplification of deviance', in R. A. Scott and J. D. Douglas (eds.), *Theoretical Perspectives on Deviance*, New York, Basic Books.

Scull, A. (1976), 'The decarceration of the mentally ill: a critical view', *Politics and Society*, vol. 6, pp. 173–212.

Scull, A. T. (1977a), *Decarceration: Community Treatment and the Deviant – A Radical View*, Englewood Cliffs, NJ, Prentice-Hall.

Scull, A. (1977b), 'Madness and segregative control: the rise of the insane asylum', *Social Problems*, vol. 24, pp. 337–51.

Scull, A. (1979a), *Museums of Madness: The Social Organization of Insanity in Nineteenth Century England*, New York, St Martin's Press.

Scull, A. (1979b), 'Moral treatment reconsidered: some sociological comments on an episode in the history of British psychiatry', *Psychological Medicine*, vol. 9, pp. 421–8.

Scull, A. (1981), 'Progressive dreams, progressive nightmares: social control in twentieth century America', *Stanford Law Review*, vol. 33, pp. 301–16.

Segal, S. P. (1974), 'Life in board and care: its political and social context', in *Where is My Home*, Washington, DC, National Technical Information Service.

Seiter, R. P. *et al.* (1977), *Halfway Houses*, Washington, DC, National Institute of Law Enforcement and Criminal Justice, LEAA.

Sellin, T. (1976), *Slavery and the Penal System*, New York, Elseiver.

Sennet, R. (1978), *The Fall of Public Man*, London, OUP.

Sennet, R. *et al.* (1977), 'Destructive Gemeinschaft', in N. Birnbaum (ed.), *Beyond the Crisis*, New York, OUP.

Shearing, C. D. and Stenning, P. C. (1981), 'Modern private security: its growth and implications', in M. Tonry and N. Morris (eds.), *Crime and Justice: An Annual Review of Research*, Vol. 3, Chicago, University of Chicago Press, pp. 193–245.

Sheleff, L. (1975), 'From restitutive to repressive law', *Archiv Européenes de Sociology*, vol. 16, p. 16.

Short, R. (1979), *The Care of Long-Term Prisoners*, London, Macmillan.

Shover, N. (1980), *A Sociology of American Corrections*, Homewood, Ill., Dorsey Press.

Smart, B. (forthcoming), *Marxism, Foucault and Criticism*, London, Routledge & Kegan Paul.

Softley, P. (1978), *Fines in Magistrates' Courts*, Home Office Research Study no. 46, London, HMSO.

Sorokin, P. A. (1937), *Sociocultural Dynamics*, Vol. II, New York, American Book Co.

Sparks, R. (1971a), *Local Prisons*, London, Heinemann Educational Books.

Sparks, R. (1971b), 'The use of suspended sentences', *Criminal Law Review*, pp. 384–401.

Spitzer, S. (1975a), 'Punishment and social organisation: a study of Durkheim's theory of penal evolution', *Law and Society Review*, vol. 9, no. 4, pp. 613–37.

Spitzer, S. (1975b), 'Toward a Marxist theory of deviance', *Social Problems*, vol. 22, pp. 638–51.

Spitzer, S. (1979a), 'Notes towards a theory of punishment and social change', in S. Spitzer (ed.), *Research in Law and Sociology*, Greenwich, JAI Press, pp. 207–29.

Spitzer, S. (1979b), 'The rationalization of crime control in capitalist society', *Contemporary Crises*, vol. 3, pp. 187–206.

Spitzer, S. and Scull, A. (1977a), 'Social control in historical perspective: from private to public responses to crime', in D. Greenberg (ed.), *Corrections and Punishment*, Beverly Hills, Ca., Sage.

Spitzer, S. and Scull, A. (1977b), 'Privatization and capitalist development: the case of the private police', *Social Problems*, vol. 25, pp. 18–29.

Stang, D. T. and Snare, A. (1978), 'The coercion of privacy', in C. Smart and B. Smart (eds.), *Women, Sexuality and Social Control*, London, Routledge & Kegan Paul.

Stedman-Jones, G. (1977), 'Class expression versus social control?', *History Workshop Journal*, vol. IV, pp. 163–71.
Steinfels, P. (1979), *The Neo-Conservatives: The Men who are Changing American Politics*, New York, Simon & Schuster.
Stevenson, C. L. (1944), *Ethics and Language*, New Haven, Conn., Yale University Press.
Stumphauzer, J. S. (ed.) (1979), *Progress in Behaviour Therapy with Delinquents*, Springfield, Ill., Charles C. Thomas.
Szasz, T. (1974), *The Second Sin*, London, Routledge & Kegan Paul.
Tarling, R. and Softley, P. (1976), 'Compensation orders in the Crown Court', *Criminal Law Review*, pp. 422–8.
Taylor, I., Walton, P. and Young, J. (1973), *The New Criminology*, London, Routledge & Kegan Paul.
Taylor, I., Walton, P. and Young, J. (1975), *Critical Criminology*, London, Routledge & Kegan Paul.
Taylor, L. (1978), 'Ethics and expediency in penal practice', in J. Freeman (ed.), *Prisons Past and Future*, London, Heinemann Educational Books.
Taylor, L. (1980), 'Bringing power to particular account: Peter Rajah and the Hull Board of Visitors', in P. Carlen and M. Collison (eds.), *Radical Issues in Criminology*, Oxford, Martin Robertson.
Taylor, L., Lacey, R. and Bracken, D. (1979), *In Whose Best Interest?*, London, Cobden Trust and MIND.
Therborn, G. (1976), *Science, Class and Society*, London, New Left Books.
Thomas, J. E. (1972), *The English Prison Officer since 1850*, London, Routledge & Kegan Paul.
Thompson, E. P. (1975), *Whigs and Hunters*, Harmondsworth, Penguin Books.
Thompson, E. P. (1978), *The Poverty of Theory*, London, Merlin Press.
Thompson, E. P. (1979), Introduction to H. Harman and J. Griffiths, *Justice Deserted*, London, National Council for Civil Liberties.
Tomasic, R. and Dobinson, I. (1979), *The Failure of Imprisonment*, London, George Allen & Unwin.
Tomlinson, M. H. (1981), 'Penal servitude 1846–1865: a system in evolution', in V. Bailey (ed.), *Policing and Punishment in Nineteenth Century Britain*, London, Croom Helm.
Unger, R. M. (1976), *Law in Modern Society*, New York, Free Press.
Van den Haag, E. (1975), *Punishing Criminals*, New York, Basic Books.
Von Hirsch, A. (1976), *Doing Justice*, New York, Hill & Wang.
Vorenberg, E. and Vorenberg, J. (1973), 'Early diversion from criminal justice: practice in search of a theory', in L. Ohlin (ed.), *Prisoners in America*, Englewood Cliffs, NJ, Prentice-Hall.
Walker, H. and Beaumont, B. (1981), *Probation Work, Critical Theory and Socialist Practice*, Oxford, Basil Blackwell.
Walker, N. (1969), *Sentencing in a Rational Society*, London, Allen Lane.
Walker, N. (1972), 'Crime and penal measures', in A. H. Halsey (ed.), *Trends in British Society since 1900*, London, Macmillan.
Walker, N. (1981), 'The Home Office's review of parole, England and Wales (May 1981)', *British Journal of Criminology*, vol. 21, pp. 274–6.
Walters, R. Cheyne, J. and Banks, R. (1972), *Punishment*, Harmondsworth, Penguin Books.
Waltzer, M. (1980), *Radical Principles*, New York, Basic Books.

Webb, S. and Webb, B. (1929), *English Poor Law History. Part II: The Last Hundred Years*, Vol. 1, London, Longman, Green & Co. (reissued by Cass, London, 1963).

West, D. J. (ed.) (1972), *The Future of Parole*, London, Duckworth.

Willett, T. C. (1964), *Criminal on the Road*, London, Tavistock.

Williams, K. (1981), *From Pauperism to Poverty*, London, Routledge & Kegan Paul.

Wills, G. (1975), 'The human sewer', *New York Review of Books* (3 April).

Wilson, J. J. (1978), *The Declining Significance of Race*, Chicago, University of Chicago Press.

Wilson, J. Q. (1974), 'Crime and the criminologists', *Commentary*, (July), p. 49.

Wilson, J. Q. (1975), *Thinking About Crime*, New York, Basic Books.

Wilson, J. Q. (1981), 'What works? revisited: new findings on criminal rehabilitation', *The Public Interest*, no. 61, pp. 3–17.

Wines, F. H. (1895), *Punishment and Reformation*, New York, T. Y. Crowell.

Wolpert, J. and Wolpert, E. (1974), 'The relocation of released mental patients into residential communities', unpublished paper, Princeton University.

Wolpert, J. and Wolpert, E. (1976), 'The relocation of released mental patients into residential communities', *Policy Sciences*, vol. 7, pp. 31–51.

Wootton, B. (1959), *Social Science and Social Pathology*, London, George Allen & Unwin.

Wootton, B. (1963), *Crime and the Criminal Law*, London, Stevens.

Yochelson, S. and Samenow, S. E. (1976), *The Criminal Personality*, Vol. 1, New York, Aronson.

Young, J. (1975), 'Working class criminology', in I. Taylor, P. Walton and J. Young, *Critical Criminology*, London, Routledge & Kegan Paul.

Young, P. (1976), 'A sociological analysis of the early history of probation', *British Journal of Law and Society*, vol. 3, pp. 44–56.

Young, P. (1980), 'Punishment and social organisation', in Z. Bankowski and G. Mungham (eds.), *Essays in Law and Society*, London, Routledge & Kegan Paul.

Young, W. (1979), *Community Service Orders*, London, Heinemann Educational Books.

Zeitlin, I. M. (1968), *Ideology and the Development of Sociological Theory*, New York, Harper & Row.

Index

effect on penal systems, 194–6
Williams, K., 209
Wilson, J. Q., 123
Wines, F. H., 3

Young, J., 6
Young, W., 179–80, 197

Zeitlin, I. M., 50